Making & Selling Culture

Making & Selling Cul

Richard Ohmann, *editor*

With

Gage Averill

Michael Curtin

David Shumway

Elizabeth G. Traube

ture

Wesleyan University Press

Published by University Press of New England

Hanover & London

Wesleyan University Press
Published by
University Press of New England
Hanover, NH 03755
© 1996 by Wesleyan University Press
Printed in the United States of America

5 4 3 2 1

CIP data appear at the end of the book

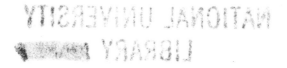

Contents

Richard Ohmann **Prefatory Note**

The project presented in this book had its origins in the late 1980s, when the Center for the Humanities at Wesleyan University (then under my direction, now that of Elizabeth Traube) turned to an emphasis on cultural studies. We organized lecture series, conferences, and semester-long colloquia around issues of cultural production and reception, meaning and identity, power and authority, cultural politics, and so on. For the fall of 1992, we set a theme, "Making and Selling Culture," that specified an inquiry into the ways cultural producers imagine or know markets — audiences — and how such knowledge figures in their decisions about what events, experiences, and products to make. Part of our design was to invite people from various culture industries to come talk with Center fellows and others about their own work, their organizations, their beliefs and attitudes.

Given the Center's very limited budget, it would have been impossible to engage consultants of stature and influence through any incentive other than goodwill. That proved enough. Seven of our visitors were alumni of Wesleyan; their generosity to the university and to the Center was extraordinary. Two consultants (Victoria Traube and Stephen Oakes) came out of sisterly affection and friendship, respectively. And one, the late Ira Herbert, came through the invaluable mediation of the Coca-Cola Foundation. These people visited us at their own expense and without stipend, spent valuable time in interviews, helped edit the transcripts, and immeasurably enriched our study, as well as making this book possible. My colleagues and I are most grateful to them. The Center for the Humanities, whose endowment will receive any royalties from this book, is much in their debt. It is perhaps worth adding that although our consultants spoke freely about the policies of their organizations, they did not speak as representatives *of* those organizations; also, much has changed in the more than three and one-half years since we interviewed them. Indeed, more than half of the nine still alive now work at different institutions.

Our other major debt is to the Coca-Cola Foundation. Its generous grant supported our work at every turn, underwrote the publication of this book, and brought us two visiting research fellows, Michael Curtin and Sarah Thornton, who participated in our study group and greatly enriched our discussions. I am most grateful for the foundation's financial support, and for the guidance and assistance throughout of its staff, especially Donald Greene and Diane Gray. Thanks also to David Jenkins for bringing our work to the attention of the Coca-Cola Foundation, and for his support of the Center for the Humanities over a period of years.

In addition to the five contributors to this volume, our study group included Karen Bock, Mary Ann Clawson, and James Kavanagh. They helped shape the project from the outset, and this book bears the mark of their inquisitiveness and helpful criticism, at all stages. Other Wesleyan faculty members and Center fellows took part in some of our discussions. Jeanine Basinger, John Biddiscombe, Paul DiSanto, and Ronald Kuivila helped interest four of our consultants in coming to Wesleyan. Patricia Camden and Jaqueline Rich worked capably and energetically with arrangements for the interviews, with preparation of the transcripts, and with all administrative necessities. Many thanks to all these people.

Each of the five study group members who has written for this volume connected the project to his or her own scholarly interests, and shaped his or her essay accordingly. But we worked closely together before writing and through the process of revision, so that this book is far more a collaborative effort than is usually the case with such collections. The mutuality will be evident not only in the common questions we and our consultants address, but in themes that appear in several essays: the paradoxical persistence and renewal of the local and contingent in an era of global mass culture; the tentativeness about cultural power in a time of media concentration and rationalization; the murky and conflicted question of ideology and bias. Thanks to one of Wesleyan University Press's readers for noting some of these themes. I hope the interlock of essays and interviews will be evident enough without further preliminaries.

One aim of the Center has been to promote, in humanistic and cultural scholarship, more collaboration than has been customary in those areas. I hope this book stands as a good example of such work, and an invitation to more.

On the mechanics of the interviews and preparation of transcripts: each consultant received in advance a list of questions from us. All lists included some questions in common, and that, along with the salient interests of our study group, explains the recurrence of many themes across all the interviews. Each interview lasted about an hour and a half, with questions coming from all in our group who wished to participate. It will be evident that we had different perspectives and interests, and for that matter disagreements among ourselves. But it proved impossible to identify all questioners on the tapes, so I have let the false impression stand that we questioned with a common voice. After the interviews, one or more of us condensed, rearranged, and edited each transcript. Then we sent it to its "author" for review and editing. Some consultants deleted small amounts of material that they found irrelevant or imprudent. Some also made minor changes for clarity and accuracy, but as printed here, the transcripts include very little that was not said viva voce.

Elizabeth G. Traube **Introduction**

. . . .

*Elizabeth G. Traube is professor of anthropology at Wesleyan University and
the current director of the Center for the Humanities. Her most recent book
is* Dreaming Identities: Class, Gender, and Generation in 1980s
Hollywood Movies. *Her research interests include the regimes of value
employed by media professionals.*

The relationship between academic intellectuals and mass-
cultural producers has long been fraught with ambivalence. As a manifestation of what Andrew Ross calls the dialectic of "no respect," its characteristics are mutual condescension, on the one hand, and a somewhat grudging
mutual admiration, on the other.[1] Among media professionals, disdain for
intellectual pretension is likely to alternate with deference for academic
credentials, whereas left-academic criticism of the culture industries has
oscillated between attacking media professionals as manipulators of consciousness and acknowledging, with mingled anxiety and envy, their ability
to provide people with meaning and pleasure, or, at least, with the resources
for constructing them.

Within academic cultural and media studies over the 1980s, pessimistic
and optimistic views of mass culture became associated respectively with
industry- and audience-focused research. At issue was the relationship between the industrial production of cultural forms and the consumption or
reception of the forms produced. Production-centered studies, according
to their revisionist critics, had overstated the power of the culture industries
to control the meaning of their products and had reduced reception to a
passive, undifferentiated process of assimilating dominant ideology. Against
the model of mass-produced culture as an ideological force that controls
and shapes consciousness from above, reception theorists defined audiences
as social subjects who actively and variably negotiate the meaning of cultural forms on the basis of their lived experience.[2]

The "active audience" model has been effective in directing attention to
how people use mass-cultural forms, but it has also contributed to a neglect
of producing institutions. John Fiske, for instance, whose work is symptomatic of a wider trend, separates the "financial economy," where culture industries produce and distribute commodities for profit, from the
"cultural economy," where those commodities are appropriated and inter-

preted by consumers. Fiske concedes that some consumers may assent to ideological meanings inscribed in cultural commodities during the process of production, but he reserves the term "popular culture" for readings that "resist" or "evade" dominant norms and values. "Popular culture," in Fiske's highly politicized and affirmative conception, is what oppositional subjects produce out of the commodities manufactured by the culture industries and, in diametric contrast to its ideologically saturated raw materials, it is "formed always in reaction to, and never as part of, the forces of domination."[3]

Critics of the consumptionist trajectory argue that any such strict separation of cultural commodities from the uses made of them is untenable.[4] This is not to deny that consumers are active participants in the creation of meaning who put what they consume to creative use. But the analytic splitting of production from consumption overstates the interpretive control exercised by consumers and understates the power of the culture industries to limit what is made available for interpretation. Moreover, historical shifts in the organization and content of industrial cultural production cannot be accounted for within a purely consumptionist perspective. Never an unmediated response to audience demand, such shifts are driven by particular industrial conditions, which are shaped by wider economic and political forces.

Michael Curtin's article in this volume provides a model of the ongoing reorganization of the U.S. culture industries. Curtin treats the massive changes that the culture industries have undergone over the last decade as instances of a wider shift to flexible modes of accumulation in an era of increased competition for shrinking profits. In the culture industries, as elsewhere, this shift is based on a multilevel dialectic between globalization or concentration of ownership and localization or fragmentation of both production and distribution. Thus, deregulation has fostered huge, competing media conglomerates, which maintain centralized control through decentralizing, flexible tactics. Rather than maintaining large, permanent creative staffs, most media corporations rely on subcontracting arrangements with a casualized creative labor force of independent producers who assemble production teams for specific projects. A dramatic and highly visible manifestation of flexibility in distribution is the fragmentation of media markets, a trend precipitated by the growing number of culture industries that are either replacing or supplementing the strategy of building the widest possible or mass audience with a strategy of targeting specific social groups.

Although not a new phenomenon, the pursuit of niche audiences through more tightly focused cultural products is increasingly practiced within those media industries once credited with the creation of a national or mass audience: the film industry, the magazine industry, and the television industry. In television, which is Curtin's focus, rapid fragmentation of the audience reflects the major networks' loss of control over distribution in a deregulated environment. Aggressive competition from new networks and cable channels disposes all competitors to attribute heightened value to smaller audiences, especially those audiences or market segments whose consumption habits make them particularly attractive to sponsors: notably, women, up-scale professionals, youth, and underserved ethnic or racial minorities. Within the marketing logic of the industry, to appeal to special groups requires the development of individuated programming, adjusted to their supposed cultural tastes and sensibilities. Known as narrowcasting, this strategy was aggressively pursued over the 1980s by niche operators like Fox, MTV, and LIFETIME, who targeted ethnic, youth, and female audiences.

Narrowcasting is also increasingly practiced by the major networks, in response to their declining market share. The networks began to experiment with more specialized appeals in the 1970s, when the notion of a "quality audience" (urban, educated, with up-scale, cosmopolitan tastes) was developed. Arguing that the financial power of the "quality audience" increased its value to sponsors and so compensated for its small size, architects of the concept used it to win network support for programs that might not attract a mass audience.[5] Over the 1980s, the networks targeted a subset of the "quality" audience defined as "working women," while also appealing to educated, discriminating viewers in less gendered terms, with a variety of shows characterized by relatively complex visual and/or narrative codes. Such formally self-conscious programs reverse television's conventional emphasis on content and are instances of a broader phenomenon that John Thornton Caldwell calls "televisuality" or "excessive style."[6] Televisuality promotes stylistic individuation as a way of appealing to specific niche audiences, inviting them to distinguish themselves from the "mainstream" in terms of ethnic, racial, gendered, generational, and class difference.

Curtin emphasizes that two tendencies characterize what he calls the "neo-Fordist" period in the culture industries. The continuing pursuit of the widest possible or "mass" audience, an imaginary entity invested with "universal" tastes, coexists with the pursuit of niche audiences, represented as social groups who have particular cultural needs.[7] The contrast is visible within firms as well as between them, since many megafirms are also niche operators themselves or else stand behind them as owners, poised to leverage popular niche artists into mass phenomena. Under the prevailing industrial conditions, whatever ideological interests the culture industries may harbor, their economic interest is to market social difference, not to erase it. As Curtin puts it, contemporary culture industries "seek less to homogenize popular culture than to organize and exploit diverse forms of creativity toward profitable ends" (197).

Yet both productionist and consumptionist approaches to mass-produced popular culture have tended to represent its ideological influence in terms of homogenization, differing only in their assessments of how successful the culture industries are in shaping social consciousness. Where the older, production-centered approach emphasized the ideological effectivity of mass culture, reception studies found active and "resistant" audiences who use mass-cultural forms to define themselves against dominant norms and values. Neither view adequately accounts for the operation of the culture industries. On the one hand, the receptionist assumption that asserted cultural differences have oppositional political value needs to be reconsidered in the light of the culture industries' heightened interest in marketing diverse forms of distinction, a point developed with reference to global markets in Gage Averill's essay.[8] On the other hand, industrial cultural production has never been a seamless process, and it can be argued that under the prevailing structural conditions, contestation and contradiction are becoming part of the routine.

Within the industry, the relationship beween managers and creative workers is one potential site of struggle. A romantic stereotype (circulated in mass-cultural texts) constructs executives as profit-minded philistines who try to stifle creative genius, but the actual dynamic is considerably more complex. As Janet Staiger observes of the film industry, inasmuch as innovation is a means of product differentiation used to recreate demand, management's interest is not to suppress creativity in the workplace but to promote and control it. Particular industrial conditions, however, contribute to the degree of latitude that creative workers have for innovation.[9] Staiger's referent is the Hollywood studio era, when the major studios employed large, relatively permanent creative staffs; in today's fragmented system, however, managerial and creative personnel more often confront each other as buyers and their would-be suppliers, who are hired for particular projects. In itself, the heightened insecurity of the creative labor market might be as likely to discourage innovation as to encourage it, but the industrial reconfiguration of the audience would seem to facilitate departures from convention. More precisely, fragmentation of the cultural marketplace heightens the uncertainty endemic to the culture industries about "what the audience wants." Against an industry convention that the "mass audience" craves the familiar and will only tolerate innovation within certain (negotiated) limits, fragmented audiences can be plausibly portrayed as especially receptive to aesthetic experimentation and/or alternative cultural values. At least, defining what particular niche audiences want is a hotly contested process and, as recent case studies of television programming trends suggest, may result in highly unstable, contradictory texts.[10] In other words, the particular images of the audience elaborated by producers are a force in shaping what will become available for consumption.

It was with such considerations in mind that the Center for the Humanities undertook a semester-long inquiry into how cultural producers conceive of audiences and interact with the audiences they construct. As a part of that inquiry, we invited a number of media professionals to campus to discuss their respective industries with a small group of interested scholars. In the preface to this volume Richard Ohmann notes that the Center's limited finances obliged us to depend on goodwill, but it was the goodwill of prior acquaintances rather than strangers, of Wesleyan alumni (some of them former students of members of the research group), friends, and relatives. That a group of academics had such abundant contacts with media professionals is not insignificant. It reminds us of the role played by the university in the integration of the so-called "knowledge class," those whose claims to status are based on possession of special knowledge;[11] it may also index the increasingly porous boundaries within that class between the academy and the culture industries. In the remainder of this introduction I reflect on the interviews collected here as dialogic interactions between academy and industry members, and especially on what strikes me as their ambivalent tone. For while we invited and, I trust, received our visitors respectfully, I would argue that the dialectic of "no respect" was also operating, in both directions.

That we academics were prone to assert our authority is not surprising. We were, after all, on our own territory (not even the veranda but the seminar room, the very heart of the academic enterprise, equivalent to the colonial administrator's office), and we also had the advantage of numbers.[12] We referred to our visitors as "consultants" (rather than by the more objectifying term "informants"), constructing the situation as an encounter between professionals in which the industry people were the experts. Yet it seemed we could not always resist representing ourselves as the experts who already understood the culture industries in ways that their members did not. Indeed, several of us (myself included) occasionally saw fit to lecture our consultants on the nature and/or consequences of their professional practices.

On the whole, our visitors were dismissive of such attempts at enlightening them. At the most, they listened politely and then returned to their own accounts. More often, they flatly rejected our interpretations. The latter, of course, varied. Although most members of our group understood the culture industries to have an ideological function, we conceived of ideological influence in different ways. The Althusserians among us emphasized the power of the mass media to homogenize consciousness, by implanting dominant ways of thinking (constructing individuals as consumers rather than as citizens; see Edmiston: 141) or by undermining their capacity for critical thought (eroding the faculties of attention and concentration through hypervisuality; see Oakes: 82–83). Others of us approached the culture industries as sites where diverse social discourses already in circulation are selectively absorbed, reworked, and relayed back to social groups; for us, ideological influence was a matter of reinflecting and reinforcing dominant definitions of social identities, and we saw counterforces at work within the media representations themselves (see Kendall: 63–66).

Neither version of ideological influence greatly impressed our visitors. Like the film majors who occasionally wander into my courses on popular culture, they insisted that media professionals are not concerned with constructing subjectivities but with telling pleasurable stories. Obviously, these models are not necessarily exclusive. My standard response to the students is that stories are vehicles for constructing subjectivities, and hence what stories are circulated is socially consequential. With our consultants, however, we tended to lapse into a misleading, insufficiently dialectical language, which nevertheless provoked interesting responses.

At numerous junctures, consultants were asked whether they saw their cultural products as either reflecting or shaping audience needs or desires (see Kendall: 62; Oakes: 82; Robinson: 155–156; Zelnick: 27). The problem with both these views, as I see it, is that they assume a prior separation of social subjects and cultural texts. Either the desires of preconstructed subjects are the source of the texts (the reflectionist model) or those desires are a product or outcome of texts (the effects model). For myself, I would prefer a more dialectical model of subjectivity as both appropriated by and negotiated through texts. But what interests me is how our consultants *used* the concept of audience in the context of our interview, the particular "audience fictions" that they deployed in confronting academic critics.

Our interviews confirm John Hartley's argument that "the audience" is a discursive construct, a set of "invisible fictions" produced institutionally, according to the needs and purposes of the imagining institutions, which include critical institutions, such as the academy, as well as the culture industries. The "actual audience" or "social subject," Hartley points out, is a discursive construct of academic critics, whose primary concern is to describe and evaluate interactions between readers and texts. The industries, by contrast, need not only to represent audiences but to enter into relations with them, in the interests of survival and profit. The problem for the industries, as Hartley puts it, is that they must talk about something to someone, but that someone is literally unknowable. Thus, the audience fictions produced in and for the culture industries are primarily designed to reassure producers that the audience is controllable.[13]

From this perspective, critical and industry fictions of the audience clashed in our interviews. Many of the media people, I would suggest, implicitly portrayed academic criticism as an overly serious endeavor, rejecting our construction of audiences as social subjects whose interest lay in how their lived experience was represented in media texts. Against this fiction, a repeatedly invoked figure defined the consuming interest of the audience as pleasure, yet many who invoked this figure of the audience denied that they were greatly preoccupied with how to please it. Or more precisely, a recurrent argument was that it was possible, even preferable, to please the audience without being obliged to know it.

Both David Shumway and Richard Ohmann grapple in their essays with the issue of what cultural producers claim to know. Shumway focuses on how the news industry uses the claim to objectivity to give value to its products. According to Shumway, journalism misrecognizes its own constructed character, representing "truth" as something discovered by eliminating distorted frames or biases, rather than as something discursively produced by following conventional procedures. A corollary, I would add, is that journalism's claim to objective knowledge depends on disclaiming intimate knowledge of the audience. News organizations represent themselves according to a public service model in which their role is to lead or inform rather than to follow. Such organizations need to imagine their audience as rational, curious, educated and educable citizens. They do not, however, need to know what the imagined audience wants or desires. On the contrary, as Joshua Gamson argues, they are motivated to resist systematic audience research, which could give the appearance that they have lost their autonomy and are pandering to the public mood.[14]

Where Shumway focuses on journalism, Ohmann surveys a range of culture industries and is struck by the "narrowness of claims to knowledge about people, and the virtual absence of claims to power over our needs and desires." In the 1890s, he argues, representatives of the nascent culture industries were less reticent. Advertisers and magazine editors, in particular, claimed to be able to shape new needs and channel them into consumer goods, whereas contemporary cultural professionals doubt whether they understand the existing needs of consumers well enough to shape products that satisfy them. Contrasted with the boosterism of their predecessors, contemporary producers' discourse on audiences bespeaks a "decline in boldness," which Ohmann connects to the development of consumer capitalism and the process of formation of what I am calling the knowledge class.

Viewed from another angle, the disavowal of systematic knowledge of audience needs may perhaps be read as a way of asserting status, by valorizing the act of cultural production and its products. In the case of journalism, as we have seen, authority is constructed by ignoring or claiming to ignore what audiences want. The truth value of the product (news) depends on its detachment from popular desires. Similarly, it seems to me, in discounting the influence of particular audience needs, that several of our visitors from the entertainment industries attributed aesthetic value to their own activities. In other words, to refuse the characterization of one's activities as rigidly determined by market reasoning is to present oneself as an artist (in the case of creative personnel) or as involved in artistic projects (in the case of managers). If I am right, and I must stress that what follows is speculative, our interviews attest to the collapse of the modernist opposition between art and mass culture.

In the modernist construction, the market relationship provides the principle for hierarchically dividing the cultural field into high and low. High culture or (genuine) art is defined in opposition to the mass-produced cultural commodity, as the realm of individual creativity and freedom against a sheerly instrumental form determined by market rationality. As a representation of the cultural field, the inadequacies of this model are now widely acknowledged in cultural studies.[15] Long since absorbed into commodity production, high art forms one more niche within an increasingly differenti-ated and decentered cultural market, while the Frankfurt School's pessimis-tic assessment of mass-cultural commodities has been modified, partly in recognition of the proliferation of high/low distinctions *within* what are viewed as popular forms. Yet in retrospect it strikes me that by largely omitting questions about aesthetic value from our interviews while encour-aging our consultants to focus on market considerations, we implicitly re-drew the boundary between art and mass culture.

If so, our visitors from the industries resisted us, employing a variety of aestheticizing discourses to represent the work they did. Mass marketers used the language of universals to construct their products as popular art. Strauss Zelnick, for instance, first denies that movies are made for particular audiences, then concedes that "niche movies" are crafted to suit particular tastes, but ranks these lower in the aesthetic hierarchy than the "movies that are great stories," which are the ones that achieve wide appeal (23). On the one hand, the model requires a fiction of the mass audience as discriminat-ing consumers who recognize aesthetic value, people who "smell quality," as Zelnick puts it (22). On the other hand, it requires discerning creators, as television writer-producer David Kendall suggests, who can distinguish those features of their own experience that transcend individual limits and transmute them into popular art.

The valued connection to the mass audience is intuitive, a matter of imaginative projection and charismatic insight rather than systematic scru-tinizing of actual preferences. This is fortunate, of course, since the "mass audience" is an imaginary and literally unknowable construct.[16] One may see the valorization of informal knowledge as a compensatory mechanism, a way in which producers adjust to their inability to know the audience they seek to reach. But it is also a productive mechanism, a way in which creative personnel and executives alike construct themselves as discriminating sub-jects who participate in a process of aesthetic production.

One should be wary of generalizing from the disdain for research ex-pressed by so many of our consultants. Had our group included a television network executive, he or she would surely have been less dismissive.[17] Nevertheless, although formal knowledge often plays a determinant role in decision-making processes, informal, intuitive knowledge about audiences is highly valued. Of our consultants the one who took formal audience research most seriously was niche marketer Nathan Pearson, and he repre-sents the *interpretation* of research as an informal, artistic, charismatic process. Thus, praise is reserved for the analyst with a "gift" for hearing the audience speak through the research (124), one who has the capacity to be "creative or artistically interpretative" (124).

Varying models of aesthetic hierarchy were also invoked. Victoria Traube (who was at the time employed in the New York branch of a diversified talent agency) offered a relatively traditional version of the hierarchy as stretching downward and westward, from off-Broadway to Broadway theater, to Hollywood movies and television. Of the television people, Kendall alternates between the dominant construction of television in general and sitcom writing in particular as essentially low-cultural forms and an emergent view of television as a site for aesthetic experimentation. Playing off the industry's ubiquitous construction of the television audience as a child, he represents himself as "someone who does a kid thing for a living," and a very good living, too (60). But the voice of the serious craftsman is also audible in reference to "Growing Pains," and he sees the success of that relatively mainstream show as having secured him the opportunity at least to pitch a more aesthetically ambitious, televisual project (70).

Neatly subverting the traditional hierarchy is Stephen Oakes, an independent producer of animation and special effects for television commercials, specializing in a style commonly used for children's advertising. Oakes works in what is generally seen as the "lowest" form of mass culture, where the need to subordinate aesthetic form to commercial aims is most strictly enforced. Whether or not that stereotype is accurate for any period in advertising, when television took aim at visually literate consumers over the 1980s, advertising became one site for stylistic excess.[18] To some of us, Oakes seemed the most restricted in his creative activity, with every phase in his work closely monitored and regulated by the ad agency that hires him (77–78). Yet with his extensive connections to the fine arts community, which he regularly taps for creative labor, and his appreciation of the formal complexity of highly condensed visual forms, Oakes came across as the most confident of all our consultants in his personal aesthetic capital. It is with that capital, moreover, rather than any claim to knowledge of the viewing audience, that he appeals to his primary audience, which is the industry buyer.[19]

Oakes's visit provoked the most acute manifestation of the dialectic of "no respect": an attack launched by one of our group on (tele)visual culture as the enemy of reason, and Oakes' response to that attack (82–84). Personally, I was suspicious of the charge, which reproduces a deeply rooted dualism, but what I want to emphasize is how slyly Oakes turned it aside. Flatly denying that televisuality had negative effects on viewers' consciousness, he went on to suggest that academics should make better use of its techniques in the classroom. In one move, he undermined the barriers between industry and academy that his critic had sought to erect, pointing instead to potential points of contact between them.[20]

At issue is not only whether academics can profit from the sophisticated visual technologies and the regimes of pleasure developed in the culture industries, although that is a valid question. Also at stake, I would argue, is whether the culture industries can profit from modes of criticism developed in the academy. While we academics and our industry guests were often at cross purposes, there may be grounds for optimism. This much is clear: under current market conditions, the industries have a mounting interest in aesthetic and intellectual complexity; the challenge for academics is to find ways of intervening in their projects.

Notes

1 *No Respect: Intellectuals and Popular Culture* (London: Routledge, 1989).
2 See, for instance, David Morley, *The 'Nationwide' Audience* (London: British Film Institute, 1980) and *Television, Audiences and Cultural Studies* (London: Routledge, 1992).
3 *Understanding Popular Culture* (Boston: Unwin Hyman, 1989), 43. See also Fiske's *Reading the Popular* (London: Routledge, 1989) and *Power Plays Power Works* (London: Verso, 1993).
4 See, among others, John Clarke, *New Times and Old Enemies: Essays on Cultural Studies and America* (London: Harper Collins, 1991); Jim McGuigan, *Cultural Populism* (London: Routledge, 1992), pp. 70–75; John Frow, *Cultural Studies and Cultural Value* (Oxford: Clarendon, 1995), pp. 60–64.
5 See Jane Feuer, Paul Kerr, and Tise Vahimagi, *MTM: 'Quality Television'* (London: BFI Publishing, 1984).
6 John Thornton Caldwell, *Televisuality: Style, Crisis, and Authority in American Television* (New Brunswick, N.J.: Rutgers University Press, 1995). On the appeal to "working women" in 1980s television, see Julie D'Acci, *Defining Women: Television and the Case of Cagney and Lacey* (Chapel Hill: University of North Carolina Press, 1994).
7 Dual appeals may also coexist in particular products. Typically, for instance, "quality programming" constructed to flatter educated viewers is also expected to offer other, less alienating pleasures for the "mass audience." In other words, as both Feuer (*MTM*, p. 56) and Caldwell (*Televisuality*, p. 255) observe, many

niche products are designed to be readable at different levels. Conversely, programs aimed at mainstream tastes may also include elements that appeal to more specialized audiences.

8 As Steven Connor puts it, "what is dominant in contemporary culture is the projection of a universe of multiple differences." See *Postmodernist Culture: An Introduction to Theories of the Contemporary* (Oxford: Basil Blackwell, 1989), pp. 186–90. Caldwell (*Televisuality*, pp. 261–262) argues that the reception theorists' model of the active, resistant audience neglected the degree to which the television industry encourages audience activity, while limiting its oppositional value.

9 Introduction to *The Studio System*, ed. Janet Staiger (New Brunswick, N.J.: Rutgers University Press, 1995), pp. 4–5.

10 See D'Acci, *Defining Women*, and Andrew Goodwin, *Dancing in the Distraction Factory: Music Television and Popular Culture* (Minneapolis: University of Minnesota Press, 1992).

11 On the concept of the knowledge class, see John Frow, *Cultural Studies*, pp. 89–130.

12 As an anthropologist, I was sensitive to the reversal of the traditional ethnographic situation, where the Lone Ethnographer ventures out into the community of the Other.

13 See "Invisible Fictions," originally published as John Hartley, "Invisible Fictions: Television, Audiences, Paedocracy, Pleasure," *Textual Practice*, 1:2 (Summer 1987):121–138, republished in John Hartley, *Tele-ology: Studies in Television* (London: Routledge, 1992), pp. 101–18. Hartley's focus in this essay is on the television audience, especially in its "mass" version. See also Ien Ang, who adopts Hartley's model in *Desperately Seeking the Audience* (London: Routledge, 1991).

14 Joshua Gamson, *Claims to Fame: Celebrity in Contemporary America* (Berkeley: University of California Press, 1994), pp. 116–118. Gamson argues that the disinclination of many media organizations to pursue systematic knowledge of the audience is variously motivated. In the case of news organizations, the more seriously they take themselves as providers of truth, the more dissonance is raised by appearing to "bow" to audience desires.

15 See, among others, Geoffrey Nowell-Smith, "Popular Culture," *New Formations* 2 (1987):79–90; Simon Frith, "The Good, the Bad, and the Indifferent: Defending Popular Culture from the Populists," *Diacritics* 21:4 (1991):102–115; Frow, *Cultural Studies*.

16 See Hartley, "Invisible Fictions," p. 110.

17 But as Todd Gitlin has noted in *Inside Prime Time* (New York: Pantheon, 1983), p. 43, the value of research to managerial personnel does not depend on belief in its accuracy; its paramount use is in regulating intra-industry relations between

the networks and the creative community, for instance, to justify unpopular executive decisions and "give the network's voice a rational sound." See also Ien Ang, *Desperately Seeking*, pp. 21–22.

18 Caldwell, *Televisuality*, p. 10. See also Martyn J. Lee, *Consumer Culture Reborn: The Cultural Politics of Consumption* (London: Routledge, 1993), pp. 148–159, on the new aesthetic sensibility within advertising.

19 The displacement of the general or viewing audience by the intra-industry audience was a recurrent theme and merits extended treatment. Clearly, the value placed on the "audience of fellow producers" helps to sustain a sense of engagement in an aesthetic project.

20 On academic hostility to the visual image see Caldwell, *Televisuality*, pp. 336–357.

Interviews

Ira Herbert The Coca-Cola Company

April 15, 1993

· ·

Ira C. Herbert began his career with the Coca-Cola Company in 1965. He held a number of positions, including president of Coca-Cola Foods (1975), executive vice-president of the Coca-Cola Company (1976), chief marketing officer (1982), and deputy to the president of the Coca-Cola Company (1986). He was named president of the North American Soft Drink Business Sector and president of Coca-Cola USA in 1988.

He died on March 4, 1995.

"Ike Herbert was the quintessential advertising man. The memorable ads created for Coca-Cola under his leadership helped move consumer product advertising to a whole new level," said Roberto C. Goizueta, chairman of the board and chief executive officer of the Coca-Cola Company. "As a custodian of the Coca-Cola mystique, his dedicated service and many contributions to the Coca-Cola Company will long be remembered."

I was born and bred midwestern, born in Chicago, raised in Chicago, went to Michigan State University and Northwestern University. Never traveled more than 250 miles out of Chicago except for the service. My secret ambition was to become the next Edward R. Murrow, and I started out to do that in journalism and broadcasting. Then I went to business school and worked in Dayton, Ohio, and Freeport-Rockford, Illinois. When I came back from Korea I decided that I wasn't going to live in small towns anymore. I went to work for an advertising agency and after 10 years I joined McCann Erickson, primarily for the opportunity to work on the Coca-Cola business. After a few years, I was asked by Coca-Cola to join the company and handle their advertising, and I did. I was primarily responsible for the development of material and strategies in advertising from roughly 1965 to 1975, and of course I was intimately involved in strategies from the agency point of view for a couple of years before that. Then in 1975 I was asked to go to Houston and become president of our noncarbonated beverage division, which is Hi-C and Minute Maid. At that time we were also a major coffee producer and marketer, primarily regional in scope, but major. And then in 1981 I came back to the corporation in Atlanta to become the global marketing director and handle advertising on a worldwide basis. In about 1987 I was asked to become president of Coca-

Cola North America. It included both the United States and Canada. I did that until I retired about a year ago.

Coca-Cola is, really, high-class marketing. We are a company that is, by any measure, highly successful, perhaps the epitome of a multinational, multicultural company. We market in 180 countries. We market in more countries than belong to the United Nations. We do business in 80 different languages. It is an enormous business, and it is a single-focus business. It is for all practical purposes soft drinks. Soft drinks, as you know, is not a high-tech business. It is a very simple business. The closest we come to high-tech is in the arena of production. How fast can we turn out product? In the original days, maybe 10 to 20 cans a minute. Now we have canning plants that spit out 5,000 to 6,500 cans a minute.

We have two areas of concentration. First, there is the fountain business, also called the "on-premise" business. The kind of drink you find in a McDonald's, a restaurant or a drug store, or any place where you go inside and drink Coca-Cola by the glass or cup. And then you have the core of our business, what we call the bottle/can business, which is a franchise operation. Around the world it is marketed and developed and invested in by mostly independent businessmen who are indigenous to the country in which we are marketing. You have Germans running the German operation, you have Frenchmen running the French operation, et cetera. Our role at the Coca-Cola Company is to perpetuate and develop a specialness about the brands that we sell, which takes the product above and beyond what is actually in the bottle itself. And so our purpose in life is to keep our system enthused, committed, and perhaps most importantly, to be able to reach the consumer, everywhere. And that word is not used lightly. When we say everywhere, we mean everywhere! Eighty percent of our profit comes from outside the United States. And it will become greater over time because we have so many, many areas that are either just being seeded or that haven't developed their potential of growth. Our history of growth certainly over the last fifteen years has been phenomenal. We have moved around the world. We are the leaders in the soft drink business. Our worldwide share of market is approximately 46 percent. It is about 42 percent in the United States. And it is about 47 to 48 percent outside of the United States. We have four global brands. By global brands I mean brands that we market for all practical purposes everywhere in the world. They are (obviously) Coca-Cola, Diet Coca-Cola, or Coca-Cola Light, depending on the rules of the country, Sprite, and, outside of the United States, Fanta, which is essentially an orange drink but is also a line of flavors.

We are a multinational management as well as a multinational company. If you were to walk through the halls of our international headquarters in Atlanta you would find Australians, and Germans, and Frenchmen, and Spaniards, and Cubans, Indians, Egyptians, Argentinians, and Britons. You would not find any Chinese, you wouldn't find any Russians, only because they haven't got there yet. I have no doubt in my mind that they will, over time. The company is multinational and multicultural, but we are monolingual. We do our business in English. No matter where you are from, if you are going to work for the Coca-Cola Company in any kind of senior capacity, you must be able to speak and communicate well in English.

We deal in a rather controlled marketing environment. That may be changing in the last month or two, but up until then the concept was that the advertising was the same and the music was essentially the same globally.

Globally?

Yes. Now, execution could be different. We developed pattern advertising that could be adjusted to fit the local environment, the local culture, the local language, and could be changed or edited as long as the concept wasn't changed — as long as the feel wasn't changed — as long as the sound wasn't changed. The feel of the commercial had to come out according to pattern. That has been highly successful for us. With the exception of two segments of the world, we are by far — and when I say by far, I mean by far — the leader. These two exceptions are the Arab countries (where we have just recently been taken off the boycott list because of our trade with Israel) and Venezuela. For some strange reason Venezuela has always been a thorn in the side of the Coca-Cola Company, one of the few countries that we don't lead. Back in '65 the Arab countries warned us that if we gave a franchise to Israel they would throw us out. I remember sitting at a meeting where our position was "We simply can't allow somebody else to tell us to whom we can and where we can sell our product." So we decided to grant an Israel franchise, even though we endangered our Arab business where we had been by far the leader.

What about the Soviet Union. Was it also . . .

Yes, but that has changed now. We have made major changes. I believe we are now the leaders in the Soviet Union. But even when we weren't the leaders in the Soviet Union, the amount of volume that came out of the Soviet Union was not big enough to be a crucial issue.

The Coca-Cola Company has probed in arenas other than soft drinks, and has done so with varying amounts of success, but has always come home to "mother." The only other business that has been maintained has been the highly successful noncarbonated beverage division that we run out of Houston. As you know, we went into the wine business and we went into the movie business and we went into the water purification business. I can't think of others, but there have been a series of those that we have tried and we have always backed off. Fortunately they have always been successfully concluded. We moved into the wine business, built it up and sold it at a profit. I don't have to tell you the story of the movie business. We got in and developed it for just about 900 million dollars, sold it for billions.

So we have been, from a financial point of view, successful in those addenda, if you will, but have never really felt at home with them. We would always come back to soft drinks.

Could you talk about the similarities and differences between North American and global marketing? To what extent do you have to be multi-cultural in your marketing inside the United States? Are the new media, with a kind of microfocus, likely to change the answer to that?

We believe we know more about our market than other companies do about their individual markets. We are very, very determined researchers. Besides all of the individual research projects that go on constantly in various segments, either having to do with geography or demographic content, we have a research project that has been going on since about 1955 with four thousand interviews a quarter. So by the end of the year we have dealt with a minimum of sixteen thousand interviews. And this has been going on now for near forty years. It is true not only in the United States but in most of the developed countries of the world. We have keyed advertising to various demographic and ethnic groups. Within that, however, the concept has always been the same. We don't change the concept. What we do is maybe change the music, maybe change the execution, certainly change the casting, but in terms of what it sounds like and what it looks like and what it is selling, at a particular point in time, we have kept it more or less patterned. Again, I am talking essentially about our global brands. The nonglobal brands are really run on a local basis. You know, the old cliché, "think globallly and act locally," was really created by the Coca-Cola Company through our franchises and local bottlers, because everything that was done, all promotions, all activity, all packaging, all sales activity, all social activities, the image of the Coca-Cola bottler as a leading citizen of the local community, has all been keyed on a local basis, overlaid with an umbrella of the global strategy. We have been dealing with various ethnic demographic groups within an overall concept. Very recently, and by that I mean within the last eight to twelve weeks, the company has moved to a more fragmented approach, based on the assumption that the media today is fragmented and that each of those groups that are targeted by that media core should be communicated to in their own way with their own message, with their own sound, with their own visualization. Just as an example, two years ago brand Coca-Cola would create a dozen commercials for the year in North America. We have just finished producing 26 and it is only April. I don't know where it is going to end.

Commercials with different themes?
There is a signature now called "Always Coke," but how you get to that signature depends on the intent of that communication. So we have really embarked on a new experiment as far as Coca-Cola is concerned. Part of the problem that Coca-Cola advertising has always been faced with has been the problem of our consumers' expectations. Until recently, well even today, Coca-Cola advertising could not go far out. The consumer would complain. We would get letters saying, "That's not Coca-Cola." We were literally so successful in establishing in the consumer's mind this icon, this image (the Doris Day, apple pie, rosy cheek, this-is-America kind of thing), that the consumer objects to things that take him beyond these expectations. I approved a commercial that we tried out in Canada because we didn't have the guts to try it in the United States. It really was far out. It didn't work. But every time we would probe that arena, it just wasn't right, it didn't fit, it wasn't Coca-Cola, and the consumer objected. So we made our "living" on the hilltops and the greens and the country sunshine. But that wasn't as true outside of North America as it was in North America itself. It is going to be interesting to see what this new approach does, and how consumers react.

For instance, is there even a possibility that you might run some commercials on pornographic pay channels?
Is MTV pornographic? I don't think Coca-Cola will ever run on the Playboy channel. Now Sprite might. We have never placed a Coca-Cola ad in *Playboy*. It is not Coca-Cola.

But you would place a Sprite ad there?
Oh yes. And have.

And what is the difference?

The fact is, it is not Coca-Cola. There is only one Coca-Cola. I would guess that 65 percent of the consumers in the United States do not know that Sprite is made by Coca-Cola. Coca-Cola is a world of its own. It is the most recognized brand in the world, and admired brand, I should say. If you take the number two brand to the 42nd brand and combine them, Coca-Cola is more admired and recognized than the number two to the forty-second brand combined. When you talk about Coca-Cola in most places in the world, it is immediately identified as a piece of America and yet there are many instances, recorded instances, where people have come from foreign countries to the United States and said something like "Oh, you have Coke here too." Because we have localized it to a point that they really feel that "Yes, it's American, but it is really ours." It is an interesting dichotomy.

Certain American products have suffered in the last thirty years from this
association with the United States. There was a report recently about the problems
that Disney is having selling Euro-Disney to Europeans, perhaps because Disney,
like Coke, is so closely identified with the United States. How do you deal with
that strategically?

Very carefully, but very low key. Very nonconfrontationally. We have found that generally speaking, perhaps because of the ingrained habit of having a Coke, there has never been a successful boycott of Coca-Cola. I'm talking about anything that lasts beyond four or five days, or a week. It just hasn't held up.

Not even in Venezuela?

Venezuela. They don't need to boycott us. They might as well have boycotted us. It is a unique situation.

It is difficult to boycott our product, and I'll use North America as an example. At any ballpark you go to, any circus you go to, most places that you go to in the United States that people view as fun or as special — you are going to find Coke there. It has insinuated itself into the lives of the people to a point where it has become — you know, it's there. One of the reasons that we made the mistake on new Coke, despite all that, was because Coca-Cola had become wallpaper. If you asked people "What is your favorite soft drink?," overwhelmingly they would say "Coca-Cola." "What did you buy yesterday?" "Pepsi Cola, or Seven Up." "Why is that?" "Oh, I don't know, I just wanted to try something different." And they had been trying something different for the last five years. Our intent was to reinvent Coca-Cola.

And for the wrong reason, we succeeded magnificently. The consumer revolted. Hysterical. An eighty-year-old lady called up the president of the company in tears: "Why have you taken away Coca-Cola?" In the discussion we found out she hadn't drunk Coca-Cola in forty years. But it was hers. We had taken away a part of her youth. And it keyed a terribly emotional uproar in the United States. That was one of the two crucial mistakes that I believe we have made. But it worked out beautifully. Sales exploded when we brought back Coca-Cola Classic.

The other: Until 1981 the leading diet drink in the world, certainly in the United States, was a drink called Tab. When we introduced Diet Coke, at the end of 1981, we became so involved with the hysterical success of the introduction that we took our eye off of Tab. We should have generated major marketing dollars to sustain both brands. And we didn't do it.

You let Fresca get away too.

Yeah, Fresca was a good brand but it was not of the dimension of Coke. The Tab brand was really a sort of second-tier brand. The first diet cola on the market was DietRite, the second diet cola on the market was Diet Pepsi, the third diet cola on the market was Tab. The name has no "Cola" in it. It had no identity, so we really had to start from a blank sheet of paper. We didn't call it Tab Cola because our franchise contracts specified we could only use the word Cola with Coca-Cola. Therefore we had a tough time getting Tab started. People didn't know what it was. In 1968, they banned cyclamate. Up until then soft drinks had essentially been sweetened with cyclamate and a touch of saccharin. The problem was that brands sweetened with saccharin only tasted terrible, awful, so most companies came out into the marketplace with a mixture, part sugar and part saccharin. Therefore the normal diet soft drink was now roughly sixty calories, as opposed to one. We did a great deal of research and found out that the diet drinker didn't really care about taste as much as they cared about calories. They wanted something cold and relatively sweet. Diet drinkers for a long time were almost totally female. We did taste-testing around the country and found out that Tab with saccharin only lost taste-tests 80/20 to Diet Pepsi. Now to those who are not familiar with taste-cuttings, 55/45 is a big win. But the diet drinker said that the most important thing they wanted out of their diet drink was no calories. And so we talked the company into introducing Tab with all saccharin and one calorie and it tasted like hell. However, it became the number one soft drink in the diet category in a matter of months and never gave it up. And it came from number three to number one and stayed number one, because we read the research right. In that case we read it right.

What about the caffeine in Coke? Do you ever advertise the lift Coke gives you?
We do not talk about lift in Coca-Cola for a couple of reasons, the most important one being that it potentially communicates something "tonic-y," almost medicinal. The purpose of Coca-Cola is pure refreshment. We don't want that confused. We don't want to communicate in any way — even remotely — that we are *trying* to sell Coca-Cola on the basis of its caffeine content.

You will never see a child under thirteen, in Coca-Cola advertising, drinking Coca-Cola — anywhere in the world. Now, you might see a child carrying a bottle and giving it to somebody. You might see a child in a family group, but they will never be drinking Coca-Cola.

So you want to disassociate it from the medicinal and from the possibly addictive?
At a cocktail party in Atlanta, I ran into a lady who was in her late sixties, who was absolutely convinced that in the back hills of Alabama, Coca-Cola managed an enormous sanitarium for Coke addicts. And there was nothing I could do to convince her that it simply was not true. She was sure that people drank so much of this stuff that they must become addicted, and therefore we had a sanitarium that treated them. All of the fables and wild stories that develop over Coca-Cola could literally fill a book.

How much of the warm, fuzzy image (in contrast to Pepsi's harder, jazzier image) is a product of geography and the culture of the mid-South?
I think that is one factor. I believe there is a more important factor. Coca-Cola really started in a drug store in Atlanta. It became a major phenomenon during World War II, when the United States asked the Coca-Cola company to supply their troops with Coca-Cola, and therefore Coca-Cola established a group of people who traveled with the troops and set up mobile bottling plants wherever the troops were. Woodruff's position was, "No soldier will ever pay more than a nickel for a Coke no matter where he is in the world." That, frankly, became the basis of the global business of Coca-Cola. Those mobile or temporary bottling plants became permanent. They were sold off to franchises and that is how the Coca-Cola business became global. And that is why we beat Pepsi Cola to the international world so badly. That is the positive side. The negative side was that

we became very arrogant. We decided that there wasn't anything that could touch us. And when Pepsi came out with "twice as much for a nickel too," Coca-Cola could have devastated Pepsi Cola in a short time by introducing a twelve-ounce bottle. Instead we allowed Pepsi Cola to get a foothold as a "private" label — the kind of thing to serve to Johnny and the kids in the kitchen, but when friends come over we'll have Coke in the living room. Now that did two things. First of all it did a great deal for Coca-Cola's image. Because Coca-Cola became the quality soft drink. It became the "living room" soft drink for company. And you served the "cheap stuff" to the kids because they didn't know the difference. But that gave Pepsi a start. And then Pepsi Cola did something very smart, and Coca-Cola didn't respond. They realized that they couldn't take on the Coca-Cola Company on a broad base, so they said, "Okay, what we need to do is to go after the kids and ignore the rest of the market. Let Coke have it. We've got to begin establishing our own image in a specific segment."

Pepsi was capitalizing on a market that Coke had essentially given them by not responding?
They hired Alfred Steele, who worked for Coca-Cola and who married Joan Crawford. Al was the guy who really triggered this strategy. They became much more aggressive.

There is a very big cultural difference between Coca-Cola and Pepsi; you see it in their ads as well as in the way they market their product, the way they deal with the trade, the way they deal with other companies. I don't mean it's necessarily good or bad, I'm simply saying it's different.

I don't think there's any doubt about it. We are a different kind of company; we attract different kinds of people. Andy Pearson, who was the operating guy at Pepsi, was said to have had a rule: "The way to succeed in this business is to drop off the bottom twenty percent of your people every year — evaluate, challenge, evaluate, then get rid of the bottom twenty percent." Coca-Cola is much more all-family. It's just a different approach to how you do business and what wins in the long run.

Part of what led to our arrogance, I believe, was this Southern gentleman-liness. "The competitors are really not important. They will go away." It was fortunate, in one way, that the competitors survived. The soft drink business could not have grown to its current dimension without the competition. I don't think we would have pushed or fought the way we did. The two of us literally exploded a market. I'm not sure we could have done that alone.

How did Coca-Cola then go about reclaiming its share of the young people's market?

It really never did. It came back to the point where we are certainly the leader again in that segment. I don't remember the numbers, but where we were 90/10 we are now 50/35 or something like that. Those are made-up numbers obviously, but we never again achieved overwhelming dominance.

What is the line between youth and the next stage in life, the upper twenties or whatever? Do they bring the brand with them as they grow older? Or do they switch over when they get to be thirty?

They do bring the brand with them. As a matter of fact, the over-fifty consumer today drinks more Coca-Cola than the over-forty did ten years ago, than the over-thirty did ten years ago. Today, the senior citizen now drinks much more soft drinks than the teenager did thirty years ago. Don't hold me to those numbers.

Per-capita consumption in the United States is over 300. That means that every man, woman, and child in the United States drinks a Coke approximately once a day. Think about the potential if we could generate twenty percent of that in China, or in India, where we are just getting back in after having been thrown out. (India insisted that we give them our formula, that the state had a right to own a part of every foreign product that was sold within the country. IBM and Coca-Cola and one or two others said "goodbye" and left. And it has only been recently that we've returned.)

You talk about age as a category. Is gender a category? Has your advertising changed to take gender into account?

It has not. Coca-Cola is approximately 53 percent male and 47 percent female. Pepsi Cola slightly reverses that. Coke is a little more masculine, but it is not significant. Coca-Cola has always been a stronger, less sweet product than is Pepsi. So, we reason that since it is lighter, Pepsi is slightly more attractive to females. But, there isn't any real statistical significance to the difference.

What about marketing — are there some commercials that are aimed at women?

Absolutely. The more emotional the commercial became, the more it was attractive to females. Many of the commercials and the advertisements that we have done have tried to generate some kind of emotional strain, some kind of emotional grab. Some have been successful and some yawns. Pepsi had a commercial starring the rapper Hammer: when he picked up a Coke he began to sing "Feelings" and everybody sort of went to sleep, and then he picked up a Pepsi and all became jazz again. It was a jab at Coca-Cola, which has always tried to find some kind of emotional hook.

You said that emotional advertising is more interesting to women. How do you arrive at that conclusion?
They prefer that over something else.

What about class? What about income and educational levels? Can you differentiate on those grounds?
Coca-Cola has always been the great middle-class. We don't show very many people in mansions and we don't show very many people in the ghettos of Los Angeles either. But we do have specific campaigns aimed at both blacks and Hispanics.

Those are the images you portray on the TV screen. What about the people actually drinking it, are rich people actually drinking Coca-Cola in about the same proportions as . . .
No. The highest per-cap user of Coca-Cola is a young man about eighteen years old, white.

Does his young black counterpart drink different soft drinks, or drink other kinds of drinks?
He drinks more soft drinks in total than does the white, but a hunk of it is a flavor. He is more likely to drink an orange or a grape or something that's sweet. He's more likely to do that than your eighteen- or nineteen-year-old male, white.

Are there now more women and minority people in decision-making decisions? And if so, has it made a difference in market strategies and advertising industries?
There are significantly more women, especially in the marketing area. To-day brand managers, marketing managers . . . I would say the majority are women. Has it made a difference? Has the approach changed a lot? I'm not sure. It hasn't changed the kinds of things you talk about or the arguing and fighting over the right thing to do.

There are significantly more blacks than there were ten to fifteen years ago but still not enough. That's going to take more time. They are in such demand, the competition for them is so heavy.

Is that for reasons of tokenism or because they have something to contribute because they are black or from that culture?

That's a very good question. I believe they have something to contribute, unquestionably. I also believe there's a political reason.

Could you say more about your research? When you interview people is it to find out how they use the product? Is it about their life-styles? Is it what they like in advertising?

It is an attempt to identify their attitude toward the product, the ambiance of the product, and their activities with the product. What do they do? How often do they buy? When did they buy it? Where did they buy it? How much did they buy? Who drank it? When did they drink it? Why did they drink it? Under what circumstances? The trick to selling Coca-Cola is to get it in the house, because it will move out. A case will move out of the house practically as fast as a six pack if it's there. If we can get three cases in the house they will go within a very small period of time. So the trick is to have consumers stock an inventory — to increase how often they drink and how much they drink and when they drink it. And in the supermarket, what do those guys push? — suitcases (which are twelve packs), or they push two-liters, which go really fast. If I get a two-liter in that house, it's gone. Especially if it's a house with kids.

So, maybe you can tell us a little more specifically what kind of thing your research tells you that helps you get that extra ounce?

It tells me what kinds of packages they buy, tells us where they like to buy it, tells us price information. It tells us . . . you name it, it tells us.

Does it tell you more unconscious kinds of things? What sorts of needs they have that they might not be able to talk about?

We probe at that. Obviously attitudinal research is a lot tougher, but we do have a lot of information on attitude.

How successful has attitudinal research been in your opinion?

I think it's thin. I wouldn't identify it as a success. It has given us indications of where and when and under what circumstances. I remember one commercial we did where we got killed because they didn't like the guy's haircut. It was a great commercial. It was a guy who was on "Thirty Something" — long blonde hair. He was picking up his twelve-year-old daughter.

She had just finished her dance lesson and he was bringing her a Coke. It was an adorable commercial, but the consumer reacted negatively to his long hair.

How do you incorporate attitudes into worldwide patterns?
In terms of our target group, which is really thirteen to twenty-nine, we have found that there are so many more similarities worldwide than differences that we can almost ignore the differences. That's what made our global pattern advertising successful, that recognition that in the last ten years teenagers in Great Britain or Germany or the United States, or some other place, had much in common.

What role has Coca-Cola played in creating a situation where teenagers, and people across the globe, are that similar, homogenized?
I suspect some. I don't know how much. We have never tried to create trend. We have tried to reflect. We try not to be ahead of the game, we try to be in the game. We try to make Coca-Cola new to each generation. That's why in the 1973 to 1974 period, when the country was in a blue funk, we came out with our campaign "Look Up America." We try to deal with situations as they exist, and respond to them.

Did your interviewers ask people at that time, "How are you feeling about your country," and so on?
Yes. "How are you feeling about yourself, what's bothering you?"

You said something earlier about keeping the system enthused. I assume you mean your own system — the distributors, franchises. Is that a part of your advertising campaign? Are you thinking, we've got to get our people on line?
There are two things that will trigger enthusiasm within the system. Number one is a first-rate piece of advertising that they like and that they sense the consumer likes and sells product. And the other one is a first-rate new product. There's nothing that will galvanize a bottler system more than a successful piece of advertising, or a successful new product.

Take one advertising campaign that you are familiar with and walk us through the decision making.
The most successful campaign that Coca-Cola has had in the last fifty years — and we've had a series of good ones — has been "It's the Real Thing."

That's because it was able to identify to the consumer — to signal — a uniqueness, a difference or specialness about Coca-Cola. It was introduced in 1968 and it lasted until I went to Houston in 1975. "It's the Real Thing" differentiated Coke in the mind of the consumer. In effect it said, hey, this is the gold standard, everything else is an imitation. But it also did an enormous amount to trigger the system, the bottler. The bottler felt that he had found a hook, something that only Coca-Cola in the soft drink business could sell. We kept jazzing it up. For example, "Look Up America" was really an adjunct of "It's the Real Thing." It was sort of an additional execution of it.

Was it after the introduction of the other Coke?
Yes. As a matter of fact it was. It was the attempt to communicate again that Classic was really the original Coke — it is the real thing — it is the gold standard. We brought it back.

How did you make that decision?
To bring it back? That was a very easy decision. We'd have been massacred had we not brought it back.

I mean the decision to bring back the advertising slogan.
Obviously we did a good deal of research. We tried to find out what would trigger, on the part of the consumer, an understanding of what Coca-Cola Classic really was. And by reintroducing, if you will, the campaign "It's the Real Thing," we were able to communicate to the consumer: This is really the same old good stuff!

Were people switching to Pepsi?
Yes, they were switching to Pepsi. And they were primarily switching because some liked the sweeter taste better. It wasn't as strong. It wasn't as . . . Remember "The Pepsi Challenge"? The reason "The Pepsi Challenge" won was because it was a sweeter drink. Now if you are doing a test where the product is delivered over a period of, let's say, thirteen weeks, over time Coke will win. But on a simple taste-test, the sweeter drink will usually win. Our feeling was, and we read the research wrongly, that the American palate was going for lighter, sweeter, drinks. And all of our indicators were slowly sliding. For the first six to eight weeks, New Coca-Cola sales were up, obviously a function of trial. Even people who never drank a Coke wanted to see what the New Coke tasted like. And then of course the hysteria seemed to take hold, and people stopped buying Coke out of principle.

How geographic are Coke sales?

Oh, very geographic. West Virginia, Kentucky, Tennessee, New Orleans, Texas, Georgia, Alabama, okay, that is Coca-Cola country. Rome, Georgia, has a per capita of 600 per person. They take baths in this stuff. I don't know what they do with it but they buy the hell out of it. Texas, I can't tell you how much Coca-Cola we sell in Texas. The West Coast is essentially Coca-Cola. Coke/Pepsi would be like a 53/47 split — very close. The same thing is true in the Northeast where it's — let's say it's 50/48 — I'm not exactly sure what it is. I think we have a lead in that part of the country. Western Pennsylvania, Michigan, Ohio, Illinois, Indiana, Minnesota — that's Pepsi Cola country — the area of the country where they call it "pop." Now central Florida is an island. Pepsi gets a split down there. In southern Florida (Miami), with the influence of the Hispanics, it comes back to Coca-Cola, because Hispanics are heavy Coca-Cola users. Cuba was a fantastic market. All of Latin America, except Venezuela! Brazil, we outsell them twelve to one. Argentina, Chile, Bolivia — you name it — the whole Latin American and Central America continent is Coca-Cola. So whether they come up from Mexico (in Mexico Coke is eight, nine, ten to one over Pepsi) into Texas, into southern California, or into Florida . . . wherever Hispanics are, you are going to find Coca-Cola a heavy favorite.

NOTE ABOUT IRA C. HERBERT

Ira C. "Ike" Herbert began his career with the Coca-Cola Company in 1965. During his twenty-seven years with the company, among several positions, he served as chief marketing officer and later as president of the North America Soft Drink Business Sector. He retired in 1991, and passed away on March 4, 1995. His views on The Coca-Cola Company from 1965 through the 1980s offer a unique historical perspective.

Strauss Zelnick Twentieth Century Fox

November 20, 1992

. . . .

At the time of this interview Strauss Zelnick was president and chief operating officer of Twentieth Century Fox, a major producer and distributor of motion pictures. Currently he is president and chief executive officer of BMG Entertainment North America, a leading media company with interests in recorded music, direct marketing, music publishing, video, and interactive entertainment. Prior to joining BMG, Mr. Zelnick was president and chief executive officer of Crystal Dynamics, Inc., a leading producer and distributor of advanced-platform video games. Mr. Zelnick holds degrees from the Harvard Law School, the Harvard Graduate School of Business Administration, and Wesleyan University. He lives in New York with his wife, Wendy Belzberg, and their two children.

Twentieth Century Fox is one of the six or seven major motion picture studios in America — in the world. The company was founded by a merger of the Twentieth Century Film Corporation and Fox Film Corporation in 1935. And the Fox Film Corporation was founded in 1915. Today the company is a division of Fox, Inc., which has four lines of business: Twentieth Century Fox, the film company; Twentieth Television, a television production and distribution company which also performs free television distribution services for Twentieth Century Fox; Fox Broadcasting Company, which is the Fox network; and the Fox station group. Fox, Inc., in turn, is a division of News Corp., which is a company controlled by Rupert Murdoch and is primarily in the business of publishing and television.

Revenues for Twentieth Century Fox come from the production and distribution of motion pictures, both our current lineup and our library. Fox has one of the three great motion picture libraries. There are about 2,500 feature films in our library. About half of those are actively licensed at any given time and generate income for the company.

The main determinants of profitability in the movie business, as in any business, are costs and revenues. There are different kinds of costs, overhead cost and product cost. In the movie business, overhead cost is important. As a very mature industry, our margins are thin, and if you spend too much in overhead, you can never make money. Fox has far and away the lowest overhead of any of the major studios. Obviously, more important determinants of profitability are on the revenue side. A rule of thumb is: "If the business side of the company is run effectively and the creative side of the company is run poorly, then you will fail. If the creative side of the company is run well and the business side of the company is run poorly, you will succeed. And if both sides are run well you will succeed greatly." So it is a unique business; if so many movie companies seem to be so poorly run, it is because at the end of the day it doesn't really matter. Of course, it matters in bad times, but if you are well run, you've planned for them. You financed for them, you capitalized for them, and you know how to get through them. Obviously, the better run you are in the good times, the more money you will collect. That is why so many things that seem odd businesswise take place in the movie business: because hits cure all ills. In the absence of hits, nothing you can do in the structuring of business can solve your problem.

How difficult is it to know in advance what your revenues are going to be?
Budgeting is an odd science in the movie business. We are actually getting better at it. Over a yearly period, you can hold still your level of production and the level of investment in production, marketing, and overhead. What you can't hold still are your revenues, unless you have a couple of sequels in a year.

You said if the creative side is run well the business will succeed. What does it mean to run the creative side well?
That is a hard question. I think that you need to have a philosophy of production and to apply it with discipline. But there is no magic philosophy. Year in and year out the studios that perform well make a lot of money on about 20 or 25 percent of their pictures. Twenty or 25 percent lose money, and the rest break even, so by definition, you wish you hadn't made three-quarters of your release schedule. So it is hard to talk about a creative philosophy that leads to success. I think Fox has a pretty good formula, but it is not very different from anyone else's formula, so it is all in the execution. Our formula is: One, all movies need to be story driven, but lower budget movies really need to be story driven; two, higher budget movies can be star driven and story driven; three, never make a movie that is neither story driven nor star driven, or an expensive story-driven movie that is not also star driven. That doesn't tell you anything, unfortunately; it all comes down to reading a script and making a decision.

How many new films do studios make each year?
Somewhere between fifteen and twenty-two.

Every couple of years certain majors say that their overhead is out of control and that the way to resolve this problem is by having more films to amortize their overhead. So they increase their volume and they end up losing a lot of money because the quality of the incremental volume is never as good as the quality of the initial volume. I believe that a studio maxes out at about twenty pictures a year, in terms of quality, unless you have more than one creative group. Disney, for example, has three studios but they are one creative group. Columbia has two studios but there is one guy at the head who at the end of the day decides what gets made.

Huge corporations that are based, or originally were based, overseas now own studios: News Corp. owns Twentieth Century, Sony owns Columbia, and MCA was recently bought out by Matsushita (now Seagram). Is overseas ownership affecting decision making at those studios?
Well, there are two issues, involvement of conglomerates in the business and foreign ownership. Let's start with conglomerates. There were two eras in the business, pre '46 and post '46. But the post '46 era didn't really have an effect on the ownership of the studios for about twenty years, when conglomerates began to take over studios. That is how long it took for everyone to get in real trouble. There is a range of reasons for the shift, including the Consent Decree, the significant decrease in the amount of production, and most importantly, the advent of television and other enter- tainment venues. So studios which pre '46 had a manufacturing facility that turned out fifty movies a year found that economically they could only turn out fifteen movies a year. It took them a long time to downsize. And then they found that, with competition from television and with talent no longer having a regular paycheck, they couldn't get away with making the kinds of movies they had made. When there were fifteen movies made a year, talent became independent and star talent became more expensive. Everyone felt that they needed to make star movies, and all of these factors together made the business much more risky, and gave studios a much lower revenue base. So the studios started taking bigger risks, without realizing it. By and large, they weren't run by businessmen, but by the old guys who had been ac- customed to a business where they could make mistakes and lose money; on balance it was still good business. When virtually every major studio almost went bankrupt in the '60s, they recognized that a very volatile cash flow was associated with the business. And so, either studios diversified and became

conglomerates themselves, like Twentieth Century Fox, which got into real estate, soft drink bottling, television, and other things, or they were bought by conglomerates. We still need to be owned by conglomerates.

The bulk of our business is distribution. Probably three quarters of our employees are involved in generating revenues. Out of the other quarter, most are involved in counting revenues, and then we have about twelve people who are involved in actually making movies. The bulk of our business is financing, distributing, and accounting. We have a huge staff that does nothing but license our pictures in all markets around the world. So to give you an idea, the video division is responsible for distributing new pictures but they are also responsible for distributing catalogue pictures. And we have those people domestically and overseas. The same thing holds true for every medium that exists and for some media that don't exist yet.

How much of the business is foreign?
The revenues on the catalogue pretty much track the product revenues domestically, so it is now basically 60–40 domestic to foreign. It will be 50–50 in the near future. It makes sense, right? The U.S. population is a small percentage of the world's population, so as we increase the quality and the breadth of our distribution, then our revenues should shift more to international revenues.

Is the international market influencing production decisions at this point? Or do you still pretty much produce for the American market and just try to make whatever you can off of the overseas market?
The international market has definitely influenced production decisions. But that has been true for a long time. Certain films still get made specifically for the American market. But, again, the creative side of the business tries not to be driven by the business side of the business. As soon as you get into formulaic decision making, you are going down the wrong path. Some people may say, "Let's make a movie for the world market; we will get a French actress, a British director, and Tom Cruise will star in it." And suddenly you are making a deal rather than a movie. That is a disaster. What tends to happen instead is we have a creative process and when it comes to a decision point you'll look at the project and ask, "Can we make this, is it commercially viable?" And one thing that may come up at that point is, will this work in international markets as well as domestic markets? For example, we made a picture called *White Men Can't Jump* even though we suspected that it would not have an international market. We made it

anyway because we thought the domestic market was big enough. We are making a picture called *Rising Sun*, which we specifically tailored to an international market in the way we cast it and the very decision to make it.

What makes you think that something is or is not going to be viable in the international market?

That's a good question, but it gets dicey because you can end up with cliches, such as, action adventures always work overseas, which they don't; or domestic comedies never work overseas, which they may. But certain things you know about. Movies starring black people often don't work overseas. That's a problem because it does influence investment decisions. But it is a fact, albeit mutable, like every other fact. I think we have an obligation to try to change it, and our studio has tried. But we have a unique ethnic population in this country. Other parts of the world are more homogeneous in their racial populations. People in Japan do not tend to go see a movie with black stars unless it is an action movie. Our black subculture, which is reflected in most of our movies, makes little sense to the rest of the world. Also, we tend to make a lot of comedies where the humor comes from ethnic issues that mean nothing overseas.

Can you identify principles that might influence success on the international market?

Sure. Anything that is really verbally driven won't work, especially comedy. You can translate most dramas, but not all. *Ordinary People*, for example, was a huge hit here. It didn't work overseas because they couldn't imagine what all these rich Americans were upset about. *Kramer vs. Kramer*, same thing. So, that is one problem. Comedies that are verbal don't translate to many cultures, and we do dub or subtitle our movies. *Home Alone*, for example, worked in Japan because it is very physical comedy, but an American comedy of manners is going to have real trouble in Japan. The bulk of our market is culturally similar to the United States, except for Japan. But Japan is our largest market after the United States.

How do movie makers think about audiences domestically?

We tend to think about it more after than before the fact. I think when you start thinking about creating something for a particular audience you are already going down the wrong path. I do not believe in underestimating the intelligence of the viewing public. I think people smell quality, so you can't take a bread and circuses approach to the audience.

Right before we make the decision to go ahead, we will ask ourselves who is our audience for this movie, and the biggest part of our market is the youth market: people under the age of twenty-five. Although all kinds of people consume movies, young people drive the business. And then there are certain ethnic groups. But at the end of the day, you make your real money when you have the broadest possible market. And you get the broadest possible market by making movies that are great stories. You may justify your decisions by thinking in terms of niche markets, but I don't think the positive decisions are really made that way. It may work as an eliminating factor. You may say, this is a great little movie but who is it going to appeal to?

In the case of Malcolm X, *budget decisions were tied to whether or not it would cross over into a wider audience. Are there niche movies that have a particular budget figure? Or are you hoping for crossover in almost every film?*
In any one year, you know that certain movies won't cross over and you make them because you think they appeal to certain markets. We thought *White Men Can't Jump* would appeal ethnically and then secondarily to a youth market, which it did. We never thought it would attract an adult market, and it didn't. You have to spend less money if you think you're niche marketing. But the nature of our business is that you spend a fixed amount of money on a product and you sell it to lots and lots of people.

What other categories are important for you in making these decisions?
There aren't really that many categories. The list would be international markets, domestic ethnic markets, and youth versus adults, and to a lesser extent, male versus female.

Could you talk a little bit about gender categories? How do movies like Fried Green Tomatoes, Thelma and Louise, *and* In a League of Their Own *come to be made?*
I think you are going to be hard pressed to find anyone who will tell you the reason *Fried Green Tomatoes* was made is because there is a big female audience out there. That picture got made because some people said this is a really great story that needs to be told and there will be an audience for it because it is a great story. And there was. Ditto *Thelma and Louise.* Does society's changing perception of women influence the kinds of movies that are made? Sure. Just like society's changing perceptions of African-Americans or Asian-Americans will be reflected in movies. And presum-

ably, movies' depiction of those people may have an influence, although I believe a limited one, on people's perceptions of those groups. But that's different than deciding to make movies for particular groups. *League of Their Own* was developed at Fox and ended up being made at Columbia. So I can tell you specifically — we were aware that it was a female-oriented movie but that wasn't why we were interested in it. We wanted to make it because we thought it was a great story.

Do you do audience studies after the fact?
Absolutely. Once you've finished a movie, you've got something that people can look at and you can actually do pretty good research on who is and is not going to like it. It doesn't necessarily tell you who is going to go to it, by the way, but it does tell you how they are going to feel about it if you can get them in the door. In other words, we can research playability, not marketability. Ever since 1920, people have been trying to figure out a formula for making a hit movie. And I repeat: there is no formula. If you go out to an audience and you research concepts, for example, all you will find out is that they will pick the concept that they are most familiar with. That doesn't tell you anything about making a movie. The problem is that no one component of a movie is a movie. I could give a script to a broad audience and say read this and pretend that Ray Liotta is in it and then tell me whether or not you are going to go see it. And Ray Liotta is not in it, now tell me whether you are going to go see it. And I would get a broad range of results because everyone has read it and put their own impression on it. But once you make a movie, your band of interpretation narrows because it's right up there on the screen, and people tend to agree on what a good movie or a bad movie is.

Sequels are popular because they are the safest part of our business. There was a period of time when sequels weren't doing well because people were making rip-off sequels. *The Sting* was a great movie, but *The Sting II* was like a TV-movie version of *The Sting*. That kind of sequel failed, but the sequels people are making today are remakes, more than sequels. The same cast, the same director, same writer — the same movie. The same movies do tend to do well. Now *Home Alone* was the third highest grossing movie of all time. And the sequel won't do that well. But on pictures that perform in the $150 million box office range, you could expect to do very nearly as well. We're making two sequels which I'm convinced will do better than the original movies. We're making a sequel to *Hot Shots* that I'm sure will do better because *Hot Shots* was released at a very competitive time. [It did do better.] And we're doing a sequel to *My Cousin Vinnie*. *Vinnie* was a good little movie, but it worked only in specific areas of the country. It worked so well in those areas that it was successful, but now the rest of the country knows about *Vinnie* and has accepted the character, and I think a sequel will be more successful. [The sequel was never made.]

I am curious about the strange space occupied by airlines and hotel pay-per-view, where you essentially have captive audiences. Does that particular segment have any kind of impact on getting movies viewed that otherwise might not be viewed? I just saw Prelude to a Kiss *on a flight, and I wouldn't have gone to see it in a theater.*

There are no markets that rescue you from failure. Your value in all markets tracks your value in your primary markets. There are some films that might do a little better in the secondary market than they ought to, for example, action pictures. But you are talking about a fifteen percent difference. Airline sales will pretty much track the success of the product. However, major studios have relationships with the airlines and we can go to them and say, "Look, this is an inoffensive film that your audience will like." Remember, the airlines don't like bad language, sex, or violence. They are essentially running TV movies. So a picture like *Prelude to a Kiss*, which doesn't have any of that and has two stars and is a sweet little picture that everyone can watch, is easy for the airlines to put on. Hotel/motel pay-per-view is different because that is essentially a softcore porn business. When you go to a hotel room and you see ten movies on Spectradyne, you'll see two softcore porn movies and eight current theatrical movies. People watch the softcore porn movies. The current movies are basically just there for show. Another interesting fact about airline sales is that movies set on airplanes where the experience is not particularly good won't sell. So, for example, *Die Hard II* didn't get sold to the airlines. *Passenger 57* won't get sold to the airlines.

When there are commercial airlines in the picture and the logo is visible, other airlines may not run it. For example, _____ Airlines is tied in to _____. So if you go watch the movie on a plane you will see that you can't make out the logo because we had to fuzz it out. Now _____ takes place on _____ and we can't really fuzz it out. There is too much of the airline in it. We can show it on _____, but that is a small part of the market. So we will actually lose out on the rest of the market unless we can figure some way to cut out the airline, which I don't think we can. We knew it up front, we tried to solve the problem and we didn't.

Did you make a deal with _____ ?
Yes. Essentially, they provided tickets.

If you didn't get much out of _____ from doing the placement, why would you identify it so centrally in the film?
Because we had a director and a writer who wanted a real airline, not a generic one. At that point it could have been any airline.

Is product placement the mark of authenticity rather than a money-generating device?
We could talk for hours about product placement. Recently, a lobbying group got very upset about product placement. They didn't realize that we *have* to put products in the movies. Movies look fake without products. We are not out there trying to run advertisements in movies. The business is way too big for that. We don't get much for product placement. In an average picture with a $20 million budget, we may get $100,000. So it is not going to change our decision one way or another.

The home video market has literally exploded now. What effect does that secondary market have on decision making, if any? What are some films that you know will do well in a secondary market that might not do well in the theaters?
Video is now our largest single revenue source. Bigger than theaters. Having said that, because video is released after theaters, the success in video tracks the success in theaters like every other market. Certain pictures outperform in video, but that would never induce you to make a picture because if it fails at the box office, video will not "fix" the failure. A movie will perform in video in accordance with its performance at the box office, which means you won't make enough money to justify the decision. However, certain genres work better in video, like action adventure. For a while, horror was working better in video. And certain genres work less well in video.

Intuitively, I would have said action adventure won't work well because you need the big screen, and intimate little movies will do better on video.
It has to do with who is renting videos: teenagers. They are not going to rent intimate little movies, they are going to rent action adventure movies. The quality of the experience isn't as good, but the rental decision that drives our business now is a teenager/young adult decision, by and large.

Although the last couple of questions made it clear how complicated a full answer will be, how do you conceptualize your product? Are there any universalizing ways that you think about what sorts of experience you are selling to people and what it is exactly that people get out of movies?

Besides providing entertainment, movies are part of the activity of dating. You can consume pure entertainment at home as easily as in a theater, but the theater offers a social experience, and there is something to be said for that. But does that influence our decision about the movies we make? Not really. Do we say, this is a great date movie? No.

Do you think at all about anxieties to which films might respond? In the case of magazines, for instance, many of the ads as well as the stories appeal to and promote anxieties such as "Do I have too much cellulite?" Is there anything comparable in movies? Do you think of people out there as having deep needs you could address, if never fully satisfy?

Well, magazines are a very different product than movies. As fiction, movies are more closely related to novels than to magazines or newspapers. And I would say there are universal themes. Most movies include love stories or a relationship of some kind. Movies that don't deal with relationships tend to have problems. But that is because human beings are fascinated by relationships.

The appeal of Home Alone *seems in part to derive from the anxieties of working parents over kids having to cope with being alone. Do current social experiences enter into thinking about movies?*

They did at the marketing stage because we had to worry about being socially responsible, but I would disagree with you. I think that movie appealed because it is great slapstick. We wouldn't have thought about being home alone twenty years ago because there weren't latchkey kids. So yes, the idea probably derived from the culture, but I'm not sure that the appeal did. I think the appeal of movies comes from the same elements that have always appealed in fiction. What we do is no different than what was done two thousand years ago. We tell stories. We just have a better medium for telling stories. To digress a bit, you might want to think about the phenomenon of interactive or multimedia. Everyone is saying how multimedia is going to completely change the entertainment business. Well, I say multimedia doesn't apply to the narrative entertainment business because the entertainment business is not interactive. It has never been interactive. It is never going to be. Games are interactive. Rides are interactive, but not entertainment. Storytelling isn't interactive. The storyteller sat there and told the story. He didn't stop the story and ask, "Should the princess live or die?" He said, this is what happens. The whole multimedia thing has to do with interactivity. People have tried interactive movies, the technology exists to do it. There was a movie made a couple of years ago where you could decide on the endings (*Clue*). The audience took a vote and you went to one ending or another. Everyone hated it. It's a game, not a movie. So I do not believe interactivity is what narrative entertainment is or is going to be about.

And yet Disney took their expertise at film making and used it to produce their amusement-park empire. Could film studios at some point put their expertise to work in the sorts of interactive games that are being debated?
Absolutely. I'm not suggesting that a new form of entertainment can't be created. I'm saying that you're not going to change the way movies are delivered. You may get smells or sounds or virtual reality or 3-D — absolutely; but I think human beings like storytelling in a certain form and there are limits on how that form can change.

I want to get to the question of social responsibility. What values enter into your decisions about making and marketing movies, and what internal or external pressures influence what can or can't be made?
It's true that we take account of the social environment within which we work. We don't only think about movies commercially. We think about them morally and ethically. The way I look at it, we have a First Amendment right to make whatever we want, but we also have an editorial responsibility. Now one person's editorial responsibility is another person's lack of responsibility. It's pretty subjective, but we do focus on questions of responsibility.

There are several points involved in the issue of responsibility. First, some people think that what we do affects society's values. I disagree. I think we've become part of the cultural vernacular but I don't think we create values. If, however, you believe we create values, then point number two is that we have a responsibility to create the right kind of values, and point number three is, why aren't you guys creating the right kind of values? I disagree with number one, thank God, because if it were true that we create values, then God forbid a fascist should take over one of these companies.

*Well, if movie people are discussing these issues, you must think what you do will
have effects.*

I think we believe we have an effect on the cultural vernacular. None of us
feels that we create values. We just feel that we have a responsibility to
do the right thing. If I said something really terrible to you, it probably
wouldn't change the kind of person you are, but it still wouldn't be the right
thing to do. Moreover, there are other influences on decision making besides putative effects. For instance, *The Last Temptation of Christ* was made
without regard to the fact that it might offend people and then it was pulled
because it did offend a small but vocal group. I'm not sure we would have
made the picture. Had we made it, I'm not sure we would have pulled it.
Probably we wouldn't have made the picture because we would have said,
this may really be offensive to people and why make something that is going
to offend people? Not that it's going to change people's minds about things.

I think you have a responsibility to think about what you are doing and
how you're portraying people and what message may be inadvertently conveyed, and to try to do what you believe is socially responsible. That is
different than saying that I am creating values and I want to make sure I
create the values I believe in. That scares the hell out of me. Luckily I don't
think it is possible to do. Once you get into the business of creating values,
you are out of entertainment and into propaganda. And people won't watch
propaganda.

What do you think about movies like JFK*?*
Pure entertainment. Specifically not propaganda, in my opinion. First of
all, it was a good movie, right? And second, it had great marketing. Stone's
whole approach to the assassination infuriated people who thought they
knew what actually happened, and the ensuing furor had a positive impact
on the movie.

*How can you separate being uncomfortable with the viewpoint from concern over
its potential effect?*
I didn't say it wouldn't have an effect. I don't believe we create values, but
we definitely have an effect. You create discussion, you create debate, you
create awareness. Lord knows, *JFK* created awareness.

*You are a participant in the cultural production of values. You tend to promote
certain things and not others.*

You are right, which is why I say we become part of the cultural vernacular. But does someone who condemns adultery go to a movie and come out saying, "You know what, it is not such a bad idea after all"? I don't think so. I think that is a value that you bring with you. I think we influence littler things, things that are on the edge, like styles of dress. People came out of *Annie Hall* saying, "Gee that looked good, I'd like to dress that way." That is what I mean by shaping the cultural vernacular. I think "values" is a word that means more to me than to other people. It certainly means more to me than to Michael Medved, who seems to believe that people walk into the movies thinking one thing and they walk out thinking another.

On the issue of gender, in The Devil's Candy, *Julie Salamon describes the making of a scene where Beth Broderick sits on the Xerox machine. According to her account, Brian DePalma was really disturbed by the scene and more generally, by the whole way women are represented in the movies. There was an article a couple of weeks ago in the* Times *Arts and Entertainment section about the ways in which women's bodies are displayed in films. In Hollywood, by and large, men have power as executives, as directors, as writers. Do you think that this leads to a certain exploitation of women? Would things change if women were in positions of power?*

Interesting. In the book, they xeroxed a man's genitals, not a woman's. I guess the answer to that question is yes. If there were more female executives in power, I think they would be more sensitive to those issues than some of the male executives are. Interestingly, most development executives are women, though. So most of the people who get a script to production these days are women, not men. There are more men in decision-making positions; there is only one woman in such a position today. But yes, by definition, where you come from influences your sensitivity to particular issues. And sex sells, and nakedness in the movies tends to mean women being naked — because men like to see women naked and women don't mind seeing women naked, but men don't particularly want to see men naked and women don't particularly want to see men naked in the movies, as it turns out.

You base that on what? Or is that sort of finger knowledge?

It is actually borne out in a lot of our popular culture. Consider pornography. Men consume pornography, not women, even though you could presumably make pornography that appeals to women. But men are the consumers of pornography in this country.

They got a lot of letters in response to that Times *article from women saying, "Come on! Women don't like looking at men? Why do you think Tom Cruise is such a star?"*

There is a difference between nudity and partial nudity. Look at the Chippendales phenomenon. Interestingly, the Chippendales don't take off their underwear. I'm no expert on the subject, but I do think there is a difference in nudity with regard to what men and women seem to want. We are talking about broad, general categories because our movies are made for the wide audience. So sure, there are lots of unserved segments of the audience who would disagree.

You said that most of the development executives are women now? Was that true when you first came into the movie business?

I would say that there are more women now, but development executives have had a lot of women in their ranks for a long time. Just like book publishing houses have had a lot of women editors — for a long time.

At what point do perceptions of macrosocial swings enter into the discussion?

I think people try to read trends, but it goes back to the first comments I made. Any time you try to do something that is driven from outside the movie you end up getting hurt. There is no doubt that certain events turn out to be bad for the movies and certain events are good. But no one is that good at predicting. I thought the presidential campaign was a good time to release *Bob Roberts*, although some people thought not. A picture called *Space Camp*, which was supposed to be released right around the time that the shuttle exploded, never got released because the timing was bad. But when you start thinking in such terms as, "Skateboarding is a real craze: let's make a skateboard movie," you tend to get destroyed. Someone once said, "A couple hundred million Americans go to the bathroom a couple of times a day, but no one wants to see a movie about it."

You think the same applies to dance craze movies?

Yes. By extension, you always get copycats. Everyone is always looking for solutions. So they say, "What worked in the past?" That has about as much success in the movie business as in the stock brokerage business. "What mutual fund earned the most in the past couple of years? I'll go with that one." And then the returns die. So *Dirty Dancing* works, we'll make a couple of knock-offs. There is a base audience and you get a few bucks, but basically, copycat movies don't work.

Sure, there are movies whose themes are related to what is going on, and I think they can have a certain influence. *Dirty Dancing* did create a dance craze; *Annie Hall* had a huge impact on the way people dressed for a long period of time.

Did movie people discuss the set of issues that have often been grouped together under the rubric of family values?
Yes, although I am not sure anyone knows what it means. Michael Medved spoke to a gathering of the senior executives at News Corp. Michael Medved, in my opinion, doesn't have his facts straight. For example, he claims that R-rated movies perform less well than PG-rated movies. So therefore why is anyone making R-rated movies? Of course, number one, he is wrong, statistically, and number two, correlation doesn't imply causation. To make that argument you would have to argue that somehow the rating of the movie affects its value, and of course there is no such correlation. The fact is that some people go see good movies, and some good movies are rated R and some are rated PG. I went back and studied Fox releases, and Fox's R-rated movies performed much better than PG over the past ten years. But does that mean that I am going to call everyone up and say, "Only make R-rated movies"? No. It just means that whoever was making the decisions about movies in that period tended to pick movies that were R-rated. And the movies that happened to perform well happened to be rated R.

Don't people want to get R ratings on their movies rather than PG?
Not really. You would rather get PG 13. A G is the kiss of death. PG is okay, but you would really like to have PG 13, because that means everyone can go see it, and no one will think it is too immature for them. But R cuts off a portion of your audience. On balance you'd rather not, but there are movies that you make that are R.

Most movies are R.
No, actually they are not. I think it is about 50–50. I do not believe that racy themes are necessary to telling a good story. There was a period of time in the '70s when everyone thought they were. That is another thing that people completely forget. Movies are a lot less racy today than they were twenty years ago. You never see male frontal nudity in a studio movie today. You did in the '70s. You rarely see full frontal female nudity today, although you do now and then. You saw a lot of it in the '70s. If you wanted to be

rated R, you had full female frontal nudity—in the late '70s particularly. That has changed.

If PG 13 is the rating that you want, to have the widest possible market, why do so many movies end up with Rs? For artistic reasons?
Because if you have more than four "fucks" in a movie, it is going to get an R.

Okay, but why have four "fucks" in a movie? Is that artistically motivated?
Because if you make [a movie about certain subcultures] you've got to have "fucks" in the movie for it to be realistic. So I guess the answer is artistic.

You remarked that the '70s were more racy than now. It seems to me that language has gone the other way. The number of "fucks" has increased.
Yes, we talk about it more now and do it less. And the stuff that is sexy is sexier.

Did anybody believe that because they gave Die Hard II an R, people under seventeen weren't going to see it?
Fewer people under seventeen go see it.

I don't think that is cutting off a big part of the market.
It is, and that is one of the issues. I sat down with a guy who runs a right-wing Christian organization that reviews all the movies and sends out a brochure and it goes to churches so that church leadership can tell their members what they ought to see and not see. It is scary, actually: they are not only opposed to sex, but they are in *favor* of violence, which I found very, very upsetting. The gentleman said to me, "I don't always think everything should be rated R; *The Last of the Mohicans*: that should have been rated PG." I said, "You see people's throats getting slit. You see blood everywhere. They tore a heart out." "Well," he said, "I didn't think there was anything wrong with that, for a broad audience." The group also found antiwar messages unpleasant. *For the Boys* had an antiwar message, so they felt that it was something that their constituency should avoid. They felt it was subversive.

There it is—and we're all part of the same culture.

Peter Sonnabend Sonesta International Hotels

September 24, 1992

· ·

Peter J. Sonnabend joined Sonesta International Hotels Corporation in March 1987 as vice-president and general counsel, after six years of practicing law in Boston. In May 1995 he was also named vice-chairman of Sonesta's board of directors. Mr. Sonnabend's responsibilities include overseeing the legal and administrative affairs of Sonesta Hotels, and participating in Sonesta's expansion activities. The company owns, operates, and licenses 18 deluxe hotels and resorts in the United States, the Caribbean, Bermuda, South America, and the Middle East. Mr. Sonnabend graduated from Wesleyan University in 1976, and from Boston University School of Law in 1980. He presently resides in the Boston area with his wife and two daughters.

Sonesta Hotels is a hybrid company. Sonesta started in the '40s when my grandfather began acquiring hotels. He was a successful business-man. He started in real estate and decided he liked to acquire things, in-cluding hotels. In 1956 he acquired a public company called Child's Restau-rants and merged his hotels into Child's to create a public company called Hotel Corporation of America, which was listed on the New York Stock Exchange. In the same year, he bought, among other things, the Plaza Hotel in New York. Soon after that, the Mayflower Hotel in Washington. Along the way, the company was associated with some of the world's great hotels: the Carlton Towers in London and others. In 1970, because the company had become quite international and was one of the larger hotel companies, the name was changed from Hotel Corporation of America to Sonesta — the word "America" was perceived as perhaps a disadvantage for companies operating internationally. Those were the Vietnam years and Americans were not looked upon so favorably abroad as perhaps we are today.

Everybody asks, "How did you come up with the name?" My grand-father had a cattle farm in Holliston, Massachusetts. He was not a rancher and not a farmer; he did it strictly for the tax advantages. His name was A. M., but his friends and associates always called him Sonny. His wife's name was Esther. So they called the farm Sonesta.

There was rapid expansion in the early '70s and there was also a recession, like now. In 1974 to 1976, New York City was an absolute basket case. You may remember the famous headline when Gerald Ford was President: FORD TO NEW YORK: DROP DEAD. It looked like the city was going bankrupt. We sold The Plaza Hotel for what was then an outrageously high price, $25 million. It sold about sixteen years later for $400 million to Donald Trump, but back then $25 million was an extraordinary price. Sonesta used the money from the sale of the Plaza to buy in stock. It was then a much larger company, and had expanded rapidly until it was in danger of losing some properties that it was developing. By buying in stock the family's interest increased from about twenty percent to sixty percent, where it stands today. But the company has become smaller. In the '70s, there was modest development. Properties were sold off; leases either expired or were terminated.

One of the trends in the hotel industry in the late '70s and early '80s was for companies not to own properties and not to lease properties, but to manage properties for others. The advantage to the hotel companies was that in managing properties and earning fees based on revenues, there was no risk. No matter how poorly the hotel performed, the management company received its fees. With a lease, of course, if you don't do well you have to come out of pocket to pay your rent. If you own a hotel, or any property, and you have a mortgage to pay, you can't say to the banker, "Well, I didn't do well this past month, let's roll the mortgage payment over to next month"; you would have to come out of pocket for the mortgage. But if you are just managing, you let the owner of the hotel worry about meeting his debt service obligations or his lease payments. This was a great coup for hotel companies.

So during the '80s we were looking for management opportunities and most of the hotels that are now Sonestas — from Portland, Maine, to Key Biscayne, Aruba, Curaçao, Egypt, and Bermuda — are management contracts. The only hotel that Sonesta owns now is the Boston hotel, in Cambridge. We lease our New Orleans hotel. The others are either management contracts or, in special circumstances, license arrangements. These are hotels that use the Sonesta name and reservation service, but we don't operate them, we don't own them, and we have no investment in them; we've agreed to let them use the name "Sonesta."

I started out as a lawyer in Boston with a small firm. I joined Sonesta about five and a half years ago as general counsel, vice-president, and secretary, and that's my title today. As an officer of the company, I get involved in development decisions, management contract decisions, I worry about a whole host of internal problems from SEC reporting, to employee benefits, to insurance, and, to a lesser extent, operations and marketing decisions.

One area of interest is what has happened in the real estate industry, particularly in hotels. As you are all aware, our industry has gone through a period now of three or four years of no growth, no development, no new hotels being created. In fact, many existing hotels are being converted to other uses or are being torn down. During the '80s, driven by the tax benefits of investing in hotels, properties were created for which there was no demand, and we are now paying the price with a tremendous oversupply of hotel rooms. Sonesta — we like to think it's to our credit, but it's probably because we didn't exploit the opportunity — was not grabbing up hotels the way others were then. We were not out there looking for any hotel — we do not operate suburban hotels, for instance, or highway hotels. Our hotels, we like to think, are a special collection, unique properties, in unique locations, and those hotels have done pretty well — even in these very tough times.

Are these always destination hotels?
Well, the resorts may be, but there are also city hotels: Boston, Portland, New Orleans. Certainly destination resorts would include Orlando, Key Biscayne, Aruba, Curacao, and the resorts we are creating in the Middle East, and of course Bermuda.

I'm interested in the story behind the Sonesta name because the marketing department could have come up with it. It sounds like "siesta" and it is not localizable. It's nicely generic. Do you hire market research firms to help you with names?
The name Sonesta was intended to create a unifying flag for our hotels. We wanted there to be a common marketing effort for all our hotels. You can only do that if they all have some common brand identification. So Sonesta was the name that was used. As I said, it's an international sounding name and we are an international company. It doesn't mean anything, and it's not going to offend anybody. In fact, people like it so much we found them using it on all kinds of things. A few years ago, I went into a market in Boston and bought twelve cans of Sonesta dog food. Not only had they taken our name, but they had copied our stylized lettering as well. It was pure piracy. Don't ask me why a company would want to pirate the name Sonesta.

And what did you do?
It happened that we had a Board of Directors meeting that day, and I put the cans right on the board room table. We wrote a very nice, but firm, letter explaining that we have service mark registration to protect the name Sonesta. This company was out of Puerto Rico and they agreed not to sell their dog food in the United States, but if you go to Puerto Rico . . .

What about the name Sonesta Beach — *the other names?*
That was really a marketing decision. The word "beach" is a selling point. It tells people who are going to a resort in Florida or the Caribbean that the hotel is on the beach. This is important from a marketing standpoint. If you have a spa or a casino, as we do in Aruba, as we do in Curaçao, it is important that you get that across in your name. We can compete better in resorts than in business hotels because the decisions people make to go to resorts are driven by different factors than when they go on business trips. If you are coming to Boston on business, you may decide that the Marriott or Hilton or Sheraton is just fine for you. They are fine hotels. They provide good service and you know what you are going to get. It is a cookie-cutter approach to hotels. And now with frequent traveler programs there are even more reasons to go to those hotels on business. But when you are taking your family on vacation, you're less concerned with frequent traveler programs and more concerned with where the resort is located, what kind of facilities it has. Is it on the beach? Does it have a pool, golf, tennis courts? Is there shopping near by? Are there things for your kids to do? We find that by having very fine hotels in good locations with unique facilities, we can compete well right next door to a Marriott, as we are in Bermuda, or a Sheraton, as we are in Key Biscayne. We can outperform them. We struggle with our city hotels. We do better with our resorts.

You're saying two things here: you have a special collection of unique properties in unique locations, but you are also saying that there is a brand name. What do you think that brand name reflects or suggests?
We like to think it suggests to travel agents, wholesalers, and to a certain extent, the public, that when they go to our hotels they're going to a place that will feature personal service, that will have very comfortable accommodations, that will reflect the area, the community. For instance, in Aruba, or Curaçao, or the Middle East, the hotels are not going to be Holiday Inns. They are not going to be Marriotts. They are not going to be boxes set on the beach or set on a hill — they are going to feature elements from the

community and from the area of the world where those hotels are located, either through decor or through facilities.

I guess what I'm saying is that we are selling experience. When you go to Aruba you don't want to think that you're in New York; you want to be in Aruba. You are going for an exotic experience. That's what we strive to provide.

Can you give us some ideas about specifically how that experience is created — for example, decor in Aruba? How do you generate the feeling that this is not simply a cookie-cutter franchise experience but something that distinctively reflects the locale?

The obvious things that come to mind for me are colors that you use. In Aruba of course they would be tropical colors. Menu items would reflect the local cuisine. Aruba and Curaçao, which are right off the coast of Venezuela, might be heavily oriented toward fish or Latin influences. Those are the types of things that you would find in the facilities. There might be local entertainment, or the hotel might provide transportation to points of interest and local attractions.

Is there a unit in the company that's responsible for making it into that kind of experience?

Absolutely. Sonesta compared to other hotel companies is fairly small, but we like to think that we provide the same services that the larger companies provide. For instance, we have in-house designers who design all our guest rooms, all our public spaces, all our meeting spaces, and for them using the local area, using fabrics from local communities is an important element of their design. You can hire outside designers, professional designers, and you may get the same product, but one advantage of having the services in-house is that these people know what would make this hotel a Sonesta.

So even though we have a unifying name for all of our hotels, when you hear the name Sonesta, if you know our hotels you will know that when you go to a Sonesta it will be a unique hotel that features decor reflective of the local community — the local experience.

Is this true of architecture as well? The New Orleans hotel is certainly idiomatic of the locality.

I'd like to say yes, but for us, because we are not actively developing hotels, we kind of take them as we find them. Often the developer or owner will come to us and say: "Look, I've got a great site. I'm creating a hotel in

Curaçao. I need somebody to operate it. Would you be interested? I know your hotel in Key Biscayne. I stayed there, and I loved it. I think you could do a good job." We take a look at it, and chances are he's already got the plans prepared, so we inherit a design.

But, in the case of Curaçao, we got in early enough. They had planned a high-rise hotel on the beach and we persuaded the developer to create a village-style hotel, low-level with no enclosed corridors. The guest rooms open up to the outside, and that's the type of thing that we think provides guests with an authentic Caribbean experience.

How much do you know about what people actually do think of the Sonesta? Is this strategy working? Do you test or measure the ideas your people have?
I'm not involved in that personally, but I'm told that we do market research. Hotel people will approach a guest at the pool and ask them questions. In this way, we develop a profile of a typical Sonesta guest, and how that person heard about Sonesta. Generally, it's through travel agents. We cultivate our relationships with travel agents, so that when you enter a travel agency, and ask, "Where should I go on vacation, I'd like to go down to Florida?" they'll say, "Well there's a great hotel there, the Sonesta Beach in Key Biscayne. It's a fabulous hotel, with kids' programs, tennis courts, on the beach. You'll love it."

We develop a profile of our guests. We know where they come from, where they heard of Sonesta. We know how the reservations were made. But we probably are not nearly as sophisticated as a Marriott or a Sheraton in our market research. It becomes very expensive to use outside companies to do market research. Through in-room comment cards, you can do some in-house market research. You don't get as much information, but it's a lot less expensive.

Are there ever negative aspects of a site that you feel the need to work around? The things that come to my mind involve either an area that is so impoverished that you really want to restrict the interaction of hotel guests with the locality or areas where the culture is so unattractive to visitors that you might need to import or create something that's not there. Do you ever run into those problems?
I'm told that Jamaica, where I've never been, can be a hostile place for foreigners. One of the reasons that all-inclusive resorts became popular was that people were concerned about leaving the hotel grounds to eat, shop, or recreate. And in hostile environments all-inclusive resorts may have resulted, like ClubMed. I'm not saying that all ClubMeds are located in

hostile environments, but I know that a number of resorts in Jamaica are all-inclusive for this reason. We don't have any all-inclusive hotels, though we've thought about it.

Let me talk about Aruba. When we were first approached by a developer, the location of the hotel really turned us off because it was right in the town of Oranjestad. It's not a typical resort hotel; it's not on the beach. Most of the great hotels in Aruba are along a stretch of beach called Palm Beach, on the calmer side of the island. But this hotel was right in the town. He was thinking of it like a Holiday Inn, like a business hotel, not a resort, and we were only interested in it being a resort. The hotel was on the harbor so it at least had a water view. It turned out there was an island about a five- to ten-minute boat ride from the site. We told this fellow that if he could acquire the island, we could create a beach club on the island and we would be able to market the hotel as the best of all worlds. It was in the town, right in a shopping center, so it provided great shopping experiences for people, and yet you had an exclusive beach club. You wouldn't be on the public beach, but we could create a fairly spectacular beach club on this island. That's what he did. We run boats from the lobby of the hotel out through a canal into the harbor and out to this island. And, frankly, some people don't like it. Some people, especially if they have kids, want to just walk down, get into an elevator, be out on the beach and not have to worry about the boat ride. But some people like the boat ride, and it is a beautiful beach club. We created two beautiful beaches there, and there is now a wonderful restaurant and a tennis court on the island. It is called Sonesta Island!

It is a very nice resort experience for people — especially South Americans. Don't ask my why. They love to go to the shopping center in Aruba. Their idea of a great vacation is to go to Aruba and shop. They are not interested in being out on the beach or playing tennis or swimming. They just like to shop and eat. There is also a great casino. The largest casino on the island is part of the hotel.

We were initially very turned off by the site, but through creative thinking turned it into something that was marketable as a great resort.

There are many different reasons to turn down proposals. For every fifty proposals we get, if one of them happens we're lucky. I would say we turn them down less because of the location than because the financing just doesn't make sense. Somebody may have a lot of money and may want the ego gratification of creating a great monument, but we know that once we start operating a hotel the owner is going to look to us to make it profitable. The owner is going to have to pay debt service, and unless we feel that we can make the hotel successful we quite honestly don't want the aggravation. One of the luxuries of being in a family company is that we can enjoy the work we do, and we can strive to have fun in our work.

One of your questions is, "What else do you think about besides profit?" Well, in a corporation like ours, there are always competing values. You try to meet the values of your shareholders, who are really the owners of the company. You try to meet the needs of your guests. You want to try to attract guests, and you have to provide a good guest experience. You have to provide a gratifying work experience so you can hold onto good employees. Sometimes these values are in conflict and you have to find a happy medium. We are lucky because we're the owners in a sense, we're the employers in a sense, and when we take our families to our hotels we're our customers. But my point is that there is more than profit involved, and one of the goals is to have fun doing what we are doing.

Have you ever made a major error either in declining to take up an offer or in deciding to develop what turned out to have been a bad idea?
I honestly can't think of any development decision that was a mistake. I could tell you about a miserable experience that we had in Cambridge. We had a 200-room hotel on the Charles River in the city of Cambridge. If you are familiar with Boston you know that the Cambridge side of the Charles River, down by the Museum of Science, was awful, it was depressing. There was a Lechmere Sales there with some warehouses, but it was not an attractive area. The city obtained an Urban Development Action Grant to create the Lechmere Canal Project, to develop the area and make it something substantial and special. In connection with that, we had the opportunity to bid on a parcel of land adjacent to the hotel. We bid on the parcel, and we won the right to develop it. We intended to create another tower to our hotel, doubling the size from 200 to 400 rooms, with expanded restaurant and support facilities, creating a beautiful hotel. At the same time, the state and city were creating new highways around the area, and a huge mall was planned directly across the street with Lechmere, Filene's, and Sears as anchors. Luxury condominiums were being built on the river. The idea was to create something not quite like the Left Bank in Paris, but an area of the city that was unique and identifiable and would draw people. They thought they could change the name to "Cambridgeside." It was a lot more attractive name than "East Cambridge." The problem is that a lot of pressure was put on Sonesta to undertake our portion of the project as a way of spurring further development, and we completed our hotel years before anybody

else. So we were alone there, operating a 400-room hotel in the middle of a construction site for about five or six years. The roadwork was delayed, and the city and state didn't follow through on obligations. The mall project was delayed. It's only in the last three years that the area has been completed. It really is quite nice. If you go to Cambridgeside you'll see that the mall is beautiful, it's successful. And the luxury condominiums are fine. The area is quite nice.

So, it was not our fault and I can't say it was a bad development decision, but in retrospect we lost a ton of money because we took the lead and the development around us was delayed.

We do make mistakes. Let me tell you about a mistake we made in Orlando a couple of years ago. Every year we prepare individual marketing plans for our hotels, because we are small and don't do a lot of national advertising the way larger hotel companies do. In Orlando we had very good years in 1989 and 1990. We were able to achieve a high occupancy and a high average rate, and we were one of the hotels Disney recommended. A company called Disney Tours, which wholesales Disney packages, recommended us as one of the hotels off the Disney property, and included us in their packages. So we were heady with success from 1989 and 1990. We prepared a marketing plan for 1991 that sacrificed occupancy for a higher average rate. I don't know why we didn't see it coming — with 20/20 hindsight you could look back and second guess yourself. We made an awful mistake because we didn't see the recession coming, or the tremendous overbuilding of hotels by Disney. Disney has added two to three thousand new hotel rooms on the Disney properties, and let's face it, if you are going to Orlando and planning to take your kids to Disney World, you want to stay on Disney property. They created a lot of new hotels, the recession hit, and in 1991 we got creamed. We achieved the higher rate but at a tremendous cost in occupancy. So that was a very bad marketing decision that we made. It has since been corrected, and this year we will be more successful than 1991, but it took us a while to recover.

We haven't developed a new hotel in a long time and we haven't taken over the management of a hotel that we regretted. Our hotels have been operated as well as they can be and have been successful. In terms of marketing decisions, yes, we make mistakes and we try to correct those mistakes as soon as we can.

What does it mean to decide to trade off occupancy for higher rate? Do you change the room configuration — upgrade something to make it worth more?

There's a fascinating dynamic that happens when you prepare a marketing plan for a hotel. You look at your competition, and you see what they charge for their rooms, and the rack rate that you hear is often far from the actual average rate that the hotel achieves, especially when there is a lot of competition. In the past few years, during this recession, you call up a hotel and you ask, "What do you get for a single room?" and they will quote you maybe $150. But my guess is the average rate may be less than $100. If you were to take the time to negotiate with them on the telephone you could probably get a rate closer to $100 than the $150 they quoted you. They don't want to lose the business, and if you don't stay there that room goes empty. If they can get $100, they are happy and ahead of the game. So you try to find that happy medium: a high enough average rate with a high occupancy to maximize your profits. Based on your competition and other factors, you try to figure out how you can get the maximum occupancy at the maximum rate.

So it is entirely technical. It has nothing to do with the product? The product doesn't change?
No, it is absolutely supply and demand.

You mention that you've done some market research. Who do you think your customers are?
The way we design our brochures and choose the models — it is an interesting process, because conscious decisions are made about the types of people that we market to. When we go into a new area, when we are marketing an existing hotel, it's more reactive than proactive; one of the things you look at is the type of people who come to that area, you look at the type of people who are staying at your competition. Are they older people? Are they families? Are they single people? Some hotels just cater to singles; some just cater to couples; some are family hotels. In Orlando, for example, you have a big market for families. Very few hotels can survive playing to one market. In Orlando we play to families. We market to honeymooners. Orlando, I think, is now the number two honeymoon destination. Hawaii is number one and Bermuda used to be number two. Orlando is very popular for newlyweds. A lot of couples go there because Walt Disney World is as big an attraction to adults as it is to kids. Epcot, Universal Studios, MGM — there is a tremendous number of attractions in Orlando. And there is a convention center. Orlando is a wonderful hotel market; it is now the largest hotel city in the country.

So you look at who comes to that area and make your marketing decisions based on that. I know our company does not try to pioneer in terms of establishing a destination that is not well known. We just don't have the marketing power to get people to go to XYZ island in the Caribbean, when no one's ever heard of XYZ island. For example, we were offered a hotel in Bonaire. Does anybody know where Bonaire is?

Oh yes!
Bonaire is a wonderful island. It has the best scuba and snorkeling in this hemisphere. But unless you are a diver, you might not have heard of Bonaire. It's very small. It's difficult to get to. It doesn't have the airlift that other established destinations have. We found it tough to sell the island, and eventually gave it up.

You've described a marketing strategy tied to the market in specific locations. On the other hand, there is also the brand name Sonesta, and the notion that Sonesta has some sort of coherent identity as a hotel chain. Is there a group of customers that you identify for the Sonesta name in general? Certain people who would want to choose a place that reflects the local culture, the local architecture, et cetera? Or who would decide, let's go on vacation — what has Sonesta got to offer? Who are those customers?
For many of our hotels there are groups and businesses. We have regional sales offices in Chicago, New York, Washington, and Atlanta that do nothing but sell to groups. They go to meeting planners, large corporations, who are planning a conference or something, and say, "Come to our hotel, we have great conference facilities. We've got meeting rooms, we've got audiovisual equipment, we are in a unique location, you'll have a great time. You'll have meetings during the day; you'll be in the casino at night." To a large extent, when you have hotels our size — generally 200 to 500 rooms — you can take groups; so a lot of our business is groups. There is also transient business for resorts, and here we market more to travel agents and wholesalers than to the public. I don't think you'll see many Sonesta ads, certainly not as many as the larger companies, in magazines that you read. We don't have the budget to put expensive ads in those magazines. We think our money is better spent cultivating travel agents and wholesalers.

You say you have your own in-house designers, and yet you want to create something of the atmosphere of the place that you are in. Do you ever use architects or designers from the area you are developing?

I don't think so, although in planning the hotel in Curaçao, we did go out and meet local artisans. One of your questions asks how we use art in the hotels. It's not so much a marketing decision as that people in the company, including our chairman, collect contemporary art, so art is very important to him. We have art in all of our hotels, original works of art in the guest rooms. We think it is one of the things that distinguishes our hotels from other hotels. Instead of a picture of a ship on the wall, or a landscape of the 1800s, you'll see a work of contemporary art signed by the artist: generally a print, but often a unique work—a drawing or painting. If you look at our public space in Cambridge, for instance, you see fabulous pieces of art. In Curaçao, our chairman and his wife, who is a contemporary art dealer, actually went to studios on the island and met artists and bought art locally to put in the hotel. It's not only for atmosphere, although we think that is very important; it's also to help support the local economy and the local artists.

Do you have any feedback from your clients who use the hotels as to how they perceive the art? Do you ever hear what they think of it?
Yes. We have comment cards in all of our rooms. People say: "Loved the art work." Sometimes we get calls from guests, asking where they can get a particular piece. It doesn't happen often, but it does happen. And if you don't like the art, chances are you are not going to write on the comment card, "I did not like the art."

Really? People love to say what they hate.
More often it's service and food and other things. But people do appreciate the art. Especially if you are at all knowledgeable about art. Then you appreciate the effort that has been made in the hotels to furnish them with contemporary art.

I'm curious about what kind of contemporary art? Which artists?
Some names that you would recognize, and others that you wouldn't because they are younger artists. But certainly Johns, Rauschenberg, Stella. Anthony Caro has a large piece in the lobby of our Cambridge hotel. There are younger artists, Katherine Porter, Cliff Peacock, Aaron Fink, I could go on and on. Established artists are more in the public spaces, and works by younger, lesser known artists in guest rooms.

It seems as if people who choose a Sonesta Hotel partly for that reason, or come back again, would be people with a certain level of education.

I think so, but our hotels probably cater to a wealthier and more upscale client than other hotel chains. I doubt you would see good art in Red Roof Inns or Holiday Inns, or in more budget-style hotels. It creates an image, and image is important, and it's used that way.

Lots of travel writing suggests that people are not only after facilities and experiences. They are also after intangibles like aura, or prestige, or a sense of fantasy — in part, the fantasy of being for the moment in a higher class than you are, or being in an environment that is more elegant than you are used to. A vacation is the time to pretend to be somebody that you are not, so that you are buying not just what is actually for sale but something beyond that. Going to The Plaza — you think of yourself as a person who is going to The Plaza. The room may be tiny. The service may be subpar. But you have still been to The Plaza. Do you consciously sell things like that?

I don't know what people who are looking for that type of experience would come to our hotels. If you carry it to an extreme, there are hotels in the Catskills and other resort areas where they have fantasy rooms — you can be a cave man, you can be a woodsman, you can be back in prehistoric times. That's not what we're about, but I know they exist. I also know there are mega-resorts in Hawaii and elsewhere, with wild birds walking the premises, swimming pools stocked with porpoises, and other unique features — trams, monorails connecting parts of the hotel. That is very much a fantasy kind of experience, but that's not the type of experience we provide. We are not the Ritz; we are not the Four Seasons; we are not some of the five-star hotel chains; we are more of a four-star hotel chain. If you were really looking for that kind of experience, you'd go to one of those other chains.

I have a question about the hotel business in general, about the boundaries between industries, and the logic of crossover. You mention restaurants, real estate, and theme parks — is there another industry that also borders on hotels? Where are the tightest connections in the big chains, the Marriotts, for example?

Of course restaurants are unique because they are really amenities to our hotels. It is a selling point for a hotel to have a restaurant. You don't have to leave the hotel. Real estate might include golf courses or other recreational developments. Or the beach.

What about airlines? Is there much crossover in that direction?

You do promotions with airlines but you don't limit yourself to one particular airline. Cruise ships are an interesting element. They provide a boating experience along with a lodging experience. Yes, cruises I would say are a related industry more than airlines.

Didn't United Airlines own Westin at one time?
They owned Westin, but I don't think they did any special promotion, where you thought of that particular hotel chain. When you think of Sheraton, you don't think of going there and getting ITT telephone service.

I think at one time they also owned a car rental company. Some corporate planners were imagining a future possibility.
The marketing opportunity is there, but it would be very odd if Marriott acquired a rental car company and called it Marriott Rental Car.

This leads to one of the questions we asked you: How have the consolidations of the 1980s changed the hotel and resort business? It seems the answer for Sonesta is that you got less consolidated. But what about the whole industry?
A lot of mergers are driven by economics. The last four to five years have been a very tough time for hotel companies. A lot of them have filed for bankruptcy. Marriott almost went under. They put too much money into their hotels under the assumption they could sell the hotels and keep the management. When the market fell apart the Japanese stopped buying and Marriott couldn't sell those hotels. Just to stay alive, some companies have to merge. Merging creates larger reservations systems. It's been said in the industry for years that by the year 2000 there will be about four or five hotel companies, because the companies with tremendous marketing and reservations capabilities will just wipe out the smaller companies. We think we have a niche, but maybe we're wrong and maybe by the year 2000 we won't exist. These are tough times.

Do you have a direct competitor in your niche? Is there any hotel company that's directly comparable?
We try to identify Sonesta as a collection of unique hotels. When I think of chains that are comparable to us, I think of Doral Hotels, or Loew's perhaps.

Hasn't Radisson been selling itself on the basis that each of their rooms is unique?
I can't believe Radisson would do that. Radisson franchises the name Radisson. They don't own most of their hotels, and they don't manage them. They are selling the name Radisson. If you make your hotel a Radisson, it

means you are part of a reservation system. Reservation feed is very important — it adds x percentage of occupancy to those hotels. I've heard these franchises described as insurance systems: you operate your hotel as you normally would and the Radisson name gives you a little cushion of occupancy. These are marketing decisions. We don't like to think of ourselves as being competitors with these companies; they are about totally different things. We are about personal service, and about managing hotels and creating value in hotels. We are not so much about mammoth reservation systems. That's a decision we've made. If we wanted to be a different company, maybe we would change all of our hotels from Sonesta to Radisson or Sheraton or Choice. These are huge systems that get chain feed. Maybe our occupancy would go up, but we wouldn't have as much fun operating the company.

Has anyone offered to buy you out? Are you a juicy plum?
No, I don't think we're a juicy plum. Occasionally, over the past few years, there have been little feelers put out, but it could hurt our business if it got out that the Sonnabend family is getting out of Sonesta. We would lose credibility with travel agents. So whenever we get those feelers we discourage them.

But let me make another point about consolidation. At the same time that we've seen consolidation in the industry, we've seen fragmentation or segmentation of the industry. Companies like Marriott have developed other brands, budget lines — Marriott Courtyards, Residence Inns. It's created a tremendous amount of confusion in the industry. Driving along the highway, you see a sign for a Residence Inn. You are going to be totally confused — is that Choice, is that Marriott, is that a Sheraton product? Is Residence Inn the one where I stay for a long period of time, or is that one where I get a low rate? Is there a restaurant in the hotel? I don't know. Is it a good place for my family? Some companies have six or seven different brands under different names, and it becomes very confusing to people.

Cookie-cutter chains market consistency. Travelers often want to know what they can expect. You are describing an organization that really tries to create a distinctive experience — whether it's the physical layout, the construction, the food, the art work, there's a continual emphasis on something that is different, that somehow reflects the environment. Yet don't there still have to be boundaries that mark off what is going too far? For example, it would be difficult to market the hotels if you didn't have air conditioning in Aruba, or if the rooms were located on

the central square of the city and one smelled the odors from the marketplace, or if
the food was too spicy, or if the art work was too avant garde. How do you manage
those boundaries? How do you decide the difference between that which is
distinctive and that which might actually drive away customers? How can you
give them something both distinctive and predictable?

You are going to expect maid service, expect there to be a telephone, expect it to be clean, expect towels, running hot and cold water — certain basic things that you have to provide because your competition provides them and because your customers expect them. And as technology changes, your customers will expect you to keep up with it. If your competition now has two telephone lines in each room, maybe you've got to have another telephone line as well. If, instead of keys, the technology for security now is to use keycards, that's what you have to do.

There are resorts that provide a totally different kind of experience; you may get a higher average rate by providing less. This past spring, I took a trip to California with my wife. As we were driving up the coast from Los Angeles to San Francisco, we stopped at a place called Ventana. It has 56 rooms, and it's in the hills overlooking the Pacific Ocean just south of Carmel. It's a spectacular setting and you really have the feeling that you are out in the wilderness. The rooms are done in clusters — clusters of units. Some are larger and some are smaller and some have whirlpools with Jacuzzi, some have fireplaces. I think they all have telephones in the rooms, but who are you going to call there? You are there for the experience of being up in the hills. It is a very quiet, serene environment. You may have daily maid service, but you are not going to get room service, you are not going to get a choice of four or five different restaurants. There is one restaurant. They get a very high average rate for this tranquil, beautiful environment and yet it is almost a camping experience! You are away from it all. It's a very popular place, a very beautiful setting. By providing less they may get a higher rate. It's an aura — the prestige element.

How do you draw boundaries when it comes to art? A lot of original pieces of art
might not fit into a hotel room, but other ones do. How do you make those sort of
decisions?

A lot of it is just cost. One of the great things about the type of art you find in our hotels is that it is of high quality — but not art you are likely to find in a museum. It is original art, and it doesn't cost much more than those fluky things you find in other hotel rooms. But cost is a major consideration. You have a certain budget. If you are planning a hotel development or refurbishing a hotel, can you make back enough money to support the cost of creating that room? The decision to put in two telephone lines, or better quality art, or tapestries on the walls, or expensive wall coverings as opposed to painting — a lot of these decisions are driven by cost and whether you can make back enough to support that cost.

How important is it to have TV in the room, particularly at the non-American locations?
There may be some very exclusive resorts with very high rates, where you are paying for absolute tranquility, and they don't have televisions. But all our hotel rooms do because our customers expect it. Even when they go to a place like Curaçao, and are going to be out of their room most of the time at the beach or at a casino or nightclub, they expect there to be a television. Even if they don't turn it on once, they expect it. They feel they are paying for it. In terms of keeping up with technology, people now expect that no matter where you go in the world you are going to be able to watch CNN. That's a given now, and you better have a satellite dish that gets CNN.

Most of us know travelers who, no matter where they are in the world, insist on eating steak. Does Sonesta cater to those people, or do you take your local color so far that when you are in Aruba you basically have to eat local cuisine?
You have to look at what your market is. If your market is Americans, you have to serve hamburgers. If your market is more South American, maybe you would serve a different cuisine. If you have one restaurant you better serve a wider range of items in it. If you've got three or four restaurants, then you have the option of specialty restaurants that serve only a particular kind of food — maybe a sushi bar, or Chinese, Italian, whatever. In our hotels, a lot of our clientele is American — though in Aruba it's maybe only twenty or thirty percent American. But that's the thought process going into planning a menu.

You say that cost of art is part of the consideration, but part of it must be something else — Johns, Rauschenberg, those are obviously valuable works?
Not necessarily the pieces that we hang. In the lobby in Cambridge there's a large Frank Stella print. There's also a large Anthony Caro sculpture which might be considered museum quality, but that's really kind of a special case: Joan Sonnabend deals in contemporary art and has either loaned a piece or sold a piece to the hotel.

But there are other alternatives in contemporary art that would cost the same but might be too eccentric or too controversial. You wouldn't put Andreas Serrano in there, right? And you might not do something as radical with your decor as the Royalton in New York. Is there some conscious mechanism by which those boundaries are set?

It is more intuitive. There may be a temptation to go way out like the Royalton did, but it's risky. It's expensive, and you are going to lose some people. If somebody came to us and said, "I'm planning a hotel and I want all minimalist or conceptual decor," Roger Sonnabend would probably think that was the most wonderful thing he'd ever heard. But he would have to say to that person, "I don't know that your hotel will be successful. I don't think it makes economic sense. I'd love to create it for you, but be prepared to incur heavy losses, because that decor, while you and I might like it, is going to turn off a lot of people."

How do you market to non-Americans, both coming to your U.S. hotels and to your properties outside of the United States? Is that done differently? Do you see yourself expanding in that market?

We have a sales office in Amsterdam, a holdover from the mid-'70s when we had a wonderful hotel in Amsterdam that we sold last year. We don't have sales offices but we have sales representation in South America. It is very important for the Aruba and Curaçao hotels. We also do a lot of South American business in Key Biscayne. We know from experience that people from South America are looking for different kinds of experiences than people from the Northeast. Shopping is very important, and playing the casino in Aruba and Curaçao is very important for Latin Americans. Not that Americans don't gamble, but there seems to be a greater passion for it in South America.

We do market research among the guests at our hotels, foreigners as well as Americans, and we have a sense of what those people are looking for, what they want. For instance, Europeans are used to larger bathrooms than Americans are. If you really want to sell the Europeans on the luxury level you've got to have spectacular bathrooms. It's a planning decision. What's your market going to be? That's always the question. Can you solidify your base market and then perhaps move outside?

I've always been intrigued by the internal dynamics of a family business. Is there a Sonesta family ladder up which people can climb?

This is a very interesting area. First, we are a family business and we like to represent ourselves to our own people as being a family business. Our employees are part of a family. And it just makes good business sense to cultivate labor and maintain labor. Now in some situations, in some positions like busboy or maid, you see a lot of turnover, and people burn out. But there was a woman who was a chambermaid at The Plaza Hotel for about fifty years, and when she retired they gave her a party — and it was the first time that she had ever been in the lobby of the hotel. The people who work for Sonesta understand that it's a family business, and that there are trade-offs to that. The good part of it is that they are part of a family and they are going to be treated with respect and dignity. The down side is that they are not going to be president of the company some day. We try to get our general managers to stay at one hotel. We don't move people around very much. We encourage our general managers to get involved in the community, to stay in the community for a period of time. In New Orleans, in Key Biscayne, those general managers have been there for ten or fifteen years or more, and they are very active locally. People know them. They are business leaders. They are community leaders. Their division heads, the people below them, are encouraged to get involved. When there are openings at other hotels, we look to people within the company before we go outside. It's less expensive, and those people have come to understand what Sonesta is all about and what our hotels are all about. So it makes sense to move them up. Unfortunately, we are not a big company. We can't promote everybody. But we do have people who have been with the company for many, many years who, believe it or not, are not family members.

It seems there is a kind of match between the distinctiveness of the hotels and the role of the family. Could you talk about that, and about the future of family-run businesses in this kind of industry?

It's a complex question; a whole industry has sprung up of family business consultants. We speak to them, we're interviewed by them, people try to sell us their services, and sometimes we hire them. Something like ninety-plus percent of all businesses in this country are family businesses. In our case, all I can say is that we have very strong leadership from the top. My father, who is the president, and my uncle Roger, who is our chairman and CEO, have been in the hotel business all of their lives. They've got incredible experience — over forty years operating hotels. So they know the hotel business very well. They are known and respected in the industry. They've got credibility. One thing that helps relationships with travel agents and other industry people is that they know you are going to be around. You're not going to be president of Sonesta one year and president of another company the next. There's longevity and there's security. So that's a big advantage for us in selling our hotels to the industry. A lot of companies have sprung up over the past few years. In the '70s there may only have been a handful of hotel companies, and now there are hundreds of companies that promote themselves as hotel operators. A lot of them are fly-by-night, and haven't been around very long. One of the things that distinguishes us in the industry is the fact that we've been around, and when you deal with us you are dealing with the same people you have been dealing with for years. And we intend to be around for a long time to come.

David Kendall Warner Bros. Television

November 30, 1992

. . . .

David Kendall was born in Philadelphia October 4, 1957 — the day Sputnik was launched into space and the day "Leave It to Beaver" premiered on CBS. Opting against a career as an astronaut, Kendall chose to pursue a career closer to the latter birth sign. He has worked in prime-time network television since 1985 when Warner Bros. hired him as a staff writer on the ABC hit situation comedy "Growing Pains." He eventually became producer of the show and in his six years there wrote over thirty episodes. Since 1994 he's been executive producer on Walt Disney Television's series "Boy Meets World," also on ABC. He is currently developing new shows for several networks and all told (as producer, writer, or director) has worked on over 240 episodes of television. He and wife Wendy Bishop live in Santa Monica, California, with their daughter Eve.

I graduated Wesleyan in '79. I was a film major and a government major. I worked in production jobs in New York City with an eye towards becoming a producer/director/writer. In 1983 I wrote and directed a low-budget feature film called *Luggage of the Gods*, a comedy. After two years of working on that movie I wanted a faster return on my efforts and decided to try television. So I sat down and wrote a sample television script on spec for the *Cosby Show*. I went out to Los Angeles for two weeks and I got very lucky: the first studio that read it hired me. So I was working in my second week in LA on this sitcom. I figured that I would be home in New York very soon because this sitcom was starring Alan Thicke* — it was called *Growing Pains*. I was on *Growing Pains* for six years, three as producer. I wrote thirty-two scripts. I am now in a development deal at Warner Bros. Television to come up with new TV shows. So I am a sitcom writer/producer.

Because of the tremendous demand for episodic shows and for scripts, if you are the writer and you do well, you can rise up the food chain pretty quickly and become a producer. I guess the bottom-line definition of a producer in television is someone who is in charge of the words. And that encompasses all kinds of things from casting to set design. Really, a producer is an extension of the writer in television. If you have enough experi-

*Thicke had just come off a high-profile failure hosting his own talk show.

ence in writing and producing, you get this kind of credential as a "show runner." Like so much in Hollywood it is perception driven. If you are around in cool circles long enough, in a cool show, and people at the network say, "Well, he's a show-runner," you are a show runner. I think of Martin Mull's great line: "Show business is high school with money."

A basic principle about network series television is that the studios sell, the networks buy. You asked what are decisions that Warner Bros. makes about programming. Basically, if they think they can sell an idea to one of the networks, they will be in business to make that idea. The studios own the product, the networks license it. When a show is produced by a studio it is produced at a deficit. In round figures, a sitcom episode costs about $600,000 to produce, $400,000 of which is paid by the license fee; the network buys two airings, a first showing and a repeat, and the studio owns it outside of those showings. Where that deficit is made up, we hope, is in foreign sales — or the pot of gold at the end of the rainbow — syndication. I was on *Growing Pains* for six years. I did 142 shows. There was another season after I left. There were 166 half-hour episodes of *Growing Pains*. It has accumulated sales of $204 million. If you figure it was deficited at around $35 million, you are talking about a nice profit! Even if you produce pilots and series that lose money, and don't make it to syndication, they probably don't lose money because of foreign sales. A studio like Warner Bros. can make $150 million off of a *Growing Pains*, and a similar amount from *Night Court*. I'm sure *Murphy Brown* will do all right. Syndication, that is where all the big money is.

Do you think about syndication early on in the process? Does it affect the way you might imagine a sitcom?
Not primarily; there are so many hoops to jump through figuring out what ideas will sell at a network that syndication is kind of low on the list. The television audience is the broadest audience you can try and hit; really the same thing for syndication, though there are more specific needs. Some rules of thumb are generally accepted, based on ratings and research — what a friend of mine calls the agreed-upon fiction of our industry. People say that in terms of picking what shows to watch, sitcoms are more female driven than male driven, and that syndication is more male and blue-collar driven. That is one kind of accepted approach. You don't really think about syndication as you are just trying to get an idea sold.

A little bit more about Warner Television: Time-Warner is this big huge thing and Warner Television is just one part. Competing with Warner

Television within Time Warner there are two other companies: Lorimar and a new production company studio, HBO Independent, an offshoot of HBO that is owned by Time-Warner. So, just within the Time-Warner family you have companies vying for spots on the network.

A trend that is an exception to the studios sell/networks buy rule is in-house production companies. A network is limited in how much they can own what they exhibit. But as the networks' fortunes and audiences decline, in-house productions will get the best time slots. They will protect their own because everybody wants to get these $200 million pots at the end of the rainbow. Before, the networks were making so much money that to take a chance and deficit a show made no sense.

A general observation on the dying days of network television: obviously, with all the competition, the audiences aren't what they used to be. A 30 share five or ten years ago could get you canceled. Now, a show with a 20 share is a big hit. I think that there will always be some form of network television, but I think they will evolve the way the dinosaurs evolved into birds: smaller, but still around. Development is still being done pretty much as in the old days when ninety-nine percent of homes using television were watching the networks. Until people figure out what the next thing is in television, they will continue to do it the same way.

About getting a show on the air, the traditional steps of development: it starts out with a pitch. A writer/producer will go and say, "Here is an idea for a TV show." You do a little twenty-minute song and dance — talk about the characters, the world, whatever — and the network will give you a thumbs down or a thumbs up. Thumbs up means they buy a pilot script. This is a chance to do in fifty pages what you think your show is going to be: create your world, your characters, tell a sample story. If they like it, you get a produced pilot: actors, cameras, guys who bring coffee, the whole big deal. You get to shoot and to have the real thing on film or videotape. When the networks make their schedules and decide what their needs are, you may get a series order, usually in units of six or twelve. If Kevin Costner decided he wanted to do a sitcom he could probably get twenty-two or forty-four episodes. To give you an idea of the odds, the networks (I am just guessing) will buy 125, maybe 150, scripts this year and make 35 pilots and order 10 or 15 shows.

There are all kinds of ways to jump through these steps. For instance, if Disney, who produced *Sister Act*, the big hit movie, wants to do it as a TV show, I'm sure they will shop it around to a network and see if they can get some level of commitment. Or if a TV star or a faded movie star decides they want to do a sitcom they can see if they can get a six-episode order or a pilot commitment or twelve episodes. Or if somebody like Sidney Pollack or John Sayles wanted to do something in television: it is funny how TV loves when people come over from the movies, like George Lucas doing the *Indiana Jones* thing for ABC.

Are there special conventions for writing a pilot script? Would it lay out the situation, try to show what an ordinary episode might look like?
Both. A pilot script is a tough thing to write because you are not just telling one story; you are setting the groundwork for a hundred episodes. You have to show a little bit of what the world is like. It's about, this is an interesting world, this is an interesting character.

What is a character? How were those characters in Growing Pains *pitched? How were they described?*
That is interesting. I think the way *Growing Pains* was probably pitched was: Remember the movie *Mr. Mom?* You see how successful Cosby has been. Okay. Here is a domestic sitcom. The wife is going back to work. She really cares about her kids but has this career drive that won't sit still. And here is this psychiatrist, this really wise, hip guy, and he is going to move himself back into the house and set up his practice there. They have three kids, one is a real wiseacre, one is kind of nerdy, and one is young and we will see which way he is gonna go. That was probably the pitch.

So it is social categories plus personality traits.
Yes.

You start with what I think of as recognized situations in society, and then you sort of filter it through other hit sitcoms.
Extrapolation is the scarcest commodity in Hollywood. You immediately have to give the person you are sitting across from an image. You say he is a Clarence Thomas type, or it's like *Designing Women* except on Mars.

When you are describing characters in this way, are you also thinking about audience categories? Are people saying, "Okay, how does this put together an audience?"
Getting a show on the air versus running a show is like the difference between campaigning and governing. When you are trying to sell your show you are trying to get this person to give you a ton of money to do what

you want to do. So they are your audience at that point. All that is in your mind is, "Do I want to live with this show? Is this something I feel comfortable with writing?" And "Do I think that people out there will watch it?" You are talking about broad audiences, but not about lowest common denominator; it is about finding universals. You are not out to make a breakthrough. You are out to set up something that will keep going and going. Producing a film is a war. One battle. Take the hill. Do everything to get through it. A TV series is about a government, a system, repeating, perpetuating, over and over again, so that people keep coming back. You basically keep getting reelected by the audience every year. A film — you do it once.

When you are trying to formulate the world and the characters, do you try to pin down who the audience might be? When somebody came up with Designing Women, *were they just thinking about the creative process or were they thinking about a particular part of the audience that they wanted to target?*
I think it was a show more targeted towards women: it was no accident that it was originally programmed on Monday night against Monday night football. The Monday night CBS comedies are counterprogramming against Monday night football, too.

Networks study who stays home Friday night, who stays home Wednesday night, who stays home Saturday night. Wednesday night is church night across the heartland. So, homes using televisions are down. Monday people are just getting back to work and dealing with that; men control the dial, coming out of Monday night football. *Golden Girls* had its glory years Saturday at nine and the thought was that older people were home and in control of the dial at that hour. I've been told blacks and other minorities are home Fridays and Saturdays so they tend to put the black shows there. People who do research for a living tell you all kinds of things like that.

How does the audience's affluence or lack of it figure in?
There was a sense in the '80s that, okay, Reagan is in, money is cool now, people will want to watch people with money. Cosby was successful and buzz word was "Cosbyesque." Cosby is about this upper-middle-class family, so upper-middle-class families will work.

Most families on TV are middle-class; the Simpsons, Roseanne, working-class families, are few and far between. How might this relate to audience?
I think what TV does best in the family sitcom is reassuring stories about middle-class family values. But also, television feeds upon itself. If *Roseanne*

breaks through, the network thinks oh, why *Roseanne* is successful is because it is about a blue-collar family so let's clone some blue-collar family shows.

There are many possible ways of subdividing the audience. Presumably a lot of lesbian and gay people watch TV but I doubt that research people think about the lesbian and gay audience.
I have never seen anything about lesbians and gays in any research.

Why would it be customary to think of the fifty and over audience or the kid audience and all these other categories, but not to think about the lesbian or gay audience?
Maybe because it is such a specific audience. Maybe because people at the corporate level aren't used to saying, "Well, let's look at our lesbian demographics — how did we do in lesbians eighteen to forty-nine last night?" I don't know.

Is Hispanic starting to become a category?
Yes, but it tends to get lumped in with black or minority.

Our visitors from the magazine and hotel industries and so on talked a lot about segmentation. Despite the fact that the TV audience is fragmenting, TV is still the medium where you turn if you are an advertiser and you want to reach a national audience. What do you think are the things that hold together a national audience?
Some things that are universal to a family or a workplace. Working along, working out your problems that come from family friction or things that happen in a workplace that everybody can identify with; family dynamics and group dynamics.

One of the stories about TV and audiences you hear is that in the '60s CBS was very strong particularly with comedies, but once TV people were presented with ratings broken down by age, ABC targeted the eighteen to thirty-four group, and their programs changed in order to reflect their new sense of their audience.
Yes. I think that that is true. CBS went for an older audience and ABC saw that they were doing well with younger people who buy the cars.

Do networks come to production companies and say, "We want a show to put on nine o'clock on Thursday that will appeal to eighteen to thirty-four year olds"?
Maybe not in so many words; they will say, "We really would like some-

thing that is compatible with *Seinfeld*; a good flow would be something with a similar type of world that keeps that same type of audience; let's look at what we have in the hopper with development, with writer deals, and with some talent deals, and see if we can get something compatible."

Or perhaps, "Such and such a show is going to end with this season; we need something to replace it."
Right. "These shows are getting old. How can we do the same thing with new ones?"

It seems to me, the way you are describing pitches and pilots, they really are about situations.
Yes, because when you are across the table from the network's people you want them to imagine the situation. If that's sold in their heads you know that you'll be in there later to do the execution, and to keep your characters real. The "world" is where character and situation merge.

I have a project in development at ABC, a script they may decide to make among their spring pilots. It comes from a lot of different influences in my life — from being on *Growing Pains* for six years, for instance. I'm known at ABC as a guy who can handle a domestic sitcom. It's a fantasy world: I go to work, I have a cup of coffee, I put funny stuff on paper, and they give me a lot of money — it's just great. On a TV show, the writer/producers are royalty, like star athletes on a team. You walk down the hall and everybody gets out of your way because you're going someplace. Six or seven o'clock comes around, someone says what do you guys want for dinner, the orders are taken, and it is brought to you. People laugh at what you say even if it's not funny . . . it's really this great, dangerous world.

After six heavy, intensive, production years, not quite burnout, but close, my girlfriend moved into my house and I was facing these adult responsibilities. I thought of that as an interesting world, a situation for a show. I envisioned myself as having a family: someone who does a kid thing for a living and then has to deal with adult responsibilities. I thought of what happens to a star athlete. You're a baseball player, a big star, and at thirty-eight you have to start your life over again. So I sold ABC a script called *The Home Team* about a thirty-eight-year-old guy who retired from sports, was kind of a clubhouse clown, indulged in a kids' game, hitting a ball with a stick, made a lot of money, was Uncle Dad to his kids for fifteen years, and now he's got to be a full-time father. They loved the idea and they loved the script. I thought that's because so many people in my generation seem to want to cling to their childhood, and here's the ultimate child, the star athlete or comedy writer. That's where that idea came from. I don't know whether that's helpful.

It is. Why did they like it?
Extrapolation. Partly it's, oh good, we like Kendall, he's got an idea that's close enough to *Growing Pains*, but instead of the dad being a wise shrink, this is a volatile jock, kind of a big kid but sweet . . . I don't know. Maybe they like it for the fact that so many of the baby boomers are trying to hang on to their childhood and here's a guy who could run and run but couldn't hide from having to grow up. Maybe they liked that. I don't know.

What do you mean by "extrapolation"?
People say, I think wrongly, writing is writing. If you can write newspapers, you can write a screenplay. If you can write novels you can write plays. A good writer can write a sitcom. I don't think that's always true. I'll borrow a story from advertising. A friend of mine's dad was up for a job at another advertising agency. They really liked him until they looked at his resumé, and they said "you have a lot of food here but we need *frozen* food." A gang comedy like at *Night Court* isn't the same as a domestic comedy like *Growing Pains* or *Family Ties*. You'll tell the agent, "Well I liked his *Night Court* but do you have something like a *Family Ties* or a *Roseanne*?" Saying that somebody can write *Growing Pains* from writing *Night Court* is risky. You can take some leaps, but for the most part, extrapolation is rare. I just sold another pilot to Fox, a kind of broader, more farcical show, which I was very happy to do because they think of me primarily as a guy who can write these eight o'clock warm-and-fuzzy family shows, and not kind of a semi-mean-spirited Fox-like show.

In making a pitch, in defining your show, when do you refer to other shows?
Almost right away. When I told my idea for *The Home Team* to my Warner Bros. executives and said I think we can sell it, the studio executive went "Sam Malone with a Home Life!" When you're going to the network: "What have you brought us today?" "It's kind of a family show. Sam Malone with a Home Life." That's your screaming headline. You don't want to make it look like it's really derivative, because nobody wants to admit that. But even if it departs from "Sam Malone with a Home Life" you want something in their heads—a seed to start growing at least close to your idea.

Would you ever pitch something by emphasizing its uniqueness?

You'd always say it is unique. You would say it is a unique twist. It is kind of like "Sam Malone with a Home Life," but it is really different, it hasn't been done before. I think TV is really reactive — to other forces, to movies . . . I don't think you have any great, original, breakthrough television. It is all about reacting to other things.

How is situation comedy changing now? What power do its own conventions retain? Big shifts happen rarely, maybe never, you are saying. But a lot of people felt that way in the early '70s, with All in the Family *and that generation of shows, there were some basic changes in sitcom conventions. Whether you agree or not, are there are shifts of some magnitude underway now, or likely to be?*

Maybe some content is changing. TV can deal with things it hasn't dealt with before. The buzz word right now is "edge." We like the show, can you add more edge to it?

What does that mean?

I don't really think anybody knows. Roseanne is a mom with edge, a little more attitude, a little bit less sweet or sentimental. I think the quest for edge is to compete with cable. Networks aren't the only places to go for your TV needs now.

Most network executives are scared and insecure, trying to keep their jobs. The only thing they know that works is something that has worked. So they will try and clone what has happened before and keep the writers and producers in the reins. For instance, people see that *Roseanne* or the *The Simpsons* are doing well: so we'll add edge. You could have in the next year a breakthrough soft show, the opposite of edge. And suddenly people say, "You know what the audience really wants, they don't want to hear edge, they don't want back-talk and sex talk. Can it be softer?" Suddenly you'd have the soft revolution. It would be, "Oh, that's great, can it be — I hate to say soft — but can it be less edgy? Smooth?"

Two related questions. First, do you see sitcoms as reflecting values that already are held by particular groups, or as shaping those values, or both? Second, is there any move now to seeing sitcoms as reflecting the fact that different groups in society have very different kinds of concerns, and not assuming that all families have the same values?

The first question is, "Which came first, the chicken or the egg?" I don't know. I don't think people will watch a show that they aren't ready to see, although with great execution you can move people along a little bit and do something bold. I don't know if *All in the Family* was really about the genius of Norman Lear or if people were ready to see something like that. Network executives are always trying to track trends and really aren't concerned with leading, just with selling space between commercials. One of the great advantages to having a hit show and being on for six years was that we could do some different stories. Not that we had great artistic pretensions, but—you know we did a show on drunk driving—we were against it. We got a lot of nice mail. When *Happy Days* did the show where Fonzy got the library card, libraries had people coming in for cards. That's fine. But I don't think that you are really going to lead social change in television.

As for different groups and different values, I still think what television does best is finding what is universal. Even though people have different values, there are some common things.

It seems to me that Roseanne *is so successful partly because* Roseanne *says things that are unexpected and rather controversial: is that a way of presenting values that are not in the mainstream? Does "edge" depart from the universal?*
Maybe. But even though *Roseanne* is edgy, it is still about a family that loves each other. Even if they are nasty and have some attitude, they are very much together. It is still a show about family values, about a family being greater than the individual parts, even though she might insult her kids. It is still about family love.

Its values were formulaic in the very earliest sitcoms. The same with its development of episodes: there is some kind of disruption; then it is resolved. Have situation comedies evolved in any meaningful way?
The form is still doing what it has been doing from the beginning, in the '50s, and back to an ancestor of TV sitcoms, the radio show, more than movies. But I think it is doing very similar things in different ways, reflecting the way people talk and what current concerns are. Maybe I can answer by talking about the way our show evolved. After *Growing Pains* became successful we had the luxury of thinking twenty-two shows at a time, thinking about character arcs and incremental growth. There was a question about giving Maggie Seaver another baby, a combination of concerns. After three or four years how do you keep a family show fresh? What is a big event in a family life? Marriage, birth, and death. For a sitcom, certainly marriage and birth—although we did kill a few people in our show too. But

birth seemed pretty interesting. We were not the first show to do it. Almost every show does that. Fourth or fifth season somehow you do birth or a relative we never heard of dying, to keep the show fresh. Also, it is, "Can we get away with it? Is that something that Maggie would do?" If we didn't feel it was a part of her character, we wouldn't have done it. These characters became so real to us that it was really interesting to throw up new challenges, with their goals and their vision of life in mind.

It strikes me as interesting that, as you pointed out, this was happening in show after show in that period. Either the career women were having first babies or the working moms were having still more babies. To what extent was there a concern to manage those characters? They could be independent, but you had to show that they were really women too, and that being women, they loved their families. I don't know how to put this, but there are lots of things that you could do to liven up the family. Can't it be grandparents, kicked out of their homes or whatever, who have to move in with the family?
It can be.

So you were responding to something you saw out there in society? This is the moment of the career woman turning to motherhood?
Imagine a bunch of people sitting around in a room saying, "Okay, we are third or fourth season, we are doing twenty-two shows. What would be an interesting thing to happen?" The executive producers at that point were guys in their late thirties and their wives were having babies. It is both, what is an emotional truth to your character, and, what comes from your own life that you can use and understand and do well?

Didn't that plot coincide with Maggie's getting a promotion? So it involved tensions between her career success and family?
Yes. Part of it was, "What have we done to Maggie's job?" And then you realize that Jason is at home. Then you think that our show isn't about their careers, our show is about the family life: we don't really use Maggie's job that well anyway. What would happen if she quits, or Jason works outside? Will this fit in? Does this seem real? We've done a hundred shows where the roles are this way. Can we reverse it? Does that make sense? Would these people do that?

It seems to me that it's not just a question of genre, because the workplace sitcoms were doing the same thing. Murphy Brown, Night Court. *So there was something about giving career women babies that transcended family sitcoms.* TV *in general was handling the character of the independent woman. And that has always been a difficult representation. Built into that character is always going to be a worry about making her sufficiently feminine.*

I don't view it that way. You are talking about a domestic sitcom, a show that takes place in three-walled sets. What drives TV is writing, about the big moments in small events, as opposed to what is more effective in movies — small moments in big events. A kind of event that manages well on TV in these three-walled sets is, "Wouldn't it be neat if she had a baby?" It is just something that is going to come up. You know, how many false engagements, weddings, have we seen on TV? What can you do with people in their lives? If the audience cares about these people, they'll care about such events.

To try a different hypothesis: it wouldn't be the New Right promoting family values and raising critical opposition to independent women? So that the people sitting around in these rooms would say, "Okay, maybe it's time to have a pregnancy here"?

You'd say that a birth is a strike against independent women?

No, the idea is that for a long time in our history the notion of career and the notion of woman were incompatible, or very hard to reconcile. Starting maybe in the '60s there were more and more women pursuing careers and other kinds of independence — sexual and social independence of various sorts. So the question is whether those new activities of women could be reconciled with the older notion of the woman who grows up, goes to high school, dates, has a family, and so on. We're wondering whether there are tensions in your representation of a woman in a show that you might try to reconcile — to say, "These things aren't really conflicts at all. You can be both."

It is just a reflection of what's going on. People who are running our shows, the people in the networks, are in the baby boom generation. One of the VPs of comedy ABC had a baby last year. I started having some meetings with her, and she was talking maternity — I mean, it's out there and it's happening. It is people you know: "My sister is dealing with this, would this be interesting for our show?" I don't see any conspiracies. It is just a reflection of life.

Let's turn it around. This executive in charge of sitcoms got divorced . . .

People say that these shows in the 1960s and '70s about single parents reflected the lives of people in Hollywood. They might want to do a show about a single parent, but they'd say, "He's not divorced, divorce is ugly, so we kill her, and that's why he's raising his boys alone." You want to kill them off and move on. You don't want, "Well they were never married in the first place," or anything like that.

What makes it okay to represent Maggie having another baby, but not to represent divorce?
Well, to me a sitcom is about reassurance, a little escapism, a little emphasizing the positive. To do a divorce in our show we would have to say, "You see all that love and that getting along for those first ninety-nine episodes, we were just messing with you. They weren't really getting along." Sometimes we would bring in outside writers to pitch us ideas. Many outside writers would say, "Maggie and Jason are having trouble and they separate for a while." We had a lot of fighting in the show, reflecting what happens in a real relationship, but if we had them separate our whole premise would have just been destroyed.

Similarly, if Maggie begins to be attracted to another woman . . .
Exactly.

So the limits of what you can represent are the things that constitute serious threats to the family?
Yes. You have to go with the premise.

Once you've launched a series and started to get some feedback, do you ever sit down with people from audience research and try and fine tune the series? For example, "Okay, we've got this sort of demographic breakdown, could we enlarge this part of the audience a little bit?" Or do you ever get studies that say, "Focus groups show this is a concern that could be elaborated"? Or is it just a group of writers batting ideas around?
The networks will of course respond to research because most of them have no faith in their own guts, in creativity, or in anything else, I think research for the most part is useless and based on self-fulfilling prophecies. We did studies twice a year on *Growing Pains* and I would always read them. Mike had a best friend, the teen character named Boner, the dumb best friend. When he was on the show the audiences said that they didn't like him at all. Then when he left, they missed him tremendously. I don't know whether people in research studies didn't want to say they liked this dumb character. On *Growing Pains* we had the luxury of being successful early on so that

whatever we were doing we were doing well. If you are kind of struggling they will look at the research and say, "You are very weak in females. Could you do a show that has more female appeal?" Most writer/producers are people who really care about and take pride in what they do and aren't going to fold instantly when somebody says that. They will think of a way to comply, just for the politics involved—"Yes, maybe we can do a more female appeal show." But very few writer/producers will do shows that are research driven.

You talk about the politics of it: do the reports give you any ideas? Or are you just reading the stuff to be able to play the game with the executives?
It has some effect. What I always liked about the research was seeing how much people liked the show. I would say, "Isn't that neat that they liked these story areas." But so much of it was self-fulfilling prophecy. If we didn't show Jason at work, which we didn't that much, it was "Audiences are not interested in shows about Jason at work." You would find things like that in the research. There isn't that much interesting to get from it. I think research is one tool and very limited.

Do you know of any shows that have succeeded after following the dictates of the network, based on that kind of research? I am thinking of a program I have been paying attention to the last year and a half, which is a drama, I'll Fly Away. *This season they have started to make changes that might have been suggested or dictated by the network. They are focusing much more on the white character and on routine family melodrama plots in the white family, instead of focusing on the interaction between the black characters and the white characters. In my opinion they are making a big mistake. Do you know of any cases where tinkering like that has actually worked?*
No, I don't. Maybe there are some, but it might work the other way, too. I think if you have good characters, a good situation, and a good world, you have to rely on that. Otherwise it will not have any emotional truth and I think people will turn it off.

So involvement of the network is in most cases not all that useful?
If the show is working, they should leave you alone.

And when it is not working, what they tell you to do doesn't work either?
Exactly. There is always this thing that they will do—especially to older shows—well, can you have new kids?

DAVID KENDALL *Warner Bros. Television* [67

Like on Cosby. Bringing in kids from the ghetto?
If you want new kids, I think you are going to watch a new show.

What about Maggie's new baby?
That was more organically introduced, slowly. Maybe I am inhaling the fumes, but I thought that worked.

Do you ever run afoul of the network censors? Were there instances when you wanted to do something and they said no?
Not really. Most of the time you are pretty good at policing yourself. If you are not condescending to the job you are doing, you are not going to want to disrespect your audience. We did a show in the third season or so of *Growing Pains*. Mike was at a party where cocaine was used; he didn't do it even though it was offered to him, and he went home. We had some trouble early on because he didn't stand up at the party and condemn them all for using it. He went home and had a discussion with his dad. I thought the scene was nice. He felt that he had screwed up in the eyes of his friends and that they wouldn't like him, which is how I think a kid thinks. The senior producer I remember on the phone with the censors saying, "That is just not how we see our kids functioning." They let us do the show. The impact was, we made the point that this was not a kind of nod that these drugs were okay; Mike was not saying it was okay for other people to use these drugs.

But there was one instance: we wanted to use the word "pee," and they blipped us on the air. Just occasionally we would do a double entendre to amuse ourselves, or hope that the adults who were watching might snicker; and sometimes we would intentionally do things to drive the censor crazy. For instance, in the same drug episode that I mentioned, we gave the guy selling drugs the same name as our censor. He said, "My parents are going to watch, they watch the show, could you not have my character selling drugs?" We changed the name and that probably bought us a double entendre in the next episode.

I am curious about gender and the "swoon quotient." In Growing *Pains or* Full House *or most of the sort of successful situation comedies, there is a safe male, youthful, very attractive for young female viewers: Scott Baio or Kirk Cameron, you know, the kids that get on the cover of* Teen *Magazine. Do you think about swoon quotient in your construction of characters?*
If you are doing a domestic sitcom, or a family show, you are going to have

kids. If you are going to have kids, you want to have some that are dealing with issues of sexuality and dating, so you are going to have adolescents. You want some attractive people playing these roles. Sometimes you have boys, sometimes you have girls. If you have someone like — God bless him — Kirk Cameron, who at fourteen was terrific, it's not, "That's great, we can have a young hunk or a teen idol here." If you are casting adolescents, you are going to want somebody appealing and attractive.

It almost looks to an outsider as a sort of sexual marketing device. It is like a convention in the genre to have these cute boys, who are very useful in helping to sell the show to an audience and to get them that additional publicity — Teen Magazine *or* Seventeen *or whatever.*

If you are lucky there are going to be teen idols. What I was proud of on *Growing Pains* was that we said we weren't going to Fonzie-ize him and make the whole show about Kirk. We didn't make it the Kirk Cameron Show. But you know, it is tough out there, and if you are going to have a teen idol, that's great.

Was it an accident?

In episode number one, which was a father-son show, the chemistry seemed right. The first time you saw Kirk you just knew he was talented and charming and very appealing — so we took the show that way, even though we made a special effort to make sure that it was really a family ensemble. If the other kids got fewer of what we called "A" stories and Mike got more, that was fine, but it wasn't like what they did on *Happy Days*, which was make it about Fonzie. Like I said, it's the difference between getting elected and governing. Once the show was underway, it was just, "What is working? what are our elements that are working here?"

We have been asking everybody about globalization. Do you have anything to say about the international audience?

Not really. I think TV is a very American product, and that's its strength. When I was in Italy last spring and turned on the TV, there was *Growing Pains* dubbed in Italian. I mean, it is out there, all over the world. I don't know just where, because that is kept from us. When I get my residual check it just says F for foreign — it doesn't tell me what country. But it is out there. It is sold internationally as an American product and I have felt no effects of globalization. It's just, "Sell us some sitcoms."

Your getting these checks is of course one of the things we mean by globalization. It would be interesting if in developing your new series you were thinking partly about the international audience, but you are probably not doing that.
No. Not at all.

Let's hear about your colossal blunder.
More than my mistake, I'd say it was ABC's major mistake on a show that I did. Last year, with a partner, Dan Guntzelman, I created a show called *Willie*. It was really a dream project. We were very excited. Willie was an eleven-year-old boy with a collection of semi-misfit kids — kind of a contemporary "Our Gang." Willie makes his own home movies on video. So part of the show would be a kid's camcorder view of the world — the shorthand would be Walter Mitty with a camcorder. So part of the show would have eleven-year-old production values and part would be a film reality. The back story was that Willie's mom has recently gotten divorced and they are moving into a new neighborhood. Episode one was the move; it's a little bit smaller than the other house, but they are going to get along. Willie goes to the new school and meets his friends. So Willie makes a little home video for his history class and gets his friends to be in it. You could see the surface story of moving to the new world, as Willie did Columbus's move to the New World.

Because we thought the show looked different from anything that had been on the air, we got Warner Bros. to fund a little presentation. We shot a sample episode, got the *Growing Pains* crew to work with us for next to nothing. The pitch was: we went in, we put a cassette in, pushed PLAY, and said, "We want to do a show that is kind of like that." ABC loved the presentation and ordered six episodes. We had to recast. We did things a little bit different. After the rough cut of episode one, and after we had shot episode two, ABC got really scared. "It isn't what we thought it was. Could you cut this differently? Are you thinking about a laugh track?" Basically they thought they were going to get *Growing Pains* rather than this.

How many people were involved?
There were three or four. The president and the two executive vice-presidents. The show that they had liked three months ago and had bought, they were suddenly afraid of. They bought a hiatus for us, gave us money to keep our crew, shut us down so that they could evaluate what they were going to do. So we had a face-to-face meeting with the studio president of Warner TV, and we got canceled face-to-face, which is a rare experience and

one I will always value: sitting in the corner office of ABC and them pulling the plug on our show. They said, "Things have changed for us since we bought it. We don't see the place for it that we saw before. We feel the show is too kid-specific in its appeal." They looked at the rough cut, got scared: it wasn't *Growing Pains*, and somehow in their mind they thought it would be *Growing Pains*. I think the show turned out great, and so does everybody who has looked at the cassettes.

Wasn't this a time when all the kid-specific shows were sinking? Like Erie Indiana?
Maybe that's true. But I never saw our show as kid-specific. I always thought it would appeal to anybody who had *been* a kid and put on a play with friends. Kids would have been the most obvious audience, but the whole literal appeal — if you have an old person on screen, old people will like it; if you have a ten-year-old on screen, ten-year-olds will like it — I don't think that is so. I don't think you watch a show because you see people in your age group. I think *Willie* was universal to anybody who has ever been a kid, but we got flushed two episodes into six, and they will never air.

You can't sell it to someone else?
We had meetings later that week with the heads of the other networks. But you go to CBS, you say, "Here is the show. Here are two episodes. What you have to do is buy this show that another network has certified as a failure already. You have to assume a two-plus million dollar debt. And then if it doesn't do well you have to explain to your upper management why you bought the show."

Doesn't ABC owe you the money for the six episodes?
ABC had to pick up the deficits for all six shows. They panicked. They flushed $2.3 million. If they had stayed on the hook and done all of the shows they would have spent about 2.6, 2.7. So for $300,000 they would have had a whole original series and six half-hours to run during the summer — I think it was a panic decision. Anyway, two-plus million dollars and it will never be on the air.

Stephen Oakes Broadcast Arts

December 10, 1992

. . . .

Stephen Oakes is a director of animation and special effects for television commercials. The style of work, frequently used for children's advertising, emphasizes fast-paced mixing of techniques. In 1981 he founded the production company Broadcast Arts, known for its work on Pee Wee's Playhouse *and MTV. Currently he is the president of Curious Pictures Corporation in New York.*

Broadcast Arts is known for a mixed-media approach to the visuals of advertising. We started off by doing a lot of the MTV logos and the on-air identities for the emerging cable systems in the early '80s. Then quickly we found out that advertisers had a lot more money than the cable companies; we have produced probably close to 1000 TV commercials as well as the series *Pee Wee's Playhouse* and a number of other pilots for series and programs.

Broadcast Arts works on the old studio system, which is a little out of fashion in terms of a way to organize a company. Ours is a very fractured industry: there are little boutiques across the country, although mostly in New York and LA, that produce commercials around one or two directors and an executive producer. We've set up a studio where we have a number of our own stages and motion control equipment and directors, and departments for editorial, and fabrication of all sorts of very wacky props and fun things. We produce classical cell animation as well, the cartoon characters. I like to boast about all the big stars I have worked with like the Trix Rabbit and the Sugar Bear, the Pillsbury Doughboy, Spuds, actually a bitch, and it goes on. Advertising brings up many issues, of filmmaking, of the entertainment side of short films, of persuasion, of communication.

We enjoy looking for the unusual projects, new technologies for manipulating imagery and surprising people; actually, novelty and sense of humor have been with us throughout advertising's history. Irreverence is part of the novelty. While I like to think of myself as something of a guerrilla filmmaker, obviously my clients are very much mainstream and they really believe advertising works. I humor them so as to have opportunities to make my little thirty-second films. Every once in a while I find out that it really does work, and that is all the more startling and rewarding.

I just finished a commercial for the old word game from Parker Brothers called Boggle. Maybe you know it. You shake a bunch of little dice with letters that you use to form words. We created a Chihuahua, a puppet, but animated it in such a way that it was fairly convincing. It wanted to go out for a walk. It is time for it to be taken out. The people are so engrossed in the game that they are ignoring the distress of the poor little dog and he is pawing at the door and doing a very embarrassing little dance to make the time pass while people are finding words like "tree" and "hydrant." So I thought—good bathroom humor—this is fun. Just days after the spot started running sales went up 17 percent for this classic game that had been sitting on the shelf.

We have anywhere from ten to fifteen commercials in progress at any one time. Our thirty-second commercials take anywhere from six to twelve weeks to do. The average budget for such a little film is $120,000 to $300,000. It is something of a big business — production itself is eight to ten billion dollars a year, just for the companies that are producing the "spots."

Broadcast Arts is one of the larger animation production companies, grossing eight million in a year. We have a staff of about 35 people, but our relationships with the fine arts community and free-lancers mean that we send out 1099s and W-2s to about 500 people on an annual basis. I like to know arts administrators because they introduce me to the up-and-coming fine artists. I help myself to their ideas and in return offer a little bit of employment. It is a nice way to go to the art galleries and be a bit of a consumer in a different way.

It is very competitive to get the work that we do. It takes a lot of cold calls and infiltrating little cliques and friendships to get these prizes because handing out the assignment to do a commercial is a really guarded moment, when the creative team at an ad agency is really displaying their sense of taste and control of who is going to do these things. So, they are coveted. And it is usually a competitive, three-bid situation.

The work is tedious. It is frame by frame. There are 720 frames in a thirty-second commercial and each one of them has to survive scrutiny. I know you are very curious as to who my audience is. My primary audience is my clients and they always have better video equipment than the public. They have a shuttle and they roll through the commercial and look at every frame. They stop and have discussions of just about every frame. The process is very intense from beginning to end with meetings about things that, of course, are quite absurd, but are all the pieces that make up the thirty-second commercial that goes on the air, influences people, and then

STEPHEN OAKES *Broadcast Arts* [73

gets imitated. We all look at past successes of advertising for raw material to regurgitate, to make something new and startling.

In the frame-by-frame scrutiny, what sorts of things might your clients stop and ask about? Do they want a different actor? They don't like the clothes? Whatever?
If they are looking at the film and saying they want a different actor there is a real big problem.

So what sorts of considerations —
Well, they are evaluating how well you did everything that you promised. If it is a product shot, you are looking at the lighting, you are looking at the color correction of the object. It is very rare that you would shoot the real thing. You always change the product to compensate for the deficiencies of the medium, which is a lovely way of saying, "Make it look better for TV." I am not a food specialist, but food comes into my work very often. For instance, in the Pillsbury commercial, I wasn't allowed to actually photograph the food. They had a guy who knows how to make steam come out of the broken roll with the right intensity and the time-lapse photography of the bake-up. The bake-up shot is what's called a mnemonic, which is any image so intense that it is a memory cue; it has very little to do with what the product really does. The client evaluates how well you accomplished each scene objective. They came with their objective and the production company is supposed to enhance it in ways they would never have thought of.

You said your budget is about $120,000 to $300,000 for a thirty-second spot. That is what you charge to the advertising agency?
It is rare that it goes below that. The advertising agency adds an agency markup, generally in the 15 percent range, plus they have charged for all the creative services, testing, and analyses, to get to the point that it was something that they even wanted to produce.

The production costs are trivial compared to the money that the advertising agency makes in the media buy. They get a commission on the purchase of air time. So the production has been allowed to escalate in costs over the last two decades. People have been upset about how fast the costs have risen. It is only recently that things have leveled off. Because of the economy, production cost controls are now an issue.

If I make a $120,000 commercial, it has probably got a media buy of three to five million. If it is a small one.

You said that you put in competitive bids. How else do you compete besides through the bids that you make?

You are anxious to be invited to bid. You don't just find out that there is a job; you are constantly showing your sample reel. And trying to know the cycles of when — Mounds candy bars are only advertised once every three years and you know they advertised last year, so you don't go talking to the Mars account this year, you wait till next year. Then you concentrate, you find out who is involved.

How many people are really competing with you? How you would sell yourself against those others?

It has gotten more competitive. I would guess there are about five or six companies in the country that could claim to have a similar look, although one company will be more into the model and clay animation and one company will veer more toward the very stylized graphic animation, like the Cappio commercial; there are maybe twenty specialties. As soon as you target a storyboard you try to show how that specialty is really our strongest suit. Then you haul out all the commercials that have anything to do with that technique and try to show the client that "we've done it already." That makes them feel very good, that it has already been done, but that yours is just a little bit different. So it has never been done, and we are going to make it that much more special.

How extensive are the specifications that the creative team gives to the bidders, both thematically and in terms of the technique?

It ranges. Smaller agencies have fewer layers to their organization, yet they all are very serious about accomplishing something specific, and therefore will give you an immense amount of briefing about what they are looking for. Generally you get a bid spec sheet that lists the mechanics — who is going to pay for on-screen talent, who is going to pay for the final post production, how many shoot days on location, what kind of insurance is necessary, things like that. Then if it is a job for Procter & Gamble, your bid package will have your scene objectives, and it will get broken out scene by scene into smaller and smaller pieces. We do our bid on a fairly standard-ized form, which is about a ten-page document that describes every warm body who will be involved and what their day rate is. The profit is clearly described, which means that you list all of your real costs with no pad in them and then you are allowed to put a markup on it. Then you have your creative fees, and it is all pretty black and white. They are trying to make it apples to apples in terms of comparing bids.

You don't describe the creative look in your bid. That comes with a face-to-face — with the director and the creative team. And the director is always chaperoned by a producer, so he doesn't overpromise. Creativity is always kept separate from a lot of the business and logistics. There is a discussion, and then a director's creative treatment, usually in writing or in drawing.

Who came up with the idea for the Chihuahua? Was it the ad agency?
Yes.

They come up with a sort of script, and you figure out how to put it together?
Yes. Sometimes it is only a script, but it is almost always accompanied by thumbnail sketches, a storyboard.

When they are looking at each frame, do they look out for race and gender and religious issues? Or is that left up to you? Are there accepted procedures for not being religiously offensive, or offensive to women, or —
Everybody. You have so many committees. A lot of people have very little to contribute creatively, but everyone is allowed to say, "That is offensive," or "I don't like that." So there is a lot of rounding off.

Is there any sort of accepted procedure for judging that sort of thing? In one commercial you have a Chinese boy and then a girl . . .
Ironically, that is not imposed by anyone. That is sort of a pseudo-enlightened way of making these households so rainbow. But the first stage for evaluating these issues of appropriateness is in the ad agency, after it sells an idea. They can do many unethical things to sell projects to their clients. But once it is sold, then it comes more into the public eye, and the storyboard, before it even gets bid, goes to the networks they intend to buy air time from. The networks have a standards and practices committee — sometimes called the censor — and they send back notes. And if you want to buy the air time you make changes; you are certainly not going to pay all that money to make a commercial and then find out that they won't play it. That is step one.

They will then tell you, "We want you to use these kinds of puppets"?
No, they will say that "you can't use that puppet" or "you can't make that joke."

Will the ad agency be specific enough to say things like, "We want you to use clay animation?"

Oh, of course. The ad agency will be involved intimately with every issue. Not only what kind of puppet, but what will be the material: are you going to use terrycloth like the Muppets, or are you going to use foam latex like Ray Harryhausen? Then the meetings begin. The committees and the meetings.

Who are your competition? Mainly other organizations like yours? Do film studios do the same work that you do? For example, Industrial Light and Magic makes TV commercials.

ILM opened up a division for commercials but I think they have had some difficulties. Ad agencies are a different sort of hoop to jump through than making movies. There is very little crossover between commercial production and theatrical long-form work. A lot of commercial directors may aspire to do feature films, but if they do commercials well, they won't be doing features; they can do better financially than a lot of feature directors in terms of day rates. And feature film people who think "I'll squeeze in a TV commercial between my big projects" are the exception. They mostly fail or find it completely repulsive.

How don't they know how to talk to ad agencies? What is it that they didn't know that made them drop out of that business?

It's many things. It is very time-consuming to build consensus among people who are not visual filmmakers. It is very hard to be told, "You actually don't know what you are doing because you haven't accomplished these objectives." Feature film and programming people are interested in storytelling, in the time that it takes to tell the story. And thirty-second commercials, which have some story to hang messages on, inhibit and frustrate a long-form filmmaker. The politics are integral to getting a successful commercial done. Film school doesn't give training for the politics.

We like to boast about being one of the strongest companies, with a lot of depth of talent; we have all these resources at our command. There are other cell animation companies that don't do model building, and there are other computer animation companies that don't do mixed-media animation. One of the unique selling points for our studio is that under one roof many of these disciplines come together for a good effect.

That brings me to our question about creativity. Given the fact that the concept is so well designed for certain market needs by the agency at the beginning, your job is basically execution. You say one of the things that makes your company so good at execution is, you are not only rummaging around, ripping off old concepts and recycling them, but also tapping another creative community, a group of artists who usually don't do commercial work. What creativity can they bring to a process that is as constricted as you describe it?

Nuances take on monumental proportions in advertising. The fact that you have done it in a different color spectrum is exciting. Colorists add a lot to the design of backgrounds for the Trix rabbit. The Trix rabbit has been around for twenty-some years. Every art director who inherits a character wants to put their contemporary spin on it. These things are very important.

What a way to go down in history. "I put a spin on the Trix rabbit." What are some other things that make your production company creative, besides color?

I had one project a while ago for Sunlight dishwashing detergent. They were so excited about taking the Lichtenstein dot pattern to talk about how there are no spots on their glasses. What we said was, "We want to do it in a multiplane fashion" — this is going to be really technical, but we took all of the drawings which would have been flat on an animation stand, we cut them out and stood them up like in a doll house. If you remember the campaign, the spots are driving Bud away from Marge, and she is pointing out the dot pattern on her glasses. It's all done in comic-book style, but with cut-out treatment; the whole thing was like a pop-up book, a pop-up book come to life. And with live action cinematography — meaning that the camera boomed down, dollied in, panned around — the room was alive, there was light coming in the window, and yet these were still images about lines and graphic conventions like the dot patterns and the color screens. So all of a sudden it was alive in a way that the agency hadn't imagined. Viewers at home were pulled out of the humdrum of another bit of cartoon animation. That was a very successful campaign. Four spots. A million dollars worth of billings. Everybody was happy. It sold soap.

How would a new look get into advertising? Maybe MTV is the kind of place that would buy a brand new look?

We did over thirty MTV logos starting in 1981. We haven't done any recently because their budgets are too low. But at first it was a wonderful opportunity, because they said, "Here is the budget; do whatever you want; just make sure it ends up with the MTV configuration, the logo." Well, that was my dream job. And we did come up with some pretty wild stuff that came from the artist's interest. We did one that was based on a woman's personal watercolors, and she was the director of it. We did some sculptural model things. We did an MTV logo made out of time lapse of frozen chemicals that did funny things during its melting. We ran it in reverse so all this glop sort of swirled together and made the MTV logo. Each one of those was like a little visual experiment. Some were more successful than others, but the stakes weren't that high. It was a kind of novelty workshop. And some of those things have gone on and been imitated.

Music videos are the other testing ground for visual treatments by young directors: we have done a fair amount of music video. In fact, ironically, the example I gave you of the pop-up book come to life was actually a rip-off of our music video for the Alan Parsons Project, titled "Nick and Sugar," for the song "Don't Answer Me." If you have ever seen that, it is a silly romance, played out in a comic-book style, all in this multiplane fashion. It won an award as most experimental, creative video of 1985.

You have a small group of people that you hire full time. Does that tend to lock you into the style that those people represent?
What's nice about our territory — mixed media — is that it embraces so many things from so many disciplines. The blend always evolves and it will be a very exciting time with the new computer technology. One of the things I'll be doing is using computers in ways such that you don't know a computer was involved. It still looks like hand craftsmanship, naive even; you know, it looks like it was done with a crayon. But it is going to have motion and a sense of illusion and animation — life put into it — because of what we can do with computers. You look at it and you say, "I could do that. That is a great idea. I could go back and with my home movie camera do the same thing."

One of our main concerns is how people in these industries think about viewers, audiences, readers, and so on. How do you talk about the people who will be watching these TV commercials? Are there audience categories that become important for certain kinds of commercials? Are audiences gendered, for example?
In the production companies, in the creative teams at the ad agencies, I would say that we don't spend much time worrying about the home viewer. It is mostly ourselves as peers. We are trying to entertain ourselves and our friends — we are trying to get away with as much fun as possible while doing the job that the brand manager has set forth for us. We only hear from the brand manager, not so much about the home viewer as about what his sales

force will think of the commercial. And many commercials that are potentially not so successful for influencing you as consumers to go to the store and purchase are wildly successful because they motivate people at a big sales convention, they rally the camaraderie, create momentum for the launch of a new product this season. That has very little effect on the home viewer.

I noticed that the Pillsbury Doughboy commercial you made for British TV is funnier and less family oriented than Doughboy commercials are in this country. So there must be some sense of what is acceptable. Do you get all of that through ad agencies? Do they say, "Look, it can be raunchier, it can be funnier, it can be a little harsher, because it is a different audience"?
British TV in particular needs to be more entertaining because their commercials are all in a block of time. So there is a tradition of more entertainment value and less hard sell. In fact, that commercial still is tainted with Americanism because of its food demo section in the center — the bake-up shot. It sticks out on English TV, although they did make the concession of letting the Doughboy have a British accent and letting him be the Dough Man — an adult voice instead of a kid's voice. Some market research showed that British women don't want to be talked down to by a little kid!

Did the ad agency tell you that? Before you made the commercial?
Yes. American women, I suppose, are listening to their kids to know what to buy. Actually, I think there is some truth to that.

If the viewing audience doesn't seem to enter into the process —
I didn't say "doesn't." It is just less on the forefront.

It seems to me that commercials for domestic products are extremely conservative in their construction of gender roles. Much more so than entertainment TV, for instance, where it is becoming commonplace to have role reversal. It is in ads for domestic products that you find the strongest reinforcement of very traditional identities. But if the thinking isn't in terms of influencing the audience, why is that not a realm of more play, a space where you start seeing all sorts of nontraditional families being imagined?
Usually the gimmick gets more attention in terms of surprising people than the backdrop of the kitchen with the two kids sitting with mom and dad. Advertisers are less likely to tamper with the definition of family.

It just seems that over and over the expectation is that the woman will be the nurturer, that the men can't take care of themselves, that they do things wrong when you send them out to shop, that the home falls apart when mom is sick.
That is a category of commercials generally called "dialogue," and I don't do dialogue. In fact, I don't really treat people like people in my commercials. I'm more involved with animation and fantasy.

You distinguish between dialogue commercials and the kind you do: do agencies make assumptions about audience that are associated with particular types of commercial?
There are traditions in product categories. For instance, in car ads you don't see whimsical, silly things like I like to do. It is very rare that I do a car ad. It's all about sheet metal and life-style things. There are traditions in product categories that tend to bring with them the stereotypes, and you don't want to rock the boat.

I'll tell you, almost every time I get a new job they haul out the historical reel for me to see. Even if we are doing something radically different, they want me to see every commercial that's ever been done for that product. I then have to justify doing something new. Will it solve the communication issue better than what was done before?

Can you define for us either the kinds of products or the kinds of audiences that make agencies think, "Ah, animation"?
That has many answers. Animation is a wonderful way to show how something abstract works. Animation is a way to avoid talent payment residuals . . . sounds silly, but if you plan to run a commercial for three years the talent payments are extraordinary, particularly if you were to have a cast of more than two or three people. There is a whole theory about critter-sell. There is one ad agency, Leo Burnett, that's wildly successful because they have the biggest corral of critters. That's Tony the Tiger, that's Jolly Green Giant, that's Snap-Crackle-Pop, that's White Cloud . . . it's all in one building. It's a wild place!

Your work seems to be a part of a trend that's really been in evidence for the last decade and a half: rapidity, the dislocation of images from structuring logic . . . do you have anything to say about what allows audiences to accept this?
The more you watch this stuff, the more you can consume it. You want more, you appreciate the technical references, the manipulation of imagery.

Every once in a while I bump into somebody who hasn't been practicing, and they look at the commercial and say "I don't get it" — and "that's really too much and maybe even offensive." It tends to be an older person, or it tends to be someone who doesn't have enough exposure to American TV.

The networks have rules that, say, for kids' advertising it might be too distracting to have scenes shorter than one second — twenty-four frames. Therefore, children's advertising for toys is abandoning the networks and going to cable and local syndication for private local media buys because if you can't do fast cuts, kids get bored. You can't stop us.

I am out to have more kids memorize my commercials scene by scene and play them back to one another, singing them as if it's a puzzle they've solved. I am working on a Kraft commercial, right now, that has so many layers that I know it cannot be understood the first time. It's a puzzle. It's like a Super Mario world. If you've never played it, and it's all been designed for people who grew up playing Mario, old Mario World, whatever . . . you're baffled by it. So most people will be baffled by this Kraft singles commercial, and upon repeated viewing there will be one-upmanship for being able to follow it.

Can you do that more with children's commercials than you could with adults?
Are adults able to sit through it?
The novelty wears off on adults faster and they get annoyed with techniques that don't have ideas behind them. Every once in a while you have to come up with a good idea to keep the adults focused.

I have a large question about whether elaborated TV languages, or visual languages like this, change us in some way or another.
I think commercials are those moments when things get louder. You can write some very intense poetry, but do you want to read four hundred pages of it? So I think thirty seconds . . . well, I like to do tens. Ten seconds is an art because you can't put too many ideas in a ten. You have to decide what your idea is — you can do a good idea in seven seconds, and then put three seconds on the end to tell you what you're supposed to remember — that's the MTV logo. The thirty-second spot is a place where you can no longer tell a good story as you used to be able to do in the sixty-second format, but you can get a strong setting, and you could probably hang three ideas plus a demo.

You're saying: we don't do anything in the cultural world ourselves; we just follow the lead. Kids no longer can pay attention for a second and I'm going to push that

further. But you are *doing something. You are making them happy. You are part of a process that's making that happen. So the fact is that you have a tremendous impact on the social world and you want to have a further impact, in decreasing the possible attention span and thinking potential of American children.*
I don't think that's decreasing; no, that's accelerating.

Not the attention span. There may be certain kinds of thinking that can only be done if you have a certain attention span.
Yes. I think people should be expected to be able to shift gears. And I don't think it's fair to say that commercials or music videos, or this genre of picture-making is eliminating the ability for the appreciation of calm . . .

But it does make it harder. If the messages they get in the social world, and the messages they learn to deal with, are specifically designed to be attractive to them on all kinds of levels, it does make it a lot more difficult. Speaking as a professor, it's hard to go into a class for a two- or three-hour lecture without using a lot of video now.
As teachers you should increase your production values out there —

We are not driven by the same economic imperative as your industry.
I think you should. That is a change in the United States that should happen. There should be an investment in the resources for teaching on a par with the resources that go into communicating on TV. Maybe it should be legislated, I don't know. Everyone is complaining about education in the United States now.

The question is really, what effect does your medium have on the ways people think? Or is it just a reflection? You said earlier, "Well, kids won't listen unless we do this to them; otherwise they just go away." That implies that children are already like this, not that what you do creates them in that way. Is that how you think about what you do?
It has to do partly with aspirations in people at certain age levels. You are almost doing the commercial for an older age that the younger kids will aspire to. It's been talked about. I don't have children of my own, I rent them.

Is children's TV deregulated?
No. It is regulated — it is self-regulated by the networks. They each have staffs, which have been cut back recently, but they are still pretty eagle-eyed.

I haven't heard any complaints of young blacks not being able to sit through three hours of Spike Lee about Malcolm X. It makes one wonder if perhaps you have to have such density of action and so many attention-grabbing things because you are, after all, giving them something they have little other interest in. My question is whether, historically, the networks have played a role in this: for example, in the move from the sixty-second to the thirty-second commercial?

You could always buy a thirty; but sixty was affordable and more was better. You can still buy two minutes.

I have been working on the early moments of the modern advertising industry in my research. A historical breakthrough, I am convinced, was when agencies began creating something that you could metaphorically call a language of advertising, which associated social tableaus with products, without any kind of reasoning about the actual use of the product. There wasn't much connection between the social tableau and the soap or cereal or whatever. I conjecture that learning that language in the 1890s and after changed somewhat how people are in the world, how they think about the world, how they think about themselves. Do you consider your project to be involved in that sort of development? Or is that a level of abstraction that wouldn't enter in?

Well, we talk about the i.d. badge phenomena all the time. "You are a Bud man." But I don't spend time thinking or worrying about how I am changing the world. I know I am in the middle of it, but there is no scheme that is talked about, except as support for individual commercials. I don't know if I can say much more than that.

We were talking about ways in which the Pillsbury commercials had to be made differently for a British market. One thing going on in the contemporary discourse of advertising is a lot of talk about globalization. Firms say they are in pursuit of a language that can transcend national boundaries and speak to audiences on a transnational basis. Animation itself would seem to be a really good place to find that construction of transnational language.

I agree.

Have you heard this kind of discourse?

I'm initiating it! I have sales people in Japan working very diligently on just that issue. A lot of people are complaining, not complaining, observing that American advertising is the best in the world. It works. It has high production values. It uses cinematography in exotic and heightened ways. People abroad love it, yet resist its imposition in their market. The ad agencies want to make better commercials by imitating U.S. styles. The British are on a par with us, or see themselves as even more sophisticated in TV advertising. I lump London and New York together—there is so much crossover in talent. People import British directors for commercials very frequently. We have more sophisticated audiences—the Italians and the Germans are still looking at glitzy techniques of the '80s and going, "Wow, give me more." The Japanese say, "Pretty soon we will be able to do computer animation as well as you." They measure it in months, I've been told.

Have advertising firms come to you and said, "We want to make a commercial that is going to work in the United States, in Canada, in Holland, in Italy, in Spain . . . ?"
Yes, but they are stepchildren, imitations of U.S. strategy. Big companies like Procter & Gamble that are globalizing want to be sensitive to the local market, so they will do their research. Johnson and Johnson will make sure there is a plastic wrapping around the BandAid box to be on a par with local packaging and hygienic expectations — even though individual bandaids are wrapped. There has to be a clear wrapper on the outside. P & G will not boast as much in Japan because to talk about your product as being better is objectionable.

Our production values and techniques are still looked at as being a model. It is just the etiquette, the social concerns, that differ.

Are there kinds of assignments that could be lucrative that you wouldn't take on for other reasons?
Can you name one that I might object to?

The Ku Klux Klan comes to you and says, "We want to do . . ."
No, they would never come to me because they would never be allowed on the air. So that is not a problem.

Plus you would be too expensive. Does the Bud commercial raise questions? Is there a danger that selling beer in a cartoon-like form might make it appeal to kids who are too young to drink? I can imagine extensions of that, that might offend you morally.
It hasn't really happened because anyone who can afford to advertise on TV is so concerned about being accepted, and not having a backlash against them, that their proposals are rounded off and safe.

By the time they get to you?

Yes. Would I do cigarette advertising? Yes. Cigarette ads were the best vehicle for fun and attitude and gimmicks; I like the rule in Japan where they can show after 11 o'clock.

Are you ever uncomfortable with the manner in which the agency is trying to represent or sell an idea?

Yes, actually some scripts I find objectionable, but I tend to put business first. You know: it is a production facility and there are other directors and maybe they want this opportunity, too. It's business.

Can you think of one that you found objectionable?

Well, usually because it is dumb. I just did a Windex ad that was so stupid. They had a concept that tested high above the norms, about a new bottle and a new formula. Both are better. The bottle has a new grip that supports your hand. And the new formula was going to be even more streak-free. It turns out that they really couldn't improve on their formula but they did improve the bottle. But they didn't want to jeopardize the test results from the commercial, so they went ahead with the same script. There was a special effect about a woman cleaning her big window. Her friend from next door comes over and says, "What are you doing?" "I'm washing my windows and it's so much better." She reaches in — fantastic special effects I got into it — she grabs the liquid and pulls it out of the bottle and there is this wobbly blob of Windex liquid: "The liquid is better and the bottle is better." But the liquid wasn't better, so she just said, "The bottle is better, see." They loved the special effect and went ahead with it.

Victoria Traube International Creative Management

December 3, 1992

. . . .

*Victoria G. Traube is senior vice-president and general counsel of the Rodgers
and Hammerstein Organization, which represents Richard Rodgers and
Oscar Hammerstein II, Irving Berlin, and works by other authors. She was
previously vice-president and head of New York Motion Picture and Theatre
Business Affairs for International Creative Management, Inc., where she
worked with agent Sam Cohn. Before that she was vice-president of business
affairs for Reeves Entertainment Group, Director of Business Affairs for
Home Box Office, Inc., and an associate at the New York law firm of Paul
Weiss Rifkind Wharton & Garrison. She is a graduate of the University of
Pennsylvania Law School and Radcliffe College.*

Let me start with the history of International Creative Management, which is something that I had to do a little research on. It kind of grew like Topsy. We are probably about a hundred agents now with an office in New York that includes a music department, a literary department, a motion picture/television department, and a theater department. In Los Angeles, we have motion picture and television departments. The current company now called ICM had two progenitors. The first was General Artists Corporation (GAC). In the early '60s MCA Universal left the talent agency business because it was also in the movie business, and back in those days there were antitrust laws. The justice department told MCA that it had to choose between movie production and its agency business. It simply closed down the agency business. GAC, one of the ICM progenitors, hired many of the agents who previously worked for MCA, which made GAC into a player back in the 1960s. In 1968 GAC acquired a company called Creative Management Associates (CMA). The principals of that company were gentlemen called Freddie Fields and David Begelman. Perhaps you have heard of them. At that point the corporate name became CMA. My boss, Sam Cohn, had been with GAC. He is now the vice-chairman of ICM. In 1974 CMA merged with another company called Internationals Famous Agency (IFA), and the corporate name became ICM, International Creative Management. IFA had come into existence when a man named Marvin Josephson (who recently gave up his controlling interest in ICM) acquired a company called Ashley Famous from Kinney. Kinney was really

Warner Bros. Ted Ashley, who was a principal at Ashley Famous, had previously sold that agency to Warner Bros. Then Marvin acquired it from Warner Bros. So, ICM is a combination of GAC and CMA and IFA—alphabet soup.

Just a little background. In the '70s ICM's parent holding company went public and turned into a diversified company, which owned, in addition to the talent agency, several radio stations, an office products business, and a brokerage business. In 1988 ICM went private again. One reason, and maybe the main one, was that Marvin Josephson, who was one of the controlling shareholders, wanted to cash out. But for a number of reasons it was also felt that the agency was at a competitive disadvantage by being publicly held, that the public market really couldn't properly assess the value of the ICM stock—the market was not equipped to deal with the business, which didn't have any assets really. The only assets of a talent agency are the agents and its clients. Moreover, there was some concern that the disclosure of management's salaries, mandated by the securities law, was a competitive problem vis-à-vis the other agencies, which are privately held. And finally, it was also felt that being a public company prevented ICM from giving its top agents the kind of equity interest in the company that you need to keep such agents. So that is the corporate history. ICM is now a privately held company again. It is controlled by three principals, Jeff Berg, Jim Wiatt, and Sam Cohn. The senior agents all have stock and will get more as time goes by.

I should also say a little bit about the other players in the talent agency business. Those of you who are interested in the movie business have all heard of CAA or Creative Artists — hereafter referred to as the enemy — and William Morris. William Morris was all but moribund until about a month ago. I say moribund, although they had huge revenues from television. They also own a big chunk of Los Angeles. But they had a weak motion picture department. However, they recently acquired Triad, a smaller agency — not one of the big three — which had some very good motion picture agents. So William Morris is now a player in the movie business again and it will be interesting to see how that works out. They are certainly pursuing our clients. Eagerly! One of your questions asked how an agency gets clients: the preferred way to get clients is to steal them. Just less trouble than bringing them up from pups. Actually, I am being a little harsh. Agents do have a bad name!

The other thing that has happened recently involves Triad, Intertalent, and UTA, three smaller agencies that were also players in the business. Ten prominent agents from Intertalent came over to ICM about a month ago, and the rest of them went to UTA. Triad and Intertalent don't exist anymore, and William Morris is much stronger in the motion picture department. ICM picked up some Intertalent agents and UTA has picked up the rest of them. It will be interesting to see how this reorganization plays out.

Let me add here that I am speaking only for myself in this conversation. These are strictly my own opinions and judgments — not those of anyone else at ICM.

Basic question: What does an agent do? The answer to that is, an agent sells. The first thing the agent has to do is to sell himself to the client. The second thing the agent has to do is sell the client to the buyer — the producer. The last thing the agent has to do is to make a deal. The deal for most agents is the least of it. Ours is a sales business. That may be the reason why agents have a bad reputation. I think that they are thought of as being even beneath lawyers in the scheme of things.

What do we offer to our clients? Why should somebody be an ICM client? The job of an agent is to get work for the client. It is that simple. In return for getting the work, the agent gets 10 percent right off the top. Rumor has it that CAA will cut its commission drastically — especially with the really heavy duty players — with the people who make five, six, or eight million dollars a picture. We will not cut our commission. [And the unions won't let you charge a commission if the artist is just getting scale — the union minimum for the job.]

In any event, getting work for the client can mean a whole range of things, depending on who the client is. If the client is an actor, especially an up-and-coming actor, it is just a question of finding the poor critter a job. They just go nuts when they are not working. It is a really rough business that way. It is one of the few businesses I know where you can't do what you do — you can't practice your craft — unless you are employed. A painter can paint, a musician can play the piano, but the actor can't act without a job. With an up-and-coming director, someone who is trying to get his first picture, the agent's role includes getting him a job, and holding his hand, and explaining to him that he is going to have to make this movie that he hates. The agent's work is somewhat different when you are talking about somebody established like Mike Nichols or Woody Allen. You don't have to get work for Mr. Allen. With somebody like Nichols it's a question of what does he want to do? He decides what he wants to do and then our job is to get him the rights and make sure he makes as much money as possible and has absolute creative control.

If someone like Mike Nichols is with your agency, is there an agreement that he won't go out looking for a project by himself? Does it mean he doesn't look, only you look?

Oh no. He looks. We send him stuff. He reads stuff himself.

Say he went to a party and met someone who said, "Will you look at something I have?" Is he obliged to say, "No, go to my agent"?

No. Of course, he can read it, but we will ultimately make the deal and take the 10%. It all comes out in the end.

To give you a sense of the sheer size of the agency and of the clients we represent, maybe I should give you a brief laundry list. Here in New York, Sam Cohn, whom I work for, represents Woody Allen, Robert Benton, Sigourney Weaver, Vanessa Redgrave, Vanessa's daughter Natasha Richardson, it goes on and on. And out on the West Coast they represent everybody from Arnold Schwarzenegger, to Dudley Moore, to Julia Roberts, to Michelle Pfeiffer. What that translates into is leverage. One of the things that a large agency brings to the table is a kind of a synergy. The ability to bring elements together. It's funny. Lawyers have conflicts, agents have packages.

What we offer our clients, in the most basic sense, is work. You can hold their hands as much as you like and as much as they like and at the end of the day, if you don't get them a job, they are going to fire you. That is just how it is. It is not about nice, it is about getting them the right projects.

As a deal-maker, what do you do on a day to day basis? I sense that the agent gets so far and then passes it over to you and you consolidate the deal.

What I do depends on the deal. It depends on the client. On major deals, Sam and I would do it together, practically every step of the way. Sometimes he'll let me make the whole deal and just give me some guidance about where he wants to be, and I talk to the client about where the client wants to be. In making a director's deal you can't say a week later, "Oh, by the way, he gets final cut." You have to consolidate it all up front — that is why those checklists. You really have to go a step at a time in negotiating. It is not like the studio sends you a contract and then you work from the piece of paper. You make a deal. You make it on the telephone, or at a meeting. You make notes. That is step one, the making of the deal itself. And step two is trying to get it written down in such a way that it actually says what you agreed to. That is the other part of what I do. I also do a certain amount of psychotherapy, general hand-holding. Sometimes I get close to being an agent but I don't really like selling. I'd rather make deals.

Do people have contracts with their agents or can they just leave whenever they like?
We like them to have contracts, which we call agency papers. We try to get people to sign them. Sometimes they do sign and sometimes they don't. Sam will never press a client to sign the agency papers. He feels if the relationship isn't there, he is not interested in keeping somebody.

Signing one of these papers is a mutual security deal? That is, they can't leave you when they get successful and they get wooed, but is it also the case that if they start failing you can't just say, "I want to stop being your agent"?
They can always leave, they just have to go on paying your commission. So the new agents who represent them have to do it commission-free until the expiration of the agency agreement. What usually happens is a practical compromise. Even if someone has signed agency papers, you with the new agent might work out a commission-sharing arrangement until the term of the papers is up. That is what we normally do, unless the relationship has become truly unfriendly. When _____ left us to go to _____, you better believe we got every last penny of our commission!

I think it would be interesting at this point to take a look at the profit participation statement I brought along [in order to explain the difference between net and gross profit participations]. Look at the total gross receipts generated by this movie—cumulatively, $103 million, so this movie did well. Then you have a distribution fee of $33 million, which just came right off the top and went into the pocket of the studio. That is the studio's compensation for distributing the movie. Thirty-three percent is an average distribution fee; the actual percentage depends on the medium. On network TV it might actually be 25 percent, or a foreign theatrical distribution fee might be 45 percent just because there is so much more work. When making a network deal, you make three phone calls. Twenty-five percent is a lot for three phone calls, but the studio is like the house in gambling. So that is 33 percent off the top. We are down to a balance of $69 million. Then you've got your distribution expenses, which ran around $35 million. They consist primarily of advertising at $21 million and prints at $8 million. That leaves you still with $34 million net. So you think to yourself, "Well, maybe there will be some 'profit.'" However, you've got $9 million in interest on negative cost [the money borrowed to finance the movie; even if the studio does not borrow the money and instead uses funds in hand, interest is charged] and a negative cost of $27 million. You see, the studio system is set up so that as an accounting matter the studio gets paid back its negative cost last. Until it has gotten its negative cost back, it is charging you interest on the negative cost. Frequently they haven't borrowed the money at all. I'll never forget Sam having a discussion with Jeff Katzenberg at Disney about this. He said, ".But you don't even borrow the money, you don't have to pay any interest!" Katzenberg's reaction was, "Hey, it's the cost of money." So, here we end up with a loss of $2 million. In other words, the net profit participants never saw one cent on this movie, which did over $100 million in distributor's gross worldwide. That is why they say there is no net. And that is why, if you can get it, you get *gross* [for your clients].

Let me talk about gross profit participation by using _____ as an example. The movie must have done $350 million world wide, resulting in maybe $2 million of net profit. What happened on _____ was that _____ and _____ and _____ were getting among them probably 30 or 40 percent of every dollar that came in at the box office after a certain point. When you are chasing that kind of prebreak gross, you never get to break even. That was Art Buchwald's complaint in his suit against Paramount and Eddie Murphy. He said, "How can this movie, *Coming to America*, have grossed $300 million worldwide and not have any net profit?" And the answer is that Eddie Murphy was getting so much out of each dollar that you never got to "break even."

This profit participation statement is dated a little more than a year ago. Wouldn't this film go on generating income?
Not much. The sequence is theatrical release, then home video within four to six months, then pay-cable, and then network, and then syndication. The foreign theatrical releases usually happen at the same time as home video. So if you look at this you will see that pretty much all of the revenue sources are represented. The only place where you might see some more money is television syndication, which is the last window.

Syndication. Does that mean it plays not on a network but on the independent TV stations?
Yes. It means sales to local stations. There is something else called first-run

syndication which is essentially an informal network: a bunch of local independent stations will agree to show a film for the first time.

How does the financing of an independent movie differ from that of a studio movie?
The financing is completely different for an independent picture. When you make a movie with a studio you get all your dough at one clip. And you pay for it. With an independently financed picture you probably raise the money by preselling distribution rights to various territories. For example, you would presell Japanese theatrical rights for — I am making up the numbers because I don't do this regularly — a million bucks. You presell U.S. theatrical for five million. I heard last week that somebody was prepared to sell worldwide rights for thirteen million, which is the budget of the picture. You carve up the world, and the buyers — the presale purchasers — sign contracts that say they will pay you the agreed-upon sum when you deliver the picture. You ask, how do you get your money? You take [the presale] contracts to the bank and the bank will lend you money against them. But the bank will also charge you interest. You won't be paying overhead, but you will be paying for the completion bond.

When a studio makes a picture the studio guarantees completion. When the picture goes over budget, the studio just digs into its pocket. That is *Heaven's Gate*. I've seen a studio abandon a picture a week into principal photography, when they are going to take a four or five million dollar bath for doing that. Once they're any further along, they usually can't do that. On an independently financed picture the completion bond is a form of insurance. You pay a fee of roughly three percent of the budget. And if you go over budget the completion guarantor has to pay the additional costs. In return for paying the additional costs, the completion guarantor gets to come in and take over production and tell the people involved what to do.

Who are bond companies?
They are essentially insurers.

Do they know about how to complete movies?
They actually have experienced production personnel. I have only seen them take over once, because generally the people making the film manage to get more money from additional investors, or other sources. The mere threat of the bonding company taking over is enough to make somebody

cough up the money. In Spike Lee's *Malcolm X*, I think he ended up putting up his salary.

Yes, and he got extra money from friends, including Bill Cosby and Michael Jordan.
The bond company was called in on a picture called _____. I don't know if anyone ever saw that movie? A real dog. A major dog. The completion guarantor had to put up the money and they sent representatives to the set and they stood behind the shoulder of the director. They said, "No, you may not do another take of that scene. No, you have to stop now." I don't think anything would have helped that picture, but this certainly didn't help it.

What percentage of major films these days are independents as opposed to studio backed?
Most really expensive films have to be studio backed. There are exceptions to that. The one that springs to mind is the Bertolucci's *The Last Emperor.* That was a while ago. There are some financiers who are able to put together something that large, but you also need Bertolucci's name.

You have told us what you offer to your clients. Could you talk about what you offer buyers, about what kind of a product you are selling?
What we offer the buyer is access. Sometimes that is new talent which we have discovered. More often the studio says, "Gee, this is a perfect project for Nichols." So they call and see if he is interested. If he is interested, then we make the deal. You don't have to do a lot of selling with somebody like Julia Roberts or Mike Nichols. At that level you're making sure that your clients get offered what they want. So you have to go out and find out what is around for them.

One of the most interesting questions you sent me was, "What is talent as a property?" It is not something that I think about in everyday life very often, but it is a good question. What I think is that talent, at least on the highest level, is not fungible. It is truly unique. I suppose there is always second best, and it is always a trade-off between the money and the talent. If you are willing to pay five million dollars to the actor, you are obviously going to get a lot more than you are going to get if you are willing to pay fifty thousand dollars.

I was wondering what "a lot more" consists of?
There really is a sense that there is somebody who is the best person for the role. That is what a director would be thinking. Who is best for this? We

recently had a situation where a director and a studio disagreed about who should be playing a part. Finally, the studio said, "All right, we will give you three weeks to find somebody better. And if we think this person is better, then you can use her, but don't count on it." My client found someone else whom he liked better and was able to persuade the studio to hire the new actress, even though they also had to pay off the first actress. So it cost them quite a lot of dough. I hope they were happy. I hope that they felt that they had gotten what they should have gotten.

When a producer, director, or studio wants one of your clients for the major role in a picture, do you ever get to say, "How about using this other client of ours in one of the lesser roles?" Is that a way that you work with actors who are coming up in the field?
I don't know the answer to that because I don't do that on a day-to-day basis. We pride ourselves on doing the exact opposite. We have a list of actors and actresses that includes everybody in a particular age category. Not just our clients. Everybody. When we are sitting with a producer trying to cast a picture, we will go over that whole list. If we have an idea for somebody who is perfect for the role but who is not represented by us, we will make that suggestion.

What is in it for you to do that?
Credibility. And we don't always do it. That happens more at Sam Cohn's level. Your average casting agent will probably submit a list of his own agency's clients. Also the big star might say, "Hey, I want to work with so-and-so." That is her prerogative.

Suppose you represent two directors who both want to direct the same project. How do you in-house manage a conflict of that sort.
A nightmare.

Does it happen?
Well, I am trying to think. Yes, I have seen it happen.

I pose the question only because it is a question in a way about talent. Do you decide which one of them is better for it? Or do you decide which one needs the job more?
The answer is, you don't decide. If you did decide you would be killed. You'd lose one client for sure. You pray that the producer has a firm opin-

ion. It is possible to get caught in a disastrous situation between clients. We had a situation where one of our director clients didn't want to use one of our actor clients in a film. He wanted that role desperately! It was a nightmare. Ultimately the director had his way, and we lost the actor.

Obviously if it were just a matter of commercial interest, an agent would want to move a client into the highest ticket films as quickly as possible. Do agents take into account any other factors, like career trajectory? Do agents advise their clients that this high-prestige project would be a better thing to do even though it pays less money than other projects? What are some of the other things that might come into play?

Really, just what you said, what would be best for the client's career. For example, Sam will sometimes advise a client to do a play off Broadway, make eight hundred dollars a week for four months. Or do a play on Broadway and make five thousand a week for six months instead of five million for a picture. (I am making up the numbers.) Doing a play in New York may be important for the client because it is prestigious. Even doing a play in a regional theater is prestigious, especially Shakespeare or the classics, or an important new play. A *good* agent will recommend that kind of thing. A good agent will also recommend a picture where the client is not going to make that much money, instead of a picture where the client could make more money but that is garbage.

So in a way, an agent is looking at a client as something to be invested in, long-term. One wants to see capital appreciation, not just short-term gain.

A good agent. Yes. A classic example is _____. He was discovered off-off Broadway by the *New York Times* and then by Sam Cohn. Sam was representing him and was orchestrating his career and arranged for him to do _____ as his first picture — an excellent choice. He is a great actor. And then he seems to have been seduced by the glitz of the people who would fly him to Las Vegas and what have you, and he ended up with managers and with another agency. And he made a string of unbelievable bowsers.

So what the agents have to sell clients is the reputation that the agents earn by having a stable of clients who have good career trajectories in the long term. If you are an agent, the short-term gain is obviously not always your primary interest, right?

Again, if you are a good agent, yes. I think a lot of agents — of course not ICM agents — don't see further ahead than next week, if that. Many of them just aren't suited to longer perspectives. They don't have that view and they are also not involved in more than just motion pictures. One of ICM's strengths is a New York office and involvement in the theater community. This is my personal predilection. But I think it is more likely that you are going to find what I will, forgive me, call art, in the theater than you are in the movies — at least in the American movies.

You've said that doing a play is prestigious and that therefore an actor might be advised to do a play to enhance his or her image as a serious artist. At whom is that image then aimed? Is the thinking that doing a play or a certain kind of movie, that maybe isn't going to be seen by that many people, will still somehow make audiences think of the actor differently? Or is the image of "serious artist" aimed at the producers?
It is aimed directly at the producers. And the critics. It is through the critics that you get to the producers.

Is there ever a point when you think about how to build the actor's popularity or appeal to audiences?
You would think about that in terms of a choice of pictures. You might, for example, not want your client to play unsympathetic roles. On the other hand, you might want your client to play a very unsympathetic role to demonstrate that she is a great actress. You know, everybody thought that she was just Little Mary Sunshine, and all of a sudden she is the Wicked Witch of the West. In that sense you might think about the audience.

It turns out audiences don't really enter into your thinking.
To some extent they do. The thinking of the artist, yes. Although some of my clients think primarily about money. But that is in a sense thinking about the audience: who will go see this picture or play?

Don't directors and sometimes actors, too, want to have a certain kind of reputation? They have ideas about what kind of product they want to make. Doesn't the agent have to take these issues into account?
Usually your client will tell you. If your client is on a level high enough to be able to control what he is making, he will know. Take someone like Woody Allen. He just wants to do what he wants to do. That is what it is about for him. He is the only director I know of who has absolute creative control. I mean absolute. The studio doesn't have script approval. The studio never sees the script. Nobody ever sees the script. And then he goes

back and he reshoots. Somebody like _____ is concerned about how he is perceived. I think a lot of them are, but I think they are much more concerned about how they are perceived by the critics and the people they hang out with than by general audiences.

Do agents think of themselves as participants in a creative, artistic process? They too are making art in some sense?
I think the good ones do. I know Sam does.

Do you think that is more true in the New York office than in the LA office?
No. Just speaking for myself, I find it incredibly rewarding when I have represented somebody whose work I admire, and made the deal for a project that I really care about. It doesn't happen that often. For example, when Bill Irwin does something on Broadway. Bill is a great, great artist. (I am sounding pompous.) I am putting together a deal now for him to do a new Broadway show. And that feels good. That really does.

Then it isn't actually all money that drives your work. There is also an ideology of art and creativity and quality that is a part of what you do. It is not just "I could make a great deal on this schlock movie?"
It depends on who you are dealing with. I think I probably live in a fairly sheltered little world. Sam is unusual. First of all, he is insistent on being in New York rather than in Los Angeles. And this is a man who goes every night to the opera or classical music or the theater. He also sees every movie. I wish I could believe most people in the business were like that. Here is a story for you. We are sitting in one of our casting meetings one day during the time that _____ was directing [a Shakespeare play] at the Public Theater. He wanted some movie actress. We were on this coast-to-coast hook-up with the agents of the West Coast office, and one of them (no longer an ICM employee) pipes up and says, "Is there a script?" What can I tell you?

It seems to me — maybe I am wrong though — that talent means something different for somebody like Meryl Streep or Woody Allen than it does for somebody who is brand new and unknown. "Talent" for Streep and Allen means not only what they can do but the whole aura, their reputation, their fame, their proven market value. By the time they get to that stage, even if they are totally worthless as actors, they are still big talent. Right? Even if they don't have any talent? How do you think about a young person, actress or actor, let's say, in terms of talent?

Does talent mean simply abilities that are recognizable to somebody? Who recognizes them if they are there? Or does talent mean that you can imagine them being Sigourney Weaver or John Wayne in twenty years?

It is an excellent question but I don't think it has an answer. Sometimes you just know. Our younger agents and even the more senior people will go to film festivals, will go see things off Broadway, or even off off Broadway, will hang out around the drama schools and the film schools.

Really?

Yes. They really do all that. _____ of our office plucked _____ out of [drama school].

How does he sleep?

Badly! There is an answer to your question about talent. We all thought he was a wonderful actor when we first saw him in _____. Also, he was so handsome. Appearance is extremely important in the business. The right appearance will make up for perhaps less acting ability. Sometimes that is just what you are looking for. On the other hand, there is the _____ phenomenon. That just happened. There is no way you could have predicted that. Who could have predicted that? Dumb luck.

When _____ finds somebody like _____ at [drama school] or whatever, is he thinking this is a person who could really be a huge star in a little while?

He is thinking, "That is a person who can make a lot of money for the agency." Or maybe not. What he was probably thinking is, "God, this man is talented, he is a wonderful actor, he looks wonderful, and I found him and no one else knows about him." The goal is to come up with a client who is going to have a great career and make a lot of money for himself and for you. But the basic thought is, this is good work. Certainly that is true when it comes to finding new playwrights, which is something else that we do.

One of the great entrepreneurs in the magazine business, which I study, was S. S. McClure, who said, talking the way you have been talking, "I know what is good when I see it." He had been a traveling salesman for a number of years and he said he knew Americans because he had talked with them all over the Midwest. Therefore, when he recognized something as good, he knew they would all like it too. I am wondering if there is some sense in which people who are identifying new talent see themselves as standing in for the big audience out there, and knowing in advance what it will like?

That is very interesting. The people I work with in New York are your ultimate elitist, establishment, liberal, whatever types. I don't think they see themselves as perceiving the common denominator at all. That may not be true of the agents in Los Angeles! It's like Potter Stewart's line about obscenity — he knew it when he saw it. I guess there is sort of a platonic ideal of someone who could be a great performer in certain things. And I guess the agents have to think that they can recognize it.

How do agents find work for the clients? And how different is the process for actors, writers, musicians?

There are agents who represent only actors. Normally someone who represents actors doesn't represent anybody else. You read a screenplay and then you make up lists of all your clients who are right for each role in the movie. Then you call the casting director or the director of the picture, depending on who you have a relationship with, and you say "how about so-and-so for this part?" And the director will say, "No, I've seen him, he's a lox." And you say, "All right," and you go on to the next name on your list. The relationship is between the casting agents and the casting director. The minute a casting director is assigned to a picture, he or she will immediately send the script to all the major agencies. It also happens on a more informal basis earlier. But in terms of getting work for the up-and-comer, that is how it happens.

For a screenwriter it is much harder. Again, there are lists that are circulated by the studios of the projects they have that need writers. Each agent is assigned two or three studios that he or she covers. They go out there once a week or whatever and they prowl around and they meet with the production executives and they say, "I have this great new kid. I have a spec script, you want to take a look." Director, much, much harder. If he has worked in the theater you can sometimes move him into movies or television. That happens. Sometimes people move out of television and into features. But that is a very rough one because someone directing a movie is being trusted with a great deal of money and nobody likes to do it for the first time.

Let's say that you have a writer who does a spec script. Do you try to sell that script? Or do you use that simply as audition piece to try and find work that the studio has already identified?

Both. Sometimes you'll get a great spec script. Unfortunately or fortunately, I don't know which, these days we're not having great auctions of spec scripts. There was a period about three years ago when you would get a script that was written on spec and it was exactly like something else that had just been a huge success, or Joe Eszterhas had written it, and you would send it around town to everybody and you would say, "You have twenty-four hours to bid." They were getting a million bucks for scripts for first-time writers. The studios have tried to cut back on that a little bit.

I'd like to ask a question about gender. What percentage of the agents would be male or female, and what percentage of the artists on your books would be male and female?

Well, let's see. I think agents might be pretty close to 50–50. Maybe 60–40 men. It is a business where women have historically done quite well. I think that is because they get to do the maternal thing with the clients and then be very fierce in protecting their cubs with the buyers. There are some really prominent women agents, two in particular, Paula Wagner and Rosalie Swedlin, who just left CAA: Paula to run Tom Cruise's production company and Rosalie to run some other very important movie star's company. We have many very substantial women agents at ICM who represent important clients.

There are probably more women agents than there are women executives in the movie business and on higher levels. There is a female role, you know, that you can fall into with clients. It can work very well. In terms of clients, I don't know. Probably, we represent more men. Certainly more of our directors and writers are male. The actors may be 50–50, but it may be 60–40. By and large the men make more money. It is a classic complaint. Meryl Streep was quoted at great length in the press about a year ago complaining about how the men made more money, and they do.

On the other hand, a client of ours, who is an enormously successful screenwriter, and has now turned her hand to directing, has got as much leverage as any other director on her level now. We can make really good deals for her. She got the opportunity to direct because she had been enormously successful as a writer. Men have come to directing in the same way. It is one way to become a movie director. (You have all heard the classic line that in the movie business the writer is the woman, the writer being the lowest of the low. The writer may not even be allowed on the set.)

Do you ever hear people who are negotiating on behalf of the studio say things like, "That movie's only got so much potential because it's perceived to be a woman's film or a black film"? Do you see those sorts of ceilings set on things as far as what's marketable? And how much negotiating power do you have?

I'll tell you where that will get played out: in the budget of the picture. When they set the budget, which tells them what they can pay the director and the actors, they will say to themselves, "If we spend more than fifteen million dollars on this movie we do not have a prayer of getting our money back because it is not going to play to that many people." The impact of race and gender doesn't get down to my level in the negotiations. It impacts on me and my clients in the parameters of the deal that is offered.

On the flip side of that, are there certain characteristics that are bankable, as with the hot market for young black directors a few years ago?
As long as their pictures make money, the studio doesn't care about anything else. It's about the bottom line.

Can a star, actor, director, or writer become big enough to succeed without an agent?
If you're somebody who's not out there looking for jobs, and people are coming to you, you still need a deal-maker. So you'd have to have a lawyer. I recently advised a friend of mine who was looking for a new agent. Although he needed an agent for movies, he did not need an agent for the legitimate theater because he was so well known in the theater that there's no reason he should pay ten percent. Everybody would come to him with everything anyway. When he wanted to do a role, he could just go to his lawyer and say, "Make me a deal and I'll pay you by the hour." You know who doesn't have an agent? George Scott doesn't have an agent. [He has a lawyer who makes his deals.]

How about Jack Nicholson?
No, he has an agent, and so does Gene Hackman. They almost all have agents. What the agency brings you is the packaging ability.

How long does it take to make the usual movie, from inception to the time it actually opens?
A studio will always have a hundred or two hundred projects in development, being written, frequently being supervised by a director. Eventually, after two or four, or ten, or forty-five drafts, the studio will either abandon the script or greenlight it. There are screen plays that have been floating around Hollywood for ten years. Famous unproduced screenplays. In fact, one of Larry Kasdan's early screenplays just got made into a movie that got panned. Most scripts just get abandoned or they go into what is called turnaround. When a studio abandons the screenplay, the director or pro-

ducer has the right to take it to another studio to see if they want to make the picture. If the other studio wants to make the movie, it must pay back the first studio all costs. The famous story about *E.T.* is that it was put into turnaround by whoever had it. I think Columbia put it into turnaround, and Universal finally made it. Studios do not like putting projects into turnaround because it could cost executives their jobs if someone else makes the movie and it is a success. So, it is sometimes very hard to get a turnaround. And they make it expensive, because by the time a script has been written the studio may have more than a million bucks invested in it. Well, that is on the high side. But a successful screenwriter, an experienced screenwriter, who makes probably $450,000 for writing the screenplay, would probably get another $150,000 if the movie were actually made. So you figure you got $450,000 for the script and a director has been hired to supervise development for another $25,000, they may have gone so far as to prepare a budget and so forth. You could have three quarters of a million dollars of costs at the point where you abandon it. And then they run overhead and interest on that. So, to pick up a project from turnaround can be expensive.

Anyhow, let's assume that the studio actually decides to greenlight the picture. There is a director who wants to make it. A greenlight means that the budget has been approved, and that the cast has been approved, and that a start date has been set. This may be anywhere from one and a half to ten years after the development process started. You generally start really preparing the film about six months before you start shooting. Preproduction is the twelve-week period before commencement of principal photography. Principal photography, depending on the size of the picture, can be anywhere between eight and sixteen weeks. Maybe twenty weeks if it is a musical or something complicated. But on an average I think it takes about three months for principal photography.

Then there is the postproduction process, which is the editing of the film. And there we try to insist that our director clients have six months for postproduction. I've seen it done in four months or less. You put on double shifts of editors and you cut around the clock, but you probably don't get the best picture that way. Ideally, you want six months. This is one of the things about which I fight most often with the studios. With somebody like ———, no problem, he gets what he wants. He gets seven months. It is something that we are adamant about, even with our younger directors — or at least if we can't win the point, we make sure the director understands the risks of the situation. In the best case, a picture could be released nine or ten months after the start of preproduction. A year is more like it.

A completely different subject: There seem to be two classes of actors. In one class there's Clint Eastwood, Arnold Schwarzenegger, Stephen Segal, the kind of people you go to see because you know what they are going to do. You go because of their already established acting personae, which don't change much from film to film. In the other class, you might find Willem Dafoe, William Hurt, whom people go to see because they want to see great acting. Does an agent look for either quality when they go scouting at Julliard? Is it the actor who decides what class she or he will fall into, or does the agent have anything to do with it?

The thing you are describing is a very real phenomenon. Clint Eastwood—of course he is partially self-invented—but he is also just a presence. I would imagine he was from the beginning, although I don't know, because I didn't see him back then. Bruce Willis got his start off Broadway. I would imagine that Bruce Willis then was just riveting. I would imagine you walked into a room with him and you couldn't take your eyes off him. You know it when that happens. I've never had the experience with an unknown. When you meet somebody who is really a big star that way, it is hard to be sure whether you are responding to something that is actually coming from them, or to your own expectations. But I think there is actually a kind of vibration from those people. This is not true of all good actors—I mean, _____, for example, _____ is just folks, and yet she is this amazing actress. Being in the room with _____, on the other hand, is another kind of experience. You really can't take your eyes off him. I think you probably know it when you see it. Wouldn't it be great to find a new one like that?

I am struck by the image of the entertainment industry as a place where real talent will be recognized and those who are recognized, at least at the highest levels, really have this charismatic quality.

Hey, I may be naive. I can't help it.

You have constructed the entertainment industry as the place where the myth of success really works. I guess I am a little bit suspicious of that. It seems to me that for every Bruce Willis there are a bunch of others who we never happen to see for one reason or another. And Bruce Willis's appeal also is something not unique to him, but rather a relationship between his type and a certain moment when that kind of fast-talking, slightly arrogant, macho was gonna play.

I would have to see it the way I do, wouldn't I? I can't say you are wrong. I will say, I think that if Bruce Willis gets himself the role in the off-Broadway play, if he gets that far, someone will find him. I think there are some actors who can't even get that first off-Broadway role and they may be blazingly talented. But if you get the first shot, and some of it is luck, you will be found. Although, of course, looks can count for as much as acting ability.

Are there people you would never think of taking on as clients, no matter how marketable, or are there deals you wouldn't make even if they looked extraordinarily lucrative?
Yes. Absolutely. It's generally not my choice. Sam definitely makes those choices. I have seen him turn down clients on the basis of their politics or just because he thinks their work is really horrible. He may say someone else in the agency can represent them. And there are actually people he wouldn't have the agency represent.

Deals we wouldn't make? We recently had an offer to do one of our clients' plays in South Africa and my first question was, "Is it an integrated house?" I was told yes it was. I went back to my client and I told him it was, but the ultimate decision was the client's, not mine.

Can you think of a major mistake you've made in making a deal?
You can make too good a deal. We made a deal for _____ in _____ that is the best damn deal that I have ever seen. Each source of revenue was in a separate pot. There were separate income streams. It was a world class deal. The picture didn't do very well, and she didn't make as much money as she thought she was going to make and she wasn't happy. It became a bad deal. Would we make that mistake again? You bet!

Nathan Pearson Broadcasting Partners

October 8, 1992

. . . .

Nathan Pearson is the cochairman of Broadcasting Partners, LLC, a media investment and management company. He was formerly a managing principal of Broadcasting Partners, Inc. (BPI), a radio broadcasting company based in New York City. Prior to the formation of BPI he was a management consultant with McKinsey and Company, Inc. In 1974 he earned B.A. and M.A. degrees from Wesleyan University in music, where his M.A. thesis was an oral history of the life and times of Texas songster Mance Lipscomb. As an ethnomusicologist Pearson worked with the Smithsonian Institution, the Library of Congress, the National Endowment for the Arts, and several state and local groups. In 1987 he published Goin' to Kansas City *with the University of Illinois Press, a history of the development and flowering of jazz in the Midwest prior to World War II. Pearson received an M.B.A. degree from Columbia University in 1982.*

Let me give an introduction to Broadcasting Partners. Broadcasting Partners is a partnership in concept, but not in legal practice. What I mean by that is that we are a corporation. We call ourselves Broadcasting Partners because my two colleagues and I who founded it think of all the people who work in the company as being our partners. And so we tend to not refer to the people who work with us as employees but rather as associates. The partners was part of the concept of the company. We were formed as a leveraged buyout in 1988. This created gigantic amounts of debt, which we regretted for a long time, but it also gave us the opportunity to go into business in a way that if it weren't for debt, we couldn't have done. We were formed around the expertise of my two colleagues, who are both career radio broadcasters. They had each been in the industry about twenty years. One had run KISS FM, which is the leading black station in New York; the other ran KISS before him and after that WOR AM, which was then the leading talk radio station in New York City. They were both very well known for their skills and we met through serendipity and got along quite well. From this came our concept of how to operate the company. We had one guy who did programming; his name is Barry Mayo. He is my partner, lives in Chicago and runs our black radio station there, and also supervises the programming for the whole company, which is a large part of what this is about. The second guy is named Lee Simonson and his area is sales and radio station operating management primarily, and he is in New York with me. He is in charge of sales training and helping to recruit and develop sales talent and sales management in the various stations. I [handle] the financial, general administrative, legal, regulatory, technological, and everything else that kind of fits in the cracks. It is a good working team. We collaborate on strategy, we collaborate on major hiring and firing at the stations, and we enjoy each other's company a lot.

We have been in business about four years and we are actively trying to grow through acquisition or merger or something like that. In this industry, and in many industries, you can categorize the companies in two or three different groups. One group in radio is that owned by much larger companies, like the ABC/Capital Cities radio stations, the CBS radio stations, the Westinghouse, ViaCom, COX, Tribune companies and so on. Those radio groups tend to be a tiny part of the parent company. In the case of ABC/Cap Cities, they have the single largest group in the whole radio business, but they account for probably less than 3 or 4 percent of Cap Cities' revenues. So, while they are big news for our business, they are tiny news for Cap Cities. And correspondingly, they get virtually no attention from Cap Cities' management, as is frankly appropriate for Cap Cities. In consequence, while Cap Cities is one of the best run media businesses in America, their radio group is relatively poorly run. The same is true of CBS. The same is true of Westinghouse. The same is true of ViaCom. Go down the list. In each case, for pretty much the same reason. So that is one group, which is a very important group within the industry, and frankly leaves a lot of opportunities for people like us.

One other group is the old-time, established mom-and-pop broadcasters, which is where the industry really has been for most of its history. There are so many radio stations, about eleven thousand total, and close to ten thousand commercial ones in the United States. There have been lots of opportunities for individual owner-operators to have a station in relatively small markets, like New Britain, Connecticut. If they got into the business long enough ago, more than twenty years ago, say, their cost of entry was very low and in many cases they can do just fine with a very small-scale business. They don't have much debt. The profits all go to them and if the profits aren't very much, it's still enough for a good living. They are probably a major force in their local town. They probably broadcast high school and college sports, and some radio programming the owner happens to like. And that is probably two-thirds of the whole industry in terms of the number of radio stations. It's a huge portion. They are not typically the major market leaders in big cities, but that's not where most radio stations are.

A third group is people like us, who are relatively recent owner-operators. This group came into business in the late seventies through the late eighties when the leveraged gearing up in America was happening and the media business became very popular for investment bankers and lenders, in part because of the very high margins that they can offer when they are run well. So a number of people got into business who were much more aggressive and they continue to be aggressive because they carry a lot of debt and are responsible to outside investors. It's kind of like a squirrel on a treadmill. You'd have to run to go forward or else you stop running and die because your debt will catch up with you. So, in general, those kinds of groups are the more aggressive, the more creative. They have less freedom, however, in terms of how they can play with their product. They tend to be the most aggressive about growth and acquisition. Within this group, our company has been lucky to be one of the best performers and we hope to continue to do that by growing. Right now we are facing a lot of struggles and strains because we have investors with different objectives. So that is the kind of general framework within our industry. Of course, there are many more subsegments, but those are the three main groups.

As for the internal structure of our company, we are a very decentralized business. We tend to believe that radio is primarily a local business. That is one of the things that is fun about it. Each one of our radio stations is locally programmed and locally managed. We believe in recruiting, training, and putting in place the best local managers we can. They then run the station as a small local business with between twenty and forty-five employees or associates. There is a local sales manager who runs the sales force of between four and twelve people, who are on the street selling advertising time. We also have a local program director and a music director with a staff of disc jockeys — usually five to seven — and an accounting office, a promotion office, and so on. One of the reasons we have done well is that we have been much more diligent and much more focused regarding recruitment than have some other broadcasters. We spend a lot of money each year doing broad, general recruiting searches around the whole industry and other industries to try to find talented people — particularly in sales management — because that is the hardest area to find talented people. When those people are doing their jobs right, we leave them alone. In our first three years of operation we were spending a lot of time in active local management because our local people were not doing so well. We had to try people, test them out, and we failed a few times. So when we failed, the people had to go and we had to kind of parachute in to take their place for a while. For example, in North Carolina, one of my partners and I were spending alternate weeks for about a year and a half going down to Charlotte to run the radio station until we found a good person to put into place. Now we have a good person in place there who has himself recruited some good people below him, and we spend very little time there. We don't need to. The same is true in Detroit, the same is true in Chicago, which in part gives us an opportunity to grow because now we have some senior management time available. So that is kind of a broad picture of the company.

Can you give us an idea of who the investors are? At one point you said they have different investment objectives and that is starting to become a problem.
We have primarily two big investor groups and a bunch of small investors. Each one of these groups is an investment fund. One, called Trust Company of the West, is a pension fund management firm based in California. They have an office in New York. They have about 30 percent of our equity and about a third of our total debt in the form of nonbank debt at higher interest rates than the banks charge. They know a lot about the radio business. They are wonderful people to work with. They are money managers rather than active investment bankers who want to control the business. So, for example, in our board structure, we have eleven members of our board — they have one board seat. They want to have a presence and be able to monitor what is going on.

The leading investor is a New York investment bank called Morgan Lewis Githens & Ahn. They came out of Smith Barney, which is a medium-sized New York investment bank. They went off on their own in 1982. In '88 they formed their first of two general investment funds, which total about $300 million. The typical time horizon for this kind of investor is three to seven years. They want to be in the business for a relatively short period. To come into it when the profitability is growing rapidly, to invest with a relatively small amount of equity and a lot of debt, and get a lot of leverage, which then allows them to get out with a large gain. That is their business. And if you can keep rolling over those kinds of new investors, that is fine for them and fine for us. Unfortunately now, there isn't much debt available, and so it is difficult to accomplish that rolling over process. These investors own half the company and run the board, because that is what these kinds of groups tend to do. They, in the jargon of the industry, want to get liquid. Meaning they want to get some real money back. We would love to have them do that. We are working with them to try to accomplish that. But, their time horizon is relatively short, so it puts some added pressure on us beyond the operations. And so what I meant by different objectives: that one group wants to get some real cash back soon because they need it and the other large group is more comfortable waiting for a while, but at the same time they have no interest in being an active player. So we have to try to balance these two not entirely agreeing forces.

You just described two interests that own 80 percent of the company. Is that correct?
Yes.

So you guys own about 20 percent.
No, about 10 percent. The other 10 percent is owned by other small investors.

Is it Morgan, Lewis that dominates the board and appoints the CEO and chairman of the board?
The chairman of the board is one of Morgan, Lewis. The operating people are us. And so I'm the CEO and one of my sales partners is the COO. My partner in Chicago is the president and the programming guy. And the titles, frankly, are a coin toss.

You said you like to give local control to stations. On the other hand, you've got the pressure from Morgan Lewis, wanting cash right away. Wouldn't that set up a conflict? They are going to want to go to a local station you have just acquired and . . .
If we were doing a mediocre job, if we weren't getting results quickly, they absolutely would do that. And I think what you are leading to is, wouldn't they want to intervene? And say, "Do something faster here; it's not getting profitable fast enough."

Some investor groups, whether it's prudent or not, just do the intervention because they like to and one of the classic bits of Wall Street jargon is, they think they can add value. There is a general conceit among MBAs, especially MBAs who have been either management consultants, which I was, or investment bankers, or lawyers, that they in general know better how to operate business X than do the operators. That's almost never true, but the MBAs like to think it because they are trained to generally oversee and manage things. And they can add a lot of insight. But you have to be mature and careful about where you add it. We've been very fortunate in that the Morgan Lewis group have realized that we know our business and so they have left us largely alone in terms of the operations. If, however, we hadn't achieved results, they wouldn't have. But the good news for us is that some groups would have intervened even if we had achieved results. But these guys are smarter than that.

Is there potential conflict over acquiring more new stations?
Yes, because to grow you have to have capital. These guys don't want to keep their capital in the business. Not because they don't like us or the business, but because they would like to get a return. So, the challenge is to preserve the business and grow it rather than sell it. One of the ways to get their capital back is to sell the whole enterprise. And right now is a very volatile time within radio — because of regulatory change, because of the economy, and various things — and there are some bargains to be had. There are people who would like to buy us.

I want to pursue this one more step. Morgan, Lewis — if they were in it in the beginning which was 1988 — at this point, their time horizon is about up, three to five years is what you were saying. So they would like to bail out with some capital appreciation, but your real growth has come from acquiring stations and turning them around. So now your major investor really wants out, with the goodies, yet the whole objective of the group and the profitability of the group comes from . . .
From finding some more stations and turning them around. Exactly right. That's the quandary. And when we started the whole business we were looking at a very different economic environment than we see now. We started in business at the tail end of the go-go eighties. Everybody thought that by 1991 at the latest we would have done a big deal in acquisition — merger or something — which would have both created growth and provided a wave for at least some cash back to investors. The economic environment has been such that it has been much harder to accomplish that. So, you are absolutely right about that conflict. We had all thought that it would never happen because we thought that things would keep going well. So that is the challenge. We are making money by turning around stations and we have proven our skill at doing that. But the investors, for good reasons of their own, want to get out.

I was wondering if you could give us some examples of the way your black adult contemporary stations serve the needs of the community? How they help build awareness of issues that are important to those listeners?

In terms of addressing the needs of the black adult audience, from our point of view, we never do enough in terms of information, hard information. The primary way we serve their needs is through entertainment, music. Prior to the creation of our [Chicago] station, adult black listeners didn't have a media vehicle that played the kind of music they tend to like to listen to. The primary black radio stations in that market, which is the third biggest in the country, and the second biggest black market in the country — after New York — were almost exclusively youth oriented. Until about fifteen years ago the tastes of young, middle-aged, and older blacks were much more congruent than they tend to be among white or other ethnic group listeners. That changed with rap. Rap became an alien form to older blacks. When we started out in business, one of our biggest claims to fame was to tell listeners we don't play rap because the older black listeners whenever they heard a rap song would turn off the radio or change the station. They just did not want it for a whole variety of reasons: musical, cultural, behavioral, and self-image. So the primary way we serve them is by playing songs they like to hear and giving them an entertainment outlet to tune into.

The second thing is through news and information. Chicago is a big news market. Relative to New York, Philadelphia, Los Angeles, people in Chicago generally care more about news than a lot of other cities — white, black, green. Especially weather. The city has horrible weather. So, weather reports are much more important in that city than most other American cities. If you are an adult black listener, you can get a good news and weather service from us instead of having to change to the all-news station. We stress that, and the other black radio station, which has a more youthful audience, doesn't. We also, as do most major black stations, sign up to a number of black news services. So we both get standard news — UPI and the Associated Press — but we also get dedicated black wire service news, which tends to have an Afrocentric view of the world. We get more African news. We also get syndicated black commentators and so on. All of that is aimed at the general needs of the audience. In addition to that, as do most black radio stations, we have a public interest program which we air on Sunday mornings. It doesn't get huge ratings but it is a very good show. It's a community panel show. We have a moderator for it and it is one of the major forums in Chicago for public servants and public issues to get raised. Our channel, by the way, was one of the ways that [Senator] Carol Braun basically came out as a major political figure two years ago. She had been in politics for a long time, but that was one of the ways she became better known in the black community, which was her springboard. So those programs are effective and do work.

I was interested in your corporate mission statement where you talked about having two primary customers for your radio stations. As a service, your customers are listeners. As a business, your customers are advertisers. Are there instances when the needs of listeners and the needs of advertisers come into conflict?
I'm trying to think if I am aware of any conflicts between listeners and advertisers and I can't think of any. We program the station for listeners. We don't program it for advertisers. Our product is to serve the demographic group we target. Our sales approach, and this is relatively unique to us, is to do a much better job in sales and marketing for our specific audience than most radio stations do. The black niche is a specialized one. So we train our account executives to be highly skilled in marketing to black consumers, whether it's radio or not. We would be happy to help to create a campaign for TV or print or billboards or whatever, because we want to be in the position of being the group that advertisers turn to in order to understand what adult black listeners in Chicago want and need and are likely to respond to and what kind of products are likely to be attractive and appealing to them. It's a huge market. One of the things we like to tell advertisers who are often reluctant to buy time on a black radio station — because black is low class, it's low income, the whole thing — is that the black population of Chicago is bigger than the population of Milwaukee. It is over one million people. There are only two viable ways to reach them: us and the other black radio station. Blacks in general have higher patterns of consumption than do whites. The group we are targeting has about the same demographic profile as listeners to an adult rock-and-roll station, about the same levels of income, the same levels of education, same kind of family structure. But they tend to buy more stuff. Per capita, they are more likely to buy a fancy car than a mid-priced car. They are more likely to buy expensive clothing, and so on. And so there are lots of areas where blacks want to be served well and where in the past they have not been. So part of our challenge is to get manufacturers and merchants to pay more attention to this market and serve it better.

For example, we have done a lot of work with airlines. Blacks travel more often than do whites in terms of income level, higher use of air travel and hotel use for leisure and so on. For example, airlines like Lufthansa, who had never thought of advertising to blacks, now do so on our station because Germany is a favorite spot for black Chicagoans to go due to the large number of black soldiers there. For example, we've done tours of black pop artists in France, Germany, and Scandinavia and done live broadcasts from Germany back to Chicago. So, we try to be creative in finding ways to do something for advertisers and listeners both. But sources of conflict, I can't think of any because we aren't for advertisers who don't want our audience. We are for advertisers who do want our audience. That is what we focus on.

This is a format that you developed and claim credit for developing. Are your partners black?
One is. The partner in charge of programming. About 65 percent of our employees are black because three of our five stations are black format stations. At those stations, probably 75 to 80 percent of all the employees are black. Finding great black people to work in those stations is our single biggest problem and biggest challenge. Especially at a senior level. General management, sales management. We have a very hard time finding qualified black sales and general management. It took us a year and a half to find a general manager of our Charlotte station because we were hoping to locate a black person because in Charlotte this is the only media source for black people. Charlotte is about 20 percent black. It's a big city and the general manager of that station automatically becomes a major leader of the black community in Charlotte. So, we thought it was very important to have the person be not only good, but also black.

In terms of starting up the company, how did you get involved in it? The other two guys already had experience in black radio.
I met them in July of '88 through a friend who was on a board with one of them and they were looking for somebody to complement their own skills. They didn't have any financial or general management background. So they were trying to find that to add to the company. They weren't looking for a partner, they were looking for somebody to work for them. I was looking for a company to run. But it turned out that we are better as a trio than any one of us would be as a solo. We all recognize that. My own background in black music, actually, is more extensive than either of my colleagues including the black colleague. I am an ethnomusicologist. My field is black music. I wrote my master's thesis on a songster from Texas. I spent eight years producing blues and jazz and folk festivals around America. I have done a major museum exhibit about the history of jazz in the Midwest. I've done a series of TV shows for PBS about jazz, a whole variety

of things. If there is one person in the company whom somebody would turn to with a question about black music, it is me, oddly enough.

But none of that music ever gets on your stations?
Unfortunately, this is one of the curses of high leverage. It is kind of along the lines of both of your questions about what kind of pressure our board puts on us. And it's not just the board. It's our debt pressure. We have to maximize every time part we can, and the way we do that is by listening to our listeners. And it's unfortunate because my black partner in Chicago is a big jazz fan, especially Miles Davis. The high point of his adult life was about a month before Miles Davis died they met by chance and my colleague had his one-year-old son with him and Miles hugged him. He said, this is a blessing. He loves the stuff. But every time we put in our research any kind of mainstream jazz, listeners say no thanks.

Listeners, or a certain percent?
Of course, a certain portion, right, thank you. That is a much more accurate way of putting it. Frankly, one of the things philosophically and culturally that all my partners and I would like to do is, as we grow, if we grow, we would like to have a lot of AM stations in our mix with FM stations. FM is where the business is now, with a few rare exceptions. We'd love to have some AM stations because on AM stations, since they don't have a lot of listeners and you don't pay much for them, you can afford to play around. You can afford to experiment and test things and do things that you think are good and fine and interesting. So, as we grow, we want to buy an AM/FM combo in every market. Just for that kind of reason.

How do your stations relate to other media? How do they relate to art? Are there black-oriented TV stations in the region that show videos? And what is the relationship between your stations and the record companies that produce for your type station?
I'll start with the medium you didn't name, which is newsprint. It's kind of sad actually. The city of Chicago has the second best known black paper in America, the *Chicago Defender*, after the *Amsterdam News*. The *Chicago Defender* is a total nonfactor in black Chicago. It has a circulation that is trivial. It's just kind of fading, as is the *Amsterdam News*, unfortunately. There definitely is black television and there is going to be more in the future. What is happening with television is what happened to radio thirty years

ago in terms of the proliferation of channels due to cable. This is what drove radio to a high degree of segmentation, which was not true in the '20s, '30s, and '40s. Right now in New York, you can hear fifty or sixty signals. That forces the radio stations to segment the audience because if it didn't, it would just be kind of a wash of sameness. That is clearly happening with TV rapidly. The only kind of surprising thing to me is that it hasn't happened faster. And it is still probably five to ten years away from really what it is going to be like. Because it's going to require more than a hundred channels before the segmentation really becomes fine. The other factor affecting TV and other kinds of visual presentations is that the cost of making the product is very high relative to radio and newsprint, which is definitely a limiting factor. I think that there is no question that in five or ten years most major cities are going to have dedicated black cable channels. It's going to be much more like radio in the future. It is not so much a threat to radio because the way it is used is different. But it is going to be much more available.

Is there any kind of tie-in?
The only kind of tie-in is that they buy advertising time from us. To get people to watch them. Most radio listenership is between 6:00 A.M. and 7:00 or 8:00 P.M. People tend to listen much less at home where they watch the TV or whatever. So, where we target most of our listeners is getting up, driving to work, while at work, and coming back from work. Most Americans still drive. And about 75 percent of all Americans tend to listen to a radio station while at work, which is very surprising to most people. Not all the time, but occasionally. So, one of the biggest things we do in all of our stations is try to attract those kinds of listeners who listen for radio contests while at work and so on. You know, secretarial pools, all kinds of things.

There is also cable radio, which has been growing recently. It started in Las Vegas about three years ago. It's basically like a pay-per-channel, noncommercial, nationally syndicated radio service. There are five to ten different formats available usually, country, rock, classical, easy listening, and so on. It's pretty good stuff. The sound quality is extremely high because it comes over on cable. It tends to have very little local content. So it tends to not be a threat to the kind of radio we do because the local content is a lot of what makes it appealing. There is no question that the number of things available to audiences is going to continue to grow. The segmentation and fractionalization is going to continue to grow. One of the advantages radio will probably have for a long, long time is that radio programs are so cheap to manufacture. You just get someone to talk and play some records, in the simplest sense. You can have local content much more readily than in a video form, which if you do it like that looks horrible.

As for our relationship to the record industry, that is very carefully monitored because of payola and plugola. It's a big legal problem if you are caught doing it. It's a ten thousand dollar fine, not only for the disc jockey, but also up the management chain. So if one of our disc jockeys was found doing it, I could be fined ten thousand bucks for each occasion. That's a lot of money. Payola and plugola still exist. They are more widespread in ethnic radio, black and Spanish radio, than in white radio because it is a more fringe business. People don't tend to pay as much attention to it. There is a well-known personality in Philadelphia, whose name I won't mention, who is widely known for still taking money from record companies. The reason why it is so widespread, frankly, is that disc jockeys have a pretty insecure life. They tend to not remain popular for very long and the pay is not great. In the old days when they could actually choose the stuff they played, they often had a lot of influence. It was easy for a record plug person to go in and say, here's a few hundred bucks, or here is a date for tonight, or here is some cocaine, whatever. That is happening less and less in the major radio stations for a number of reasons. One is that it is a real problem to get caught, because it could be the end of the whole company. For example, if we were caught once, there would be a big fine. If we were caught two or three times, the FCC might yank all of our licenses. And of course it would put the whole company out of business, and it's a $70 million investment that's gone. That would be a big problem.

The other reason is that in most major-market radio stations, the disc jockeys have absolutely no say in the content of music played. It's completely removed from them because it is so highly programmed and so highly researched. So we give the songs and the sequence to all of the disc jockeys in all of our stations all of the time, with a few rare exceptions. In those rare exceptions we carefully monitor what they do. Now, the plug people can still go to the program director and try to influence him or her, but if we ever find any of our people having even a Coca-Cola bought for them, they are fired immediately. It still exists, but we try very hard to avoid it.

You talked about the record industry and said earlier that your stations sometimes sponsor musical art groups who are clients of record companies. So how does that relationship work?

I am not going to be able to give you the best answer there is because I'm not intimately involved with that process in our company, but I'll tell you what I know. Or what I think I know. In the case of that tour, which was primarily at military bases in Germany and some other places, it was kind of an all-star adult black tour. People like Luther VanDross, Sade, and Anita Baker and that kind of stuff. I don't believe we paid anything for the artists. I think the record companies sponsored that entirely and we were cosponsored by I think American Airlines, Lufthansa, and Mercedes Benz. They are black advertisers. It was a real breakthrough on several counts for us. All of those artists were already very well established, core performers for our demographic. When we launched the station and did our first bit of audience research they were in that core group of people who had been established for those listeners for five or ten years or more. So there were probably twenty or so artists who are like that and it's more a question of who's available than I want this one rather than that one.

For example, in Michigan, we for the last three years have done a summertime boat cruise — a cruise for women only. This is a very popular promotional thing we do there. It's a contest on air. We take a boat out on the Detroit River to the lake there. We have a popular recording artist who is on the cruise, the Chippendale dancers, and we have about three hundred seats available.

The black Chippendale dancers?
Well, you never can tell. The way you get a seat for this cruise is you have to listen to the station — fax or mail in your name on a card — listen during the working day, from 10:00 A.M. to 3:00 P.M. You have to be listening when your name is called. We obviously are doing this to increase listenership. It has a phenomenal effect on listenership. We have twenty thousand faxes from people who want to be chosen, or more. It's a huge number, it's very popular. The first year the artist we had was Michael Bolton, who is very popular. We were lucky. We were in touch with a bunch of record companies and basically said, who is available, who would appeal to these kind of people? Bolton hadn't really hit it yet. So it was blind luck, because after we signed him, before the cruise, he had his first hit. This past year the artist was Eddie Money, who was popular about five years ago and is not so popular now, and we were actually having a hard time finding artists because the more popular ones, you know, Michael Bolton scoffed at being on a cruise with three hundred women. But, frankly, our need was to find somebody who we could hire at a below-scale price who would be appealing

to our audience. It really has been a matter of what was available rather than what we wanted in all three year's cases.

I guess I'm actually less interested in how the artists get picked. Here's an instance. I think it's true that the main purpose of touring or public appearances by artists is to sell records.
It used to be almost entirely the purpose. Now, for example, the Stones and the Grateful Dead make a lot more money from touring than from record sales.

Merchandise.
And ticket sales.

Here's a place where radio stations and record companies can in fact work together without being scrutinized. So it's really only plugola, where that relationship looks suspicious?
Except plugola is putting in a plug for something.

An un-paid-for plug.
Right. Which we don't do. So if a concert tour is coming through or something like it, we will actively seek to get paid to advertise that concert tour. If we don't get paid, we won't talk about it, even though it might appeal to our core audience. In the case of these tours, there is a quid pro quo going on. We get the artist cheap, the artists get a lot of exposure, the artist probably gets their full scale, because what we don't pay is made up by their company. Their airfare and accommodations are paid for by Lufthansa and, you know, American Airlines, and Mercedes Benz. And the quid for us is that we get a show to broadcast live from Stuttgart that our listeners are really attracted to. So there is compensation. It's clearly established on all sides of that transaction.

Sanctioned compensation?
Yes. You are absolutely right about that being a different, but entirely proper, way for that kind of thing to happen. And it happens all the time. So a record company, for example, that wished to be more aggressive about doing that and wished to sponsor performing artists and do those kinds of tours with radio stations could get a lot of special coverage. But they would have to pay for it too because they would have to be sponsoring the artist. But that definitely is a way to get that to happen.

You also don't play the songs —

Actually, not to a higher degree than normal. For example, in the case of Detroit, Eddie Money is not a core artist for us. We play some of his songs, but not a whole lot. The frequency of play of Eddie Money on our radio stations did not go up.

You probably mentioned his name.

Oh, absolutely. Which was part of the deal. We paid for that three hours. He was, by the way, great. He was great to work with. The whole thing was to get our listenership up. So it was a promotional vehicle and we had a whole stack of sponsors for it who helped to compensate us for it. But you are right, that is definitely a way that a clever, creative, and aggressive record company can get more people to pay attention to its artists than one who doesn't do that.

Does it make any difference to radio stations to be operating in a city such as Chicago or New Orleans that has a very active club culture? Does that set different parameters either in terms of homeward bound listeners or others?

Clearly, in a city that has a lot of club culture, we get a lot of advertising from the clubs. When we get that advertising it's usually cash up front because clubs come and go all the time. Even in Chicago, the Regal Theater, which is one of the best known black venues, is cash up front because it's show biz. I would love it if we had, for example, radio shows featuring local artists performing live. We don't do that. There are Los Angeles stations that do that, but we don't own them. So in LA, for example, I know that the very active club culture there does influence one rock radio station and that's one of the things they feature, and one of the sources of their popularity. It's kind of interesting, though, in Chicago where there is still a pretty active blues club scene but the patrons are even older than our core audience. Chicago also has a huge blues fest each year and the audience is mostly blacks over fifty and whites of all ages. The core listenership for us are blacks between twenty-five and fifty-four, and most of those people don't listen to blues. It is not part of their lives. It isn't even part of their childhood — it's part of their parents' childhood. So Chicago's blues club culture, which I personally love, isn't especially relevant to our audience.

Do you have a national program director? Or are music selections made locally?

There are a lot of companies that have national program directors and we don't, in part because we strongly believe in the local nature of the programming. My programming partner works with the local stations every two or three months when they get their next stage of audience research. He sits down with them, tries to interpret the results, and tries to think about how it relates to what they are playing and what they are saying on the air. What they say is crucially important. The disc jockeys have a very big role. It is not just in choosing the kinds of songs played. It's what they say and how they say it. Some of them get paid a great deal. There are some Johnny Carson-type people in radio who get paid close to that kind of level because of their skill at presentation. Howard Stern is a great example. Howard Stern in the most recent rating book is now the number one morning talent in New York and Los Angeles. First time that's happened in the recent history of ratings. That's amazing, and he's getting paid a lot of money for that.

Where we may have outside influence occurring is in the taste and judgment of our program directors, and that taste and judgment is monitored regularly through research. Because every time a new song enters our playlist, it gets put on our roster of research songs. Every week in our Chicago and Detroit stations and every two weeks in Charlotte, we do a telephone survey of about ninety members of our core listening audience. They are chosen randomly from several thousand. Then during a ten- to fifteen-minute call we play fragments of several new songs and we also ask some questions about the station they listen to, do they like the morning show, and that kind of stuff. So when a new song enters the playlist, within three weeks we have a very quantitative sense of what our audience thinks about it. And if they don't like it, it comes off right away. So, the opportunities for abuse and fraud are mitigated. But frankly, there are thousands of songs released every week, every month. Choosing the right ones is tough. For every song our program directors cleverly choose, there are probably three dozen that could do just as well that they didn't hear.

You use Billboard *and the trade magazines?*
And the guy listens to music all the time. And goes to nightclubs all the time to hear stuff played.

What is the meaning of local, given the use of Billboard, *et cetera? Do you find that there really are significant local differences between the Detroit station and . . .*
When our Chicago station WVAZ launched this adult black format, we got copied right away by a lot of stations around the country and they did

medium well in various cases. They didn't do well as often as they could have because they very rarely paid for local market research. However, about a year and a half after we launched this format, the ABC satellite music network, which is the biggest satellite music distributor of what is called long form programming, added ours to its dozen or so services and called it "the Touch." We don't get paid for that, because you can't copyright a format. But my colleague Barry Mayo is a paid consultant to them, and the payment we get is primarily in-kind services from them. Basically, much of "the Touch" is what we play on WVAZ. They have their own disc jockeys to cover the stuff, but the songs, the rotation, the whole thing, is pretty much us. Our audience research is aimed totally at Chicago. In a couple of markets our satellite service has beaten locally programmed services doing similar kinds of things. That usually doesn't happen. Usually if you have a locally programmed equivalent, it will beat a satellite service, which is why I would tend to say you can prove that localism exists because you can often match a heavy-metal satellite service versus a heavy-metal local service. And the heavy-metal local is going to win. The heavy-metal local one wins because local people talk about it on the air and they tend to feature local clubs and advertising. They talk about local things happening and they play some locally popular songs. I'm not sure why our black adult satellite service has done so well. I think it's probably because the alternatives are not as carefully done. For example, in New Orleans, which is a big black market where "the Touch" is the second highest ranked station in the market, with the first ranked station being a young black station. I think that if somebody was doing local research on what the New Orleans adult black market wanted it would destroy the satellite service. But one doesn't exist, so satellite is doing very well.

The other kind of thing about localism versus nationalism is in talk radio. Talk radio is the single most rapidly rising part of the radio business right now. Even more than country music, which is the most rapidly rising in music radio. This is especially because of people like Rush Limbaugh and Howard Stern. Rush Limbaugh never plays a song, and he is carried now by over five hundred radio stations around the country. This is a national service. There is nothing local. Howard Stern is local to New York, but really a national show. It's kind of harking back to the old days of Jack Benny and Burns and Allen, which were national shows. Those things work, I think, because individuals who can be that charismatic on the air are rare. It is relatively unlikely to find a local person who is as humorously rude as some people find Howard Stern. I don't, but a lot of people do. So those are unusually talented people, kind of like Johnny Carson. There are not very many local nighttime TV programs that are as regularly funny as Johnny Carson was. In terms of music, however, if something is done locally and carefully, it will beat something that is done nationally and regionally. And there are differences. Our Charlotte radio station isn't comparable to our Chicago one because it is more youth oriented and our Chicago one is adult. But if you compare our Charlotte one to our competition in Chicago which is youth oriented, the playlist is quite different. In Charlotte, for example, we don't play _____. We don't, both because Charlotte is a relatively conservative black market and he doesn't think that kind of song would go over very well. He does play some Ice-T numbers and some rap, but not a whole lot. "Cop Killer" also was not played by the youth-oriented Chicago station that is our rival. It was played by a fringe AM Chicago black station that was trying to make a name for itself. Some black radio stations around the country that play that kind of music want to make an attitude for themselves. To say, "I'm bad." So they might play it. But "Cop Killer" sold very, very well and most radio stations didn't play it. It does vary locally. Our program director in Charlotte doesn't think it fits with the local culture. That is his judgment. But in Los Angeles, it might be much more a part of the local culture. In our adult station in Chicago, Prince had a song that came out recently called "Sexy Mother Fucker," which is a very explicit Prince song. We didn't play it because we didn't think that our Chicago audience, which is obviously an up-scale sophisticated audience, wanted to hear it. Now, the song was played in Minneapolis in the quasi-adult black station there. It was played in New York on BLS. Different points of view about what the audience wants.

So these weren't ever made part of your biweekly home surveys?
No, the program director just never chose to put it on. It was his censorship but calling it censorship is kind of loaded. I think it is probably not entirely appropriate because he really does have to choose from thousands of songs. I really think judgment is a better term, because politics aren't really part of it, it's taste. It's his taste, and that is part of what we hire him for — having taste that understands what his audience wants.

How are your demographic studies done? Is it strictly controlled by the central office or is that also local?
In terms of how the studies are done, one of the strengths of my black partner who is in Chicago is at the structuring and interpretation of audi-

ence research. My poor analogy is that he is like a conductor with a score, and his score is the research, the raw data. He is very good at hearing in his head what the research is saying the audience wants to hear. That's more of a gift than a skill, frankly, and it's not just about black music. I've seen him do it in country and white rock and roll and all kinds of things. He is also skilled at articulating what he hears in his head to somebody else. So he is heavily involved with the structuring of the questionnaires for various studies. In terms of field research, the corporate office gets involved in audience research on several levels: one is that we insist that there be audience research studies done. At our Michigan station, in our first year of operation, the general manager there didn't want to have them. She thought they were a waste of time. We said, "Sorry, I don't think you've got it. We've got to do some studies" — glad we did. We mandated that. And because that general manager wasn't enamored of them we pretty much took charge of the structuring of it with the program director. In the case of stations that are running pretty well, while we insist upon a certain minimum level of research per year done in our music playing stations, we get less and less involved the better the stations do. But for every study result, my programming colleague goes to that station and sits in on the presentation of the findings. We have one firm we try to use in all cases if they're available. So the study process itself is not all that local in technique. And interpretation is done by a consultant from the research firm and by my programming colleague and by the program director locally.

While it's locally originated it doesn't mean that the person actually came from that locale originally . . .
The program director in our Chicago station by the way is a black guy and his music director is is also black. But this program director got his training in country music in Rochester and he probably is, all things said, a better country programmer than a black programmer although he's black. And in fact one of our weaknesses in our Chicago station is that all of the key programming people there are very good at quantitive analysis and interpretation of research, but they are not all that flamboyant or creative or artistically interpretative. So they actually are not as good as we'd like them to be at hearing what's going to be good next. At some point we may make a change in that staff because we don't have somebody who's good at picking up on what's going to be a popular taste or trend. In Charlotte, the opposite is true of the program director and of his colleague the music director. She is very intuitive about that kind of stuff. She's won for two of the last three

years the black music director of the year award in *Billboard* because she is very good at picking up tastes and trends in Charlotte. And that's a gift. It's a gift that is quantitatively identifiable after a year or so by seeing the person's hit rate in the audience research.

From the very beginning, government regulators distinguished broadcasters from common carriers (such as the phone company) because broadcasters were supposed to do something different than just be a conveyor of messages. Do you as a broadcast group have a vision of something you would like to communicate to your audience? Do you editorialize? How do you choose issues?

The quick answer is no. We don't have a corporate point of view. We don't editorialize on a corporate level. A good example happened a couple of years ago when Harvey Gantt was running for the Senate in North Carolina. Harvey Gantt had been the mayor of Charlotte. I know him. Our station knows him. He works with us a lot. I was for him and I'm not for Jesse Helms. It is my own point of view. My colleagues and I talked about whether we were going to do any editorializing on our black radio station, an obvious place to support Harvey Gantt. A very strong point of view of one of my colleagues was, "Look, this is a Charlotte radio station. We aren't from Charlotte. We don't know what Charlotte wants, thinks, or needs. We've hired our general manager and staff there to know that and to do that. If our general manager wants to come to us and say 'I really want to make an editorial statement and here's what I want to do,' let's listen to him, but I don't think we ought to go in and say, 'Look, why don't you do an editorial on Harvey Gantt.'" In fact, the station manager never did. He's no longer the manager there, but it is not because of that. I definitely would have. I have very strongly felt points of view about lots of things and I would love to have a bully pulpit. But my two colleagues have appropriately tempered me by basically saying, "I'll strangle you if you do that." It's a local business. We definitely want to have the opportunity to understand what our local stations wish to do from an editorial point of view because we'd like to have the opportunity to comment on it before it goes on the air, if it's something that troubled us personally. But, that has come up very rarely. So, if I were a general manager locally, I would be doing that all the time. But the general managers we have do a very good job. They don't feel that is their role. Rather, they have the kind of Sunday morning show I was talking about and other news shows in which they give a forum to various points of view on major issues. Frankly, they often select people for those forums who would not be on mass market forums, like, for example, Louis Farrakhan. He is definitely not a guy who any of us think is honorable or admirable. He has been on our radio station because there are blacks in Chicago who wish to hear him. And there have been others with opposing points of view who have also spoken. But that's the way in which our editorial stance is expressed.

In terms of a corporate philosophy in a grander and a larger sense, it's very capitalistic. We believe that we are just a little bit better at the execution of the business than are most other broadcasters. Our vision is to build a corporate partnership with all of the people in it being partners and eventually shareholders. In any given market we want our partners to do a good job at identifying a particular market segment and serving it well and serving the advertisers well. We also want them to have a fun and satisfying and lucrative career path. That is our vision. The differentiating factor mostly is the skill of the local people we put in place and nurture. So, also, part of the vision is to have this reservoir of talent within our company that we can tap and use, and help to grow and mature and be more effective. The vision is not expressed in terms of having a cultural impact on our listening audiences because we don't have a point of view about what kind of audience we want to serve. In any given market we want to find out where there is an unserved niche and serve it. Also, the niche must be large enough and with demographics such that we think that we can make a viable business of it.

Having laid out that philosophy, it would seem to me that the message would be very clear to the local talent, not to have a philosophy except one that is capitalistic in orientation. In other words, they know how the company is structured. They know who rises in the organization. And they know the values that you just laid out here. And those values say don't bring Farrakhan on, don't be controversial, don't take a hard stand—be a community leader but be a community leader that enough people like so that they keep tuning in to the station.
Well, the tuning in, you're absolute right. We want them to keep tuning in. There is no question about that. In Charlotte, for example, the career path for our general manager, I hope, is to stay in Charlotte. We've talked about that with him. That's his hope too. His goal, thus far at least, is not to rise up the corporate ladder per se, although he is a young guy. He likes Charlotte. He moved there from New York. Being a community leader, or being the general manager of a very profitable radio station in Charlotte can have a lot of permutations. For example, we have an AM radio station along with our FM station that we just kind of use to warehouse various programming.

The only reason we do that is because his staff is still very young. He frankly doesn't have a mature enough staff, nor is he mature enough to really handle the operation of a wholly second separate radio station. Within a year he probably will. He very much wants to turn that AM radio station into a community-focused black radio station. It won't make any money probably, but we strongly support that point of view. We think Charlotte needs it. So he wants it to be largely news, talk, information, local sports, some fringe programming for the black community in Charlotte, and so on. That's part of his vision of being the local owner-operator of the black outlet Charlotte needs.

In Chicago, if we had an AM radio station, it probably wouldn't mean as much because there are a number of other radio forums for that kind of thing to happen in a much larger city. In Chicago there are probably enough other program niches that if we had one or two other radio stations that probably isn't what our vision would be there, just because the audience is different and the size of the audience is different. In Michigan, our station is a white adult rock-and-roll radio station. With more radio stations there, again, the white marketplace is abundantly served by all kinds of information and vehicles and various things. But the guy in Charlotte sees a real need for a lot of information to be available to his community that is not normally available. We have told him to wait six months before you launch that because we don't think you have a seasoned enough group to do it. We don't want you to overextend yourself. We don't want you to run so fast you fall down. But once he is stronger at running, we really hope he does that. So, it does vary a lot place by place. I think there is, I hope, a lot of room within our vision for doing what is locally interesting and creative and valuable, but it's local.

This is maybe a more of a cultural studies question than a media question. You've seen all sides of American music in what you've done over the years and there are these kinds of complexities about the American music structure that nobody has adequately described yet. Do you have any sense of how the American music environment works after you've seen so many different sides of it — of the interactive forces in a kind of structural way. Do you have a kind of overview of it yet?

Well, I probably don't, but I do have a sense of some of what I think structural problems and issues are that I would like to have addressed or changed or altered. It's difficult for a relatively fringe form of culture, music or whatever, to get an adequate forum or distribution venue. When I was living in Kansas City I was very friendly with the people who ran the biggest creative record store in town, and even they were hard-pressed to stock the unusual titles because their inventory cost was such that even with the return policy that all record companies have, they couldn't afford to use their space for something they would sell once every six months. Likewise, how do you refresh, revitalize, nurture, expose an audience to things that are interesting, culturally relevant to them, or just different, when they're fringe enough that none of the main media sources are going to promote them or provide a venue for them. It's a tough problem. Another aspect of this problem is confronted by one of the other groups I work with in New York, called Young Audiences. Its mission is to try to expose children in the New York City school system — a million children — to music, art, drama, whatever, when for almost twenty years now there's been virtually none of it in the school system because of budget cutbacks. It's part of the question of how do you develop the cultural awareness of the nation, especially in a nation that has such extraordinary cultural riches, when the funding sources are dwindling rather than rising — things like folk festivals helped that. There are a million and one ways to do it, and as you know I spent all of my years before business school trying to do precisely that — to try to expose more people to more different kinds of things. And it's wonderful for me, and fun, and it worked some, but it's tough. To some degree the free market works and to some degree Alan Lomax is wrong. His big concern regards "greying out" of the cultural world, but I don't believe that this "greying out" is occurring. But at the same time there are a lot of very powerful forces at work to homogenize and, more importantly, to make it difficult to have access to things unless there's a powerful motivation to go and seek them out. One of the things the FCC wanted to do was to increase the number of radio stations. They were hoping that more broadcasters would come out doing more of the unusual, the less common kinds of things. Unfortunately, what happened is there are more people who wanted to make money than there were people who wanted to come into the sector to be creative. There's ethnic radio in every major city and it's largely through paid programming, as I think you know. But unfortunately the cost of access, even in radio where there are eleven thousand radio stations, the cost to buy a radio station in most towns is so high that you can't afford to buy one and then not program to a large audience, a relatively large audience. In New York, for example, an interesting thing just happened in terms of that. I can't remember the call letters of it but a station that has been one of the leading ethnic radio stations in the city for a number of years was just bought by somebody new. And this is paid programming—they have a Polish hour, the Polish group pays for it, a Slovak hour, an Afghani hour, and whatever—all in a day. This guy has quadrupled the rates because he bought the station and he wants to make some more money. The rates have gone from a hundred and some bucks an hour to four and five hundred bucks an hour. Several of those ethnic groups dropped out. Several bought more programming. The Chinese and Korean groups have bought more programming because they're better established, they have more financial resources and so on. Some of the West Indian groups and others have dropped out. That's a shame and I guess in a mode of a hundred flowers blooming, there are lots of ways to nurture cultural awareness in the broadest possible sense. I think one of the sad things is that when public support falls away that aspect of the safety net also falls away and I think it tends to make for a relatively more sterile environment. That's not in answer to your question . . . it's a problem and the kind of broadcasters we are don't help the problem because we can't. But it's a quandary because it is a business and the business does serve a real need.

Did we fail to ask you any tough questions?
One of the questions that we didn't touch on was: Is there an audience that is too small to be served?

Or too poor . . .
And the answer is yes and no. It all depends upon what kind of distribution vehicle you have, what your objectives are for it, and what your cost of maintaining it is. For example, Flying Fish Records, a company that's run by an amateur ethnomusicologist in Chicago, has found a great niche for itself in taking second-tier rock and folk artists and making some money on it, and also doing a whole bunch of really fringe artists that were suiting his taste—very creative and very interesting. He had his own taste and he followed it. In local radio stations, there are a lot of ma-and-pa radio stations. One of the things I wish the National Association of Broadcasters would do is have seminars for them on how to be more creative about what they offer to people locally. That's perhaps one way that things like this could get out more. In the field of record distribution and manufacturing I fear that it is kind of hopeless, frankly, because it's so deeply crooked.

But we always complain that the conservative effect is on media—that they put out thousands and thousands of records and only this many get played on radio . . .

Well, they are absolutely right. The building that I use to live in in New York had a guy that worked for the alternative distribution part of CBS records, which is now owned by Sony. I talked with him about what radio stations he would try to get his stuff played on across the whole United States. There were only about twenty commercial radio stations that he thought he even had a shot at, and about three hundred college radio stations. That's where he got it done. WESU and the WESU's of the world have an enormous role. I think one of the things the FCC could and should do is to shift more of the dial to public radio because that's really where the nurturing of unusual and interesting things is happening now.

Mark Edmiston Jordan Edmiston Group

October 1, 1992

· ·

Mark M. Edmiston has been a domestic and international consumer magazine publishing executive for thirty years. He began his career with Time, Inc., *after graduating from Wesleyan. He held senior positions at* Life, Newsweek, *and* Saturday Review. *He was founding director of* Hippocrates *(now* Health*) and founder of* Civilization *magazine. In recent years, he has been an investment banker specializing in media properties.*

For the past five months I have been a partner in a firm called the Jordan Edmiston Group. It is an investment-banking boutique. It's a boutique in the sense that it specializes in a narrow part of the world of business, publishing: predominantly consumer magazines, although we have done book publishing, newspapers to a small extent, and database publishing operations, which are the new hot button.

About forty percent of our work is advising businesses on how to manage their properties. This frequently leads to acquiring or starting up additional properties because of holes in their strategy, if you will, or to the divesting of properties. We also do that for them. So in those ways we tend to be a broker. We will find a buyer; we will look for property that fits a particular company's portfolio and then try to acquire it for them.

For example, we are working with a European company. It is called "Euromoney Limited." They publish a number of periodicals, the principal one being a magazine called *Euromoney* that focuses on world financial markets. It has very few subscribers, no more than fifteen thousand altogether, but they tend to be ministers of finance, people like that. The company is constantly looking to see what other services it can provide. One area they noted was large private bank loans. When you borrow for your car, there is a posted rate, but when you borrow $10 million to finance a new factory, the rates are negotiated. There is a company in the United States that is able to get information about those loans, and we are now trying to arrange partial purchase of that company by the Europeans. Our job, the added value we bring, is to try to make everyone comfortable in that environment. This is not a publicly traded company; you can't just go out and buy stock in it and say, "Thank you very much, I own 30 percent of your company." So you keep working back and forth. This will probably take us six months, both here in the United States and also in London. We try to understand the businesses of our clients better than they understand themselves. We are on the outside so we are able to see the forest without worrying about how many trees there are.

Previously I was at Times-Mirror Magazines, a very interesting little operation, about $250 million in size. It was invented by assembling properties that already existed into a group that was focused on middle American males. This is the first time that somebody set out to do just that. They had *Popular Science Magazine*. They acquired *Field and Stream*, *Outdoor Life*, *Skiing Magazine*, and *Golf Magazine*.

When we talk to advertisers we talk about the audience, the number of readers. That is what we are selling. The audience is estimated by two outside services, MRI (Media Research Inc.) and SMRB (Simmons Media Research Bureau). They compete with each other, with different numbers unfortunately. Most advertisers do not want just men, they want men of a certain age range, a certain income range, or a certain family situation. With Times Mirror Magazines, the index is almost a hundred. We are America in that sense.

What does it mean, the index is a hundred?
A hundred is the U.S. average. They are slightly more educated; they read, after all. They are slightly more likely to live in cities than the average population. But that's all, very slightly. In terms of age, in terms of income, in terms of family composition, they are almost exactly the American average.

Tell us a little of what you know about middle American males.
Twenty-five percent have some college education. Fifty percent are non-professional; various technical fields, some high skilled, down to zero skills. Income: $37,000; family with two children, the more traditional family. I can't tell you whether both spouses work; I assume they do, but I don't know that, and I don't know religion. That's not researched. About 10 percent black; in the case of the hunting and fishing magazines, lower. Blacks are not readers of hunting and fishing magazines. It's like ice hockey, few blacks play ice hockey, because generally you can't find an ice rink in the middle of a major city. What reaches a black audience is *Popular Mechanics*, *Popular Science*, those are big circulation books. *Popular Science* is 1.7 million and *Popular Mechanics* is 1.1 million.

There must be a percentage of women who read these magazines?
It ranges from 10 percent on the outdoor books to 30 percent on the skiing books.

This company has been relatively successful in taking this very broad niche and trying to focus on an area that has not been served before. When they go to find advertisers, they are not going to get Corvette, but they are sure going to get trucks, they're going to get four by fours. They get tobacco, because that is a downscale habit in the United States. They are doing reasonably well with clothing, rugged clothing — either outdoor clothing or specific clothing for hunting and fishing and stuff like that. Times-Mirror Magazines is a very different kind of company than any one that I know of because it was constructed for a purpose. It had a marketing strategy before it had the magazines. They are very old magazines. The average age of the nine magazines in the portfolio is 67 years. *Popular Science,* believe it or not, has been continuously published for 116 years. *Field and Stream* and *Outdoor Life* will be 100 years each in about 3 or 4 years. One is 95 and one is 97. *Ski* and *Skiing* are younger, but so is the sport.

If the demographics are all similar, why maintain the duplicates? Ski and Skiing, Field and Stream and Outdoor Life?
When I was first interviewed to go to work there, I asked exactly the same question. I assumed there was a lot of duplication, but there is hardly any in the audience: 10 or 11 percent in the case of the outdoor books and about 7 percent in the case of the skiing books.

The same demographics? Just different people? Why?
Part of it is the General Motors approach to selling cars. We'll take a Chevrolet and we'll call it a Pontiac. Not really much different in price, but it gives people another opportunity.

Skiing, for example, is slightly more technical than *Ski.* If you are starting out, I would recommend you read *Skiing* because it's going to give you a little bit more detail about boots and bindings and skis and such. *Ski Magazine* is slightly more life-style. It will tell you more about where you might go skiing, a skiing adventure. But they both cover the same things. It's a Chevrolet/Pontiac situation.

The same is true of *Outdoor Life* and *Field and Stream.* It's thought that *Field and Stream* is more of a fishing magazine and *Outdoor Life* is more of a hunting magazine: it really isn't. The impression is probably a historical leftover, like that of *Time/Newsweek*. *Time* is thought to be conservative and *Newsweek* is thought to be more liberal. At one time that was true: Averell Harriman owned *Newsweek* and Harry Luce owned *Time*. But now they are indistinguishable.

Let me talk a little bit, in very general statements, about the magazine business. It is unusual in that you have to balance the needs of the advertiser, who pays nowadays probably 60 percent of the total cost of operating a magazine, and the reader, who pays about 40 percent. So at first you might think that the advertiser gets to say what the magazine will be like. However, the advertiser is not interested in the magazine, he is interested in the reader. So you have to start with the reader. You are constantly balancing these two things. This is also what makes magazines most attractive to nonmagazine people looking for a business proposition. Many large businesses are in magazines, around the world, because they have two sources of revenue — very important — and you are able to move back and forth between them. When there is a long recession, as there is now, advertising tends to dry up and you'll notice magazines raising prices to the subscriber. If you subscribe to any magazines you are getting price increases right now: publishers are testing them out. As the recession ends, they go back to the other side. It's a balancing act, or a sort of a wave.

When you say "reader" do you mean people who read or people who subscribe?
People who read. That is where we have the information. Most magazine publishers do not have demographic information about their subscribers and newsstand buyers. They don't bother. The main reason they don't bother is that the audience numbers have in the past thirty-odd years become the only important number for advertisers and also a more accurate reflection of the magazine, because a subscriber could be male or female but that doesn't tell you anything about the reading patterns. It could be that the husband got the subscription notice in the mail. His wife said, "Yes, I'd like to read that," so *she* sends it in with *his* name on it.

So you do have figures on how many people read an issue? Is it two? three?
On the average it's more like five to one. Remember, most of these are households with children and these are sports that the family participates in. You also get copies in barbershops, on airplanes, places like that. The studies show something like thirty-five readers for every copy put in an airplane. Copies going into homes will probably have no more than two and a half readers.

Circulation figures are important for newspapers though, aren't they?
They are the game, for newspapers. Newspapers are valuable to the advertiser if they deliver everybody, or as near to everybody as they can, or everybody in a major class, in the case of, say, the *New York Times*. It reaches all people who make any kind of money in the New York metro area. But in most cities where there is one newspaper, the whole idea is for the newspaper to deliver everybody. In recent years the industry has come up with cheap little periodicals that are delivered once a week to everyone who doesn't order the newspaper. The publisher can go to the advertiser and say, "We can actually put your ad in everybody's home, even if they don't buy the newspaper." With newspapers, it's more like 90 percent of the revenue from the advertiser, 10 percent from the reader.

According to Theodore Peterson's Magazines in the Twentieth Century *(quite an old book now) the percentage of people in the country who read magazines at all in 1955 was 70 to 80 percent. Do you think things have changed very much since then?*
I know they haven't. They are just about the same. But there are a lot more magazines, so the number of readers per magazine has gone down. The big magazines are gone. *TV Guide* at one point had a 20 million circulation. It's now 15. *Reader's Digest* had 17 million, now it's 13. And *Life, Look,* and the *Saturday Evening Post* are defunct. Those magazines were being sold toward the end of their lives, even adjusting backward for inflation, for about nine cents a copy. I started with *Life Magazine*. We had one of those wonderful sayings: "Lose money on every copy and make it up in volume." And we did!

Like everything else in American society, we are more crowded with magazines. In the past ten years two thousand magazines were launched. That's the post office number. I don't know the names of them. We track in the industry the magazines that are audited by the audit bureau of circulations or the BPA, Business Publications Audit. Those two groups cover something on the order of six hundred titles. The other magazines are tiny ones that may be local and regional.

Will there ever be another general magazine with a large circulation?
No. Not in our lifetimes. I have a theory actually: it's the baby boomers; it's the generation that wants to do their own thing. Specialized magazines are theirs. No matter how specialized your interest, we'll give you a magazine. Will our society come back together again after this generation passes from the scene? I don't know.

Has the appeal of reading magazines changed from the days of the really broad magazines?

Yes. The general circulation magazines basically reported on shared experiences. We had in this country at that time a sense of shared experience. Now each person thinks of himself or herself as virtually unique. Therefore we are moving toward one issue for me and copy for you. For example, *Newsweek* announced a plan by which you may subscribe to the magazine and then for a couple of extra dollars customize your subscription by getting more of certain editorial content in your copies of *Newsweek*.

Then there is selectronic binding. Printing has been just a mechanical process. You could change things, but it was a matter of lifting out things and then putting in more things, stopping the chain. But selectronic binding is like the Japanese car assembly line process: each magazine coming through is different, and so it enables a magazine like *Newsweek* or *Time* to have maybe four hundred different versions of a given issue.

And I think the next step will be more editorial customizing. There is nothing really to stop that process from going all the way, actually asking you what you want, what news you are interested in.

All right, you are interested in news, but you're not interested in all the news. You really don't care what happens in Japan, so we will give you our Ex-Japan edition. We don't even mention Japan. And that can be done. This electronic binder will do it. There are publishers of special interest magazines that are looking at that.

Is there any attempt to customize for male and female audiences?

That is an interesting question. I have been in several meetings thinking about that. I guess because most of the people at the meetings were males we didn't know the answer. Are women skiers different? Yes, they wear different clothes. Perhaps in some ways they look at the sport differently than men do. But is that enough to base a magazine on? We don't know. A lot of publishers are thinking about that. There is a magazine just launched, *Golf for Women*. It's published by the *New York Times*. They have a magazine called *Golf Digest*, the number one golf magazine. It's read by a lot of women, but they are saying, even though 30 percent of our *Golf Digest* readers are women maybe they want a separate magazine. So they hired a woman golfer as the editor and they have a panel of professional women golfers who are the advisors and they are going to see what happens. And we'll find out in about a year.

Is there a point of diminishing returns, when a magazine describes such a narrow realm of experience that people won't buy it? It's not worth the two dollars?

Yes. Of course. When they publish a magazine specifically for you, and you are the only person in the world that is interested in it, then you probably wouldn't pay the price. But as you get narrower in interest, you tend to have more intensity of interest: the person is more likely to pay the extra money. There is a point where the lines cross over, but it's much lower than one would think. Take canoeing. How many canoeing people are there in the country? Let's look at the total potential audience. One hundred thousand, maybe? The fact is that they can produce a magazine for that, and then divide it up into kayaking and canoeing, and say, okay, we are going to specialize a little bit more.

Another example: *Ms Magazine* tried for 20 years and lost money every year trying to sell advertising. They kept running into the political problem of advertisers not liking the editorial content. A year ago the then new owner said, "Well, if you people really think this magazine is important to you, we'll publish it and we won't take any advertising at all." I know for a fact that it made one million dollars in the first twelve months. It was the first profitable year they ever had. There is now about 75,000 circulation, which means there are 75,000 people who are paying fifty dollars a year to get *Ms Magazine*.

Are there potential readerships that are simply not worth reaching by market calculations?

I thought about that. At first my answer was yes but now my answer really is no. There *are* groups who are not reached. Young urban black males have traditionally not been reached. However, there are two magazines coming out, one from Los Angeles and one from New York — hip-hop magazines — aimed at urban male blacks. They will get a lot of other readers, too, but that is the primary audience. So I think the answer is probably no. Magazines can be produced very very inexpensively, so with not a lot of money you can pretty much go after any target you want. The more intense the interest, the more that person is willing to pay for it — the smaller you can go. There are successful magazines with twenty or thirty thousand circulation. Basically, magazine publishers are constantly looking for underserved areas, seeking out those places where no one else is. It's a feeling among magazine publishers that if you are first in a category you will remain the winner for a long, long time. *Time/Newsweek*, for example. Whoever starts first is likely to hold that position.

How would you characterize what is happening at the New Yorker? *What do you think their chances of success are in obtaining a younger, upscale audience, the kind who will buy the Calvin Klein jeans and the Levi's? Those ads never used to be in the* New Yorker. *And, have they decided to write off fifty-year-old, sixty-year-old, and seventy-year-old loyal readers?*

It's called "repositioning." And it's very very difficult. Few magazines ever successfully carry it off. But to quote Harry Luce again, "A magazine is for a generation." You have something that fits a generation. But because it fit so well, it can't fit the next generation. The next generation just doesn't get it, can't figure out why anybody would want to read that.

Tina Brown could very well lose the fifties, sixties, and seventies and not get the younger readers. But she is one person who has actually repositioned a magazine. *Vanity Fair* was started by Condé Nast and it failed. It was just an embarrassment. They brought Tina Brown in and she basically rebuilt it under a tremendous amount of pressure. She is probably the one editor in a position of responsibility, that I know anyway, who really is in tune with that twenties and thirties generation — that particular yuppie twenty-something group. She got away with Demi Moore nude and pregnant, and was considered to be shocking but classy. But her successor put Madonna nude on the cover and everybody said "Yuk." Tina Brown does seem to be able to do it exactly right. Her argument why the *New Yorker* needs changing is that the staff had begun to resemble people trying to preserve flies in amber.

The magazine was outrageous when it was started. She argues that it should be the '90s version of that kind of magazine. Very difficult to do. Some magazines have succeeded. News magazines are now sixty years old, seventy years old. They change. Originally they had no reporters or photographers on staff. They had rewrite men. Basically they would take newspaper stories and write them up cleverly. Now they do all original reporting. They reinvented themselves and they carried it off successfully.

What about Reader's Digest?

Reader's Digest is not a magazine but a direct-mail list-gathering service. They test their articles. They actually have a panel of readers to whom they send out articles, and ask them to read them and rate them, and then they pick the highest ranked ones. That's the magic of *Reader's Digest* — plus it fits behind the toilet seat.

Are magazines repositioned for one of two reasons: readers are getting two old, or they are sliding down market?

They tend not to slide down market as much as they become less attractive to the advertiser — and also die. That is part of the problem. You can't just stay with a generation because they do die. People stop reading magazines as they get older. They don't read your magazine or anything else. So if you are not constantly bringing in younger people then as your audience gets older and older, the cost of maintaining a circulation goes higher and higher. At some point it becomes uneconomical to continue to operate if you let that happen.

So you don't reposition because of the wrong audience, an audience that is less affluent?
It's not an income issue. The only example I know of repositioning for affluence is *Sports Afield*, and they failed utterly. The magazine is a direct competitor of *Field and Stream* and *Outdoor Life*. It's owned by Hearst. It was the third magazine, with about a 1.1 million circulation. (*Outdoor Life* is 1.5 and *Field and Stream* is 2 million.) They tried to become a British sporting magazine, dropping the circulation to a half a million but with better demographics. Well, their demographics are the same, but there are only half a million people. They failed totally. That was a pretty tough one to do in the United States — as opposed to England, where there are more class sports.

Why did Town and Country *change format? There doesn't seem to be a big difference in the substance of their articles.*
It is a repositioning attempt. *Town and Country* is read only by stout women with pearls and blue dresses. The publishers thought they had to do something to get a younger and flashier group. More pictures showing younger people and showing people of color. That was pretty breakthrough stuff. Seriously, that is one of the things they were trying to do, but they felt that the new editor did the cosmetic without trying to adjust the editorial.

How does the youth market fit into the aging process of audiences? Instead of tracking a specific generation along, do youth magazines regularly say goodbye to older readers and usher in new generations by targeting them at a certain point in their lives?
That is the normal way of managing it. *Seventeen* magazine has very few seventeen-year-olds that read it. They constantly have to regenerate by getting twelve-year-olds to start reading it. There is fragmentation there, too. *Seventeen* used to be *the* magazine. Everybody read it. Now, there is

Sassy magazine, which has a very different approach. That forced everybody to move in a different direction. G & J redid *Young Miss* magazine; they called it *YM*. Those three magazines are targeting subsegments of the twelve- to fifteen-year-old female readership.

Traditionally, I think, young women have been a bigger market than young men; do you see that distinction breaking down?
No.

Women's magazines seem to work a bit differently from men's, which tell men about activities they are already involved in. Women are interested in travel and cooking, but they are not going to go on those culinary tours of Europe. You are not the one who's buying the high-fashion clothes; the typical Vogue *reader isn't wearing the clothes that are there. It seems that those trying to address women have assumed they must offer fantasies of who women* want *to be.*
Absolutely . . .

Much more self-helpish, but not practical self-help. You are never going to look like the person who steps out in Vogue. *But you could try this belt . . .*
Exactly. Women historically have not had as many opportunities as men; men have to learn practical things to lead the world and women can fantasize.

But magazines in general are cheap.
Entertainment, an easy way to dream. I get sailing magazines to fantasize. Not, "I'd love to have that boat, that trip to Tahiti sounds great." I'm never going to go to Tahiti, and if I really think about it I don't want that damn boat because I know what it would require me to do if I had it. The magazines feed a fantasy.

I want to go back to the question of television. It could be argued that in the '50s, '60s, '70s, television was the media space to which lots of people would go for something like a common culture. Now television itself is segmented — it's more and more apparent that that process will continue. If it does, how would you anticipate the magazine business responding to the further specialization, not just of broadcast television, but of all the other kinds of screen experiences?
We'll complement that process. There is a magazine I helped start for the black entertainment network, for black teens. It is promoted through tele-

vision. Discovery Channel has known as well that it's not just the program listing: the idea is to have a print complement to that narrow-band, narrow-casted program. That is what we are trying to do. What does it lead to? I don't know. When I put on my citizen hat I get very worried. I think there is clearly a breaking down of any consensus in the country.

That is a market-driven process, driven by a desire to sell certain things more efficiently. Right? The result is precisely that there are no general interest magazines. Now it's easy to avoid controversy by talking to people about skiing. Or fishing, right? And the commercially driven magazines are going to get the space on the newsstands, get out in the public sphere. This accelerates a process whereby people don't know how to sit down and talk about something for more than ten minutes and they don't know how to deal with something that is controversial. Television doesn't want to do it. This is a process that is driven by the demands of advertisers and it does have a social effect.

It accelerates it, but I don't think it causes it. When they ask, what is marketing? the easy answer is putting yourself in your customer's shoes. What does my customer want? Not, what can I sell to my customer?

Only the question is framed in a way that eliminates a whole set of concerns — you're describing a person as a customer, not as a citizen. To ask what does a customer want? — I don't want to think about this person except as a customer — is to produce that effect and to have a whole social process dominated by people and by institutions quite deliberately doing nothing else but that. Then you create that effect in the public sphere; you create people who are constantly being addressed as consumers. If the only thing you hear all day is, buy this, buy that, buy this, buy that, if that is 90 percent of what is being asked of you, what kind of person are you going to be? That's different from saying to you, let's think about this together; this is a problem that is going to cause controversy, but let's think about it.

I understand what you are saying, but I don't accept your conclusion. Commercial media do not think of themselves as having a requirement to do anything to change the readers, either to make them more enlightened or less enlightened. They really are looking at them from purely a commercial standpoint: what is it that will get this person to pay money for this magazine?

Why is this different than *Life* magazine in 1940 or the *Saturday Evening Post* in 1912? It's always been that way.

It was different before the 1890s when magazines started selling audiences to advertisers. Prior to that, magazines had only to satisfy the readers who paid money for them.

That's right, and they tended to be very local, not national or influential.

They were influential within a certain class range. Magazines like The Atlantic *and* Harper's *reached people in the same way that maybe the* New Republic *does now.*

Or the *National Review*: basically preached to the converted. They were products of that class and they talked to that class. There was never any attempt to break outside of it, to be more general. *Life Magazine* in its heyday had 25 million readers in a country that only had 175 million people. That's a pretty significant impact. That was not a class magazine. *Life* tried to broaden those boundaries, to treat people as Americans. That's where I disagree with you. I see so many other things beside the market process breaking up public space: language differences, geographic fragmentation, the loss of shared values. It's hard to find something that everybody agrees on. Try to think of what Americans would agree on.

Finding something everyone agrees on is different from having public spaces where people talk about what they disagree on.

People don't want to talk about that anymore. That's the problem. What they want to do is watch Morton Downey, Jr.: confrontational, in-your-face politics. I'm not going to defend the magazines. They are in for a buck and that is what they do. There are magazines on the newsstands like *Soldier of Fortune* that recruit people to kill people — domestically or foreign, they don't care. There is out-and-out pornography on the newsstand that is sold to make a dollar. A great deal of cynicism is involved in some of these decisions. But I also believe that media, even broadcast television, are not powerful enough anymore to form opinions.

Another of our visitors said that because of this commercial logic in the media industries, essentially nobody cares about content anymore, except as it draws the attention of audiences, delivers a particular group that advertisers want. Do you agree with that?

Yes and no. There are those, and more so in a recession, who are doing that, but there are still many who would not. For example, in all of the Condé Nast magazines, editorial is incredibly important. Si Newhouse happens to own the company, so he can do anything he wants with it. Another private company is Knapp Communication: *Bon Appetit* and *Architectural Digest.* The editorial is very fine. And those are the magazines that are doing better in this environment than the guys who are whoring, the ones who are saying run an ad and I'll say something nice about your product. I think there were probably always guys who would do that. And there are more of them right now, but I honestly don't know whether this is a long trend or simply a response to a very difficult economic environment. People are desperate: I'll sell out before I close up the shop.

Advertisers are very, very important, but only a few times have I ever seen an overt conflict with an advertiser. Once at *Newsweek* we did an article about chocolate and in it was a comment that Americans will buy anything if it is marketed hard enough: "Look at Campari; it tastes terrible yet people drink it" — well, Campari was an advertiser, and they got really angry. They said, "It does not taste terrible, you guys don't know what you're talking about," and they canceled the advertising for about a year. They advertised in *Time* and it was terrible. My position at that time was that it had been a gratuitous comment. The story was about chocolate, not about Campari, or even alcoholic beverages, and it was unfair to pick on Campari because you, the writer and/or the editor, just happened not to like Campari.

Do market considerations come into conflict with the aims of writers, visual artists, design people, et cetera? Clearly there are a lot of people working for magazines, who have creative values that we might call aesthetic, and they want to do things, can do things, and they come into some kind of interaction with editors and publishers and perhaps advertisers. I wonder if you could talk about that.
Let me describe my experiences with *Outdoor Life* and *Field and Stream*. In the time that I was there we redesigned both magazines and refocused the editorial. We didn't change the direction but refocused it.

That cover on *Field and Stream* is a very good example. That is the first woman to ever appear on the cover of *Field and Stream* in forty years. She's not alone but she's there.

The audience for both magazines had been pretty consistent. We were not trying to make them younger, but we felt that the audience was not getting what it really wanted, which was more about the fun of the sport. If you are a hunter you understand that killing animals is not the purpose of hunting. It's the consequence of hunting but it is not the purpose. Persons who like hunting really like the adventure: tracking, the skills and the tests that you put yourself through. We are spending a lot more time talking about that. Also ten years ago there were almost no female hunters. Now there is a noticeable group, roughly 10 percent. I said we've got to open up the editorial to recognize that. So just by putting a woman on the cover we say that it's okay to be a girl and go hunting. The cover is not trying to do anything more than that. But in terms of trying to manage creativity it was a dialogue, perhaps a negotiation: the editors on the one hand and myself on the other with some support from our research people, going back and forth. Editors will only get their backs up if they are being told what to do. Generally they will try to work (obviously!) with the people who employ them. The *Field and Stream* editor felt very strongly that we were going too far too fast. So we had a negotiation that went on for some time. I think the editor began to believe. My job was to open his eyes to what I thought was a new environment. I was not a hunter or fisherman so I was coming in fresh and looking at this and trying to understand it, and that was my reaction. But managing the process is most difficult. Often you have to take a chance on losing in order to win. The editors, too, they've got to take some chances and that sometimes will irritate advertisers.

I was looking at two of the Times-Mirror *magazines: the titles run up the page and across. The graphics violate the columns. Nothing is longer than a couple of inches. Pictures are scattered, and superimposed in some cases. It struck me that there is something like a* TV *aesthetic here. What do you think the effect of* TV *has been on design?*

Those are designed with a television mentality. The people who did those designs are in the television generation. The art director of the ski book is about thirty. The art director of *Outdoor Life* is maybe thirty-four, thirty-five. They are reacting to their own sort of aesthetic. There is also a theory that the stories have to be shorter, they have to be illustrated more, pictures can tell the whole story. All magazines are becoming more visual, as are all newspapers. *USA Today* is a prime example. Even the *New York Times* is finally going to run its color presses. Color, big pictures, and tighter, shorter stories. In the *New York Times* now you have a little column on the right in the business section, for example, that runs one-paragraph stories. So is it that the people doing the designing are a part of the generation and are imposing their aesthetic on the world, or are they reacting to it? I can't really answer, but the theory is that they are reacting to what is out there. Readers want that, and respond favorably to it.

You're describing a domain of publishing where people who are ostensibly journalists seem to have very little trouble moving with the sort of market logic that you are describing. Are magazines very different from the New York Times?

No.

I can't imagine someone who writes for the New York Times *having somebody walk in the door and say, "Listen, there's this audience that we really want to target and so we should run a whole series of stories to start shifting things in their direction . . ."*

They do it all the time: Sports Monday, Science Tuesday . . .

I have in mind the journalists in the hard news section of the New York Times. *Are you saying that people who cover Washington, trade relationships with Japan, and so on will accept the dictates of market research or of advertisers, and skew coverage of these subjects?*

Those subjects tend not to get you in much trouble with advertisers. There is an acceptance that if you are going to report on the world news you are going to report on the world news. A guy may have a favorite country, and you say something nasty about it . . . But it's not usually that personal. It's business news of one sort or another that gets to be a problem.

American Express pulled all their advertising out of the *Wall Street Journal* for a while when they did an investigative story on their bank in Switzerland.

What about Paramount canceling its advertising in Variety *after an unfavorable review of* Patriot Games?

Variety is a trade magazine, and trade magazines are creatures of the industry they report on. That's a very different kind of situation from that of a consumer magazine, which should be and pretends to be independent of advertisers.

Aren't Ski *and* Skiing *dependent on the industry?*

We'll never say in those magazines that skiing is a terrible sport.

Or that it has a bad environmental impact on mountains?

It does actually, snowmaking drains the creeks.

But you wouldn't have a story on that problem in Skiing?

Actually they have done that. *Times-Mirror Magazines* has a very strong commitment to conservation, and so they did bring it up.

Will the magazine criticize specific products of advertisers?
They'll do a test of twenty-five skis and if three skis from Rossignol are just terrible, they won't say anything. The way to get away with that morally is, "Well, what we tell you about the other skis you can trust. You are going to go out there and you are going to get a great ski." But we won't tell you that the Rossignol ones are terrible.

It's more that kind of thing, selective silence. These magazines don't sell out and say your ski is great if you'll buy an ad, I assure you. They will not tell you something untrue. And also Rossignol has made great skis for many years; this year they had a bad batch, so let's give them a break.

Self-censorship comes in many varieties: for instance, unquestioningly accepting a general ideology about what's good and bad.
Absolutely, no question about it. Journalists, including magazine journalists, tend to be more left than the general population. Vice-President Agnew was correct. There is a Washington/New York axis. These people read the *New York Times* and the *Washington Post* first thing in the morning, and the *Wall Street Journal*, they watch the channel 2 WCBS television news at night, and so there tends to be a consensus formed rather quickly as to what is important and what is not. The most important medium in the country, as far as that is concerned, is the *New York Times*. I wake up to WCBS radio (an all-news station in New York) and I love it: I listen for a half hour or so and then go down to the train station and pick up my *New York Times* and there is the front page with all the same stories on it. The radio journalist has gotten up early, read the *New York Times*, and then reported its stories. The *New York Times*, I do believe, sets the agenda. I know it does for *Newsweek*, and I know it does for *Time* as well. So there is that kind of self-censorship. Also, I think most journalists in the mainstream press think of themselves as patriots, as good Americans. So there is this idea, maybe unconscious, that we have an obligation to look on the American side a little bit more favorably. We will presume that the United States was right and not wrong.

I notice a theme in some of your questions: how much do the culture mongers — we who publish magazines — how much do we influence society? I think it is the other way around. People do a thing; then it is discovered; and then it is brought to a wider audience. I was absolutely stunned a couple of Sundays ago — the style section of the *New York Times*: white child wearing black clothes. The baseball hat turned backward and baggy jeans and all that. That started a long long time ago in the ghettos, and it slowly evolved. People started hearing about rap music. Rap music has been around for a long time, and all of a sudden people became aware of it. That's where the media made a difference. But I think if the media try to force a look the way the old fashion magazines used to, they really can't do it any more. No longer is haute couture going to determine what women wear. I think that media, and specifically magazines that I know the best, must go with the flow. It's good if you can get a little ahead of the wave. You want to be riding down the front of the wave, not the back.

If you get too far in front of the wave, you just sit there and nothing happens. Bruce Springsteen appeared on the cover of *Time* and *Newsweek* in 1976 in the same week. It's the only time that a popular music star was on the cover of both magazines at the same time. And then what happened to him for the next five years? Nothing. He disappeared. He was an '80s phenomenon. The exposure and the fact that he was on the covers — was reported in newspapers, it was on television: look what *Time* and *Newsweek* did. He disappeared. It was too soon. We couldn't make Bruce Springsteen happen. And he couldn't get any better publicity than that.

Dennis Robinson New Jersey Sports and Exposition Authority

October 23, 1992

. . . .

Dennis R. Robinson is executive vice-president and chief operating officer for business operations of the New Jersey Sports and Exposition Authority. A Harvard M.B.A., a master's in sport management from the University of Massachusetts, and a B.A. from Wesleyan, along with stints at the National Football League, the University of Houston, and Southwest Conference, provided the background and training for him to oversee the finance, operating and capital budgets, administration, human resources, strategic planning, and construction areas of Authority management. In his spare time, Dennis is overseeing the development and implementation of a master plan for the redevelopment, with a private partnership, of the Meadowlands site to prepare it for the twenty-first century with new attractions.

I graduated from Wesleyan in 1979, and was on the football team for four years. I decided that I would go into the sports industry, combining my interest in athletics with my interest in the business, and I've been lucky enough to be able to do that. I attended the University of Massachusetts and received an M.S. in sports management. Then I interned for the National Football League in New York, in the broadcasting department. I did some legal work involving the antitrust litigation with Al Davis when they were trying to move the Raiders from Oakland to Los Angeles. From there I went to the University of Houston and served three years as assistant to the athletic director; I was there for three years during the heyday of Houston athletics. We went to a number of bowl games, and participated in three final fours, so it was a very exciting time to be in Houston. I became assistant commissioner of the Southwest Athletic Conference for four years, and coordinated all of the television, radio and marketing. I determined I didn't want to be in college athletics my whole life; I attended graduate school at Harvard, and received an M.B.A., and then I landed with the Meadowlands Sports Complex in strategic planning and development work, and that is where I am today.

I am involved in all aspects of the Sports Authority. In New Jersey the Sports and Exposition Authority is a governmental agency. Established in 1971, it was actually the brainchild of the *Newark Star Ledger*, which ran a a story in 1967 about what a great idea it would be to bring the Yankees to

New Jersey. At that point the Yankees were having problems with safety and transportation and the stadium itself was run down. Various negotiations, underground discussions between business people in New Jersey and the state, took place. As it turned out, the Yankees squeezed some concessions out of the City, which owned Yankee Stadium, and decided to stay. But in the meantime, discussions started to take place with Wellington Mara and the Mara family who owned the Giants. They were second-class citizens at Yankee Stadium, playing football in a baseball facility. As it turned out, the Giants decided — if we can get our own facility, why not. The Mara family agreed to sign a thirty-year lease, and the Sports Authority was founded. The authority immediately went to find the money to put this whole deal together. That is an interesting story because it shows how important these initiatives are to municipalities and states.

The state wanted to build the complex, as most cities and states do, without taxpayer dollars. The state treasurer at the time was dealing with people who wanted a license in northern New Jersey for thoroughbred and harness racing. He said, "Why should we let the private sector make all the money? Why don't we build a racetrack under the auspices of the Sports Authority and use the revenue both to sustain the operation and to amortize the construction bonds." Giants Stadium and the racetrack? It was very innovative: the whole sports complex was really created on the back of racing. So the Authority set out to issue three hundred plus million in bonds to build both facilities. Needless to say, New York City was not pleased with this whole concept. Nelson Rockefeller was governor, John Lindsay was the mayor, and David Rockefeller was the chairman of Chase Manhattan Bank. As I've heard it told, they had tremendous influence on the financial and political communities, and it is said they tried to undermine this whole project three times. The first time they tried it they convinced two rating houses not to rate our bonds. If you can't get a rating on a bond, obviously your interest rates go through the roof; you are basically selling junk bonds, which can make the project financing unfeasible. So Governor Cahill pledged the backing of the state of New Jersey. It wasn't a state contract bond, per se, but it was a moral obligation bond; if the Authority could not make its payments the state would pick up the difference. That was enough to get the bonds rated.

So the Authority went out again and this same group of politicians and financial people started floating phony stories that New York was going to build the same kind of facility in Queens, to try again to undermine the credibility of the bonds. The bond issue was delayed a second time. On its third attempt, this same group actually dissuaded some of the underwriters (who had precommitted to the bonds) from buying them — and these were AA-rated bonds, high-quality investments. Some of the underwriters pulled out and the Authority was $50 million short to finance the $300-million deal. This was twenty-four hours before the bonds went to sale. And so the politicians and business community in New Jersey got together and within twenty-four hours came up with the $50 million to underwrite the rest of the bonds: Prudential, First Fidelity Bank, and United Jersey Bank were key players. That incident brought the New Jersey financial community into its own and out from under the shadow of New York. In essence, the sports complex has served that purpose for New Jersey as a whole. New Jersey was always the bedroom community of Manhattan or Philadelphia; today, because of the sports complex, we are the regional center of the sports world, and you could argue the concert and entertainment business as a whole. We do considerably more concerts than Yankee Stadium or Shea Stadium — we are actually the leading stadium concert destination in the country. We don't have Broadway and Radio City, but nonetheless New Jersey came out from the shadow of New York City in many respects. Something we all look at as entertainment is extremely valuable for economic development. The Cahill administration moved forward on this project because this part of northern New Jersey was nothing but a swamp at the time; Hudson County and southern Bergen County was a decaying part of New Jersey and the state needed something to revive it.

Let me throw out a few statistics. Today the sports complex generates some $950 million of annual economic benefits for the state of New Jersey through jobs, ticket sales, concessions, parking revenues, restaurants, gas stations, hotels, you name it. The Sports Authority employs the equivalent of 3,000 full-time people. We have 280 full-time salaried staff and then of course a lot of part-timers, which include ticket collectors, ushers and concessions people, security and cleaners, and so on; and some 6,000 additional jobs are directly related to the existence of the complex: people that supply goods and services to the complex, the entire New Jersey racing industry (breeding, farming, horse sales, and so forth). And we are the centerpiece of the racing industry in New Jersey.

In what important ways if any does the Authority's relation to the state of New Jersey make it different from a private sector corporation? What difference does it make that there isn't a bottom line in the usual sense?

Well, I wouldn't say that's true, that there isn't a bottom line. Unfortunately, we are accountable to more than just stockholders: we have more constituencies to manage. In fact, we play out our business in the media every day. The *Bergen Record* and the *Newark Star Ledger* both have beat writers that are at every board meeting every month; they cover every story, every promotion, every deal we cut. We have the public to deal with, the bond holders, the administration that changes every four to eight years, the legislature, our board, which is politically appointed, the media, our franchises — the Jets, the Giants, the Nets, the Devils.

You returned excess revenues up to 1986 but haven't since then: is that a result of general economic conditions?

Yes and no. First of all, from a purely business perspective, if you were running a private entity you would never totally leverage the organization. Even the worse-case LBO is not a hundred percent leveraged. Even back in the beginning of the Authority I could have told you it didn't make sense to leverage the organization 100 percent. It constricts your ability to invest in new businesses, to be able to grow and become and remain profitable. What happened is that back in 1977-'78-'79 the race track alone was returning over $40 million after expenses. The Authority said, we're making money, so why don't we use that revenue and build an arena, utilizing some state-guaranteed bonds, with first call on revenue of the operation. They did it again, on some state guarantees, but basically first call on the revenue of the operation. The Authority built a $95-million arena, Brendan Byrne Arena: twenty thousand seats — seating more than Madison Square Garden. Attracted the Devils and then the Nets and so forth. So again, a 100 percent leveraged deal with very little flexibility as to the cyclical nature of the revenue stream. Everything was hunky dory until about 1986–87 and then there was a downturn in the racing industry nationwide, due primarily to the growth of casino gaming and lotteries. New Jersey in the early seventies had a lottery that was practically nonexistent. Then the Lottery expanded their distribution and every mom-and-pop store in New Jersey sells lottery tickets now. And then the casino industry in Atlantic City: there were maybe two or three casinos at the time, now there are twelve. So the gaming industry as a whole grew rapidly in New Jersey. Before casinos, racing was the only legalized form of gambling and we benefited tremendously. So we had a highly leveraged capital structure and what became a highly cyclical revenue stream. For example, one year you have fourteen stadium concerts, the next year you have six. So in 1992 we had to restructure our debt because the racing revenues were down significantly. We still have $22 million in annual debt service plus $2½ million for taxes to the Borough of East Rutherford.

You described quite interestingly the fight between New York and New Jersey at a very high level. Is there really so much in it for either of the two states?
Absolutely. It's a billion dollars in economic activity a year because of our sports complex. New York just gave $40 million to Morgan Stanley because they produce something like $100 million of economic activity a year, with their four thousand employees on Wall Street. It's the same competition that exists in business, whether you are selling toothpaste or another product. The promotional side: who ever thought about New Jersey as an entertainment center, internationally, regionally, or nationally, before the existence of the sports complex? No one. The economics, in my opinion dictate everything. The world is grounded in economics.

It would be as if New Jersey put out a bond issue to build the Empire State Building so that Morgan Stanley could come and occupy it.
That's right. You can quantify the benefits of any tax incentive package, whether it's International Paper staying in Arkansas under Clinton, or GTE in Camden, or keeping the Campbell Soup Company. What kind of income tax are you going to lose over a thirty-year period by taking three thousand employees with a $50-thousand average salary, and moving them out? Just discount that revenue stream and look at your up-front investment; that's how you determine whether it's a good investment or not. The same is true for any kind of economic development.

You have mentioned some similarities between your product and other products. In sports, how do you think about what the product is, how it fits into people's lives, and with what other products it's in competition?
It sounds simple, but it is a complex question. If you define sports as an enjoyable diversion, you can look at your competition as just about anything else that fills that role. I think it goes deeper than that, though. I think sports fulfill a number of basic needs. To give you an example: when you are selling makeup, you're not selling eyeshadow or rouge or lipstick per se, you're selling the ability for women to feel better about themselves. Some people who are a little more cynical about products of that nature say you are selling hope. So, you go down four or five levels below the product

itself. It is really the need you are fulfilling. Sports, I think, fills the need of affiliation. Everybody wants to feel like part of a group, whether it is your neighborhood, your family, your school, your team, the gang that you are in. Everyone wants to have pride in something, whether it's their personal accomplishments or the accomplishments of other people. Everyone from the truck driver to the board chairman is an expert in the sports business: "It's a lousy trade, bad hire, cut that guy, why didn't you substitute him then, you didn't pull the pitcher when you should." I mean people really get involved, no matter what socioeconomic class they belong to. I call sports the great equalizer.

One of the things that interests us about identification and affiliation concerns gender. Given the range of sporting experiences that you deal in, can you talk about the ways in which some of them address distinctions of masculinity and femininity?
I thought this was one of the most fascinating questions you posed, but it's a question of stereotypes. Sports is masculine, and so forth. You are starting out from an assumption that there are stereotypes involved. I suppose in some respects there are. Traditionally, sports have been male. But then traditionally, working out of the home was male oriented. Traditionally, smoking was male. Traditionally, wearing pants was masculine. It seems to me that the definition of masculine changes over time. Yes, it is slow to change, but look at women's rights and how they have changed over time. It used to be that women were supposed to be passive, that was their gender role. Women in the workplace today are not passive, nor should they be. They are aggressive, they are ambitious, all those things that women were not supposed to be. You are now seeing a transition, I think, in the sports industry. Women's participation in athletics has just skyrocketed since the sixties, and their interest in watching sports has increased significantly as well. Societal transitions eventually impact the sports world. Basketball is a perfect example: the audience is about 60–40 now, men to women.

Home audience or ticket-buying audience?
The television audience, which is more indicative of the following. Economics affect the live audience more.

As far as the live audience goes, do you have any idea what the split is?
I think in college basketball it is close to 50–50 or 60–40. Even the live audience in NBA basketball is almost that. The reason it's not quite so close

is simply that a lot of corporate sales are involved. Football is more male oriented, as is professional hockey.

College hockey is different. There is not a lot of fighting in college hockey; there is a lot of finesse, a lot of skill. In pro hockey they are battling it out with their fists.

Some say that football inculcates competitive values and teaches how to operate in the business world, that it's not simply a diversion but also a sport in which people learn socially central skills: is that why it's more male coded?
You are talking about participation, which is very different from spectatorship. I will give you an example. Have you heard of Donna Lopiano? Donna Lopiano was one of the most highly respected women in the sports industry. She went to Southern Connecticut, was a great softball pitcher. She went to Southern California, got her Ph.D., and ran the University of Texas women's athletic department. Now she is the president of the women's sports foundation that Billy Jean King created. She said to me, when we were talking about women in sports, that the women who have participated in a team sport are the best to work with because they know how to work as a team and they know how to work with people. I can understand that because I played football for fourteen years, and to this day I call back experiences, draw upon the confidence — physically, mentally, emotionally — sometimes daily, certainly weekly.

Earlier you said that basketball has a significant women's audience. You have a team, the Nets, and my sense is that they don't regularly sell out.
That's absolutely the truth.

Might just be a way to go: there are lots of women who follow basketball but have never gone to a game of some kind.
I disagree. I would say that any woman who follows basketball has gone to a game.

You are sitting at a table where two women out of four say they follow basketball, but haven't been to a game. Do you make promotions? Are you going to give up on forty percent of your audience? I think this involves recoding the space. People tend to think of arenas as coded male, places where men are more at ease, more welcome, more comfortable, just as there are certain bars that women wouldn't walk into.
You mean how we set up the facility? Give me some examples.

Space in bathrooms would be a specific example.

That's a good one. Bathrooms are an issue we deal with every day. We have a commitment from the president on down about the bathrooms in our places. We installed changing tables in the bathrooms, we've put more stalls in there, we have conveniences, we have attendants in our bathrooms throughout every event; they are constantly cleaned during every event, especially during a family show like the Ice Capades or Disney on Ice. We have a commitment to the needs of women. We have also increased the variety of items that are in the concession stands. Now you have grilled chicken sandwiches, you don't have just the pizza and the beer and the popcorn. We have salads that you can take to your seats. These types of things appeal particularly to women. Traditionally, I guess, these spaces have been coded male, but as more and more women become more and more interested in sports, people like us are going to move more and more to appeal to them.

The other thing would be promotions: special prices, women coming in groups, something like that.

We do a lot of promotions at the race track, and we do particularly target women for the restaurants. Women don't want to go eat with Joe Schmo smoking a cigar. Pegasus is a first-class restaurant overlooking the track, New York skyline, it's very romantic; waiters in tuxedos; we have a restaurant that is less formal downstairs, but with equally nice service. We target women through magazines, to see if we can get them to say, "Hey Joe, let's go out to dinner here." Or if Joe says, "Why don't we go to the track?," she says "The only way I'm going is if you take me out to dinner."

It sounds as if you don't do surveys as to who comes to the games? Is that right?

No, that is wrong. Let me set the context. We are not primarily responsible for marketing the Nets or the Devils or the Giants or the Jets. However, we publish things like *The Front Row*, which promotes everything that we have at the complex. We *are* primarily responsible for certain types of shows that we produce ourselves. The kickoff classic, the first football game of the year: we own that event. We are primarily responsible for promoting our racing product. We coproduce some shows, which we promote. The franchises have their own marketing departments and we try to help them any way we can, but we are not primarily responsible.

Do you ever try to create a particular kind of new audience?

A marketer targets groups who have a predisposition to use the product.

We don't create markets. It's the old chicken and the egg. If there is a sport, an event, that we know appeals to women, if we believe they are pre-disposed to be an audience, we will target them. No question about it. But we have finite marketing dollars. To pull in a market that is tough to convert, the amount of money you would have to spend is incredible. A perfect example: do marketers create a need for people to have whiter teeth? No. They depend on a need that people have to look good. People are naturally concerned about their looks. Then they want to have whiter teeth. If they are concerned about having bad breath, they want a paste with a breath freshener. The toothpastes will have the same formula, color, taste, but most importantly, the product positioning will be different. We don't create markets; we fulfill needs. Madonna is another example: did Madonna create the sexual revolution in this country? No way. Did rock bands create the drug culture in this country? Absolutely not. Did they hop on to changing mores in this country? Or the rebellious need of American youth at the time? Absolutely. But did they create it? I don't believe it, not for a second.

People always had ways to clean their teeth, right? But at a certain point, corporations encouraged people to go from whatever means they were using to clean their teeth before to using this new special product. There was an intervention, not simply a reaction to a market but an effort to shape people's daily living patterns. Now regarding gender, are you saying that as women get more interested in the sports, the sports industry is just going to respond? Or, is there a consciousness among people in the industry that there is this potential other market out there that needs to be tapped?
Again, do we create markets? I don't think we do. Do we shape them? Do we tap into an interest? Absolutely. I'm trying to think of a product or a service that didn't really fulfill a need in which a marketer created a need.

It's one thing to have clean teeth and another thing to have very white teeth. That is in some sense a new social idea.
But the need to look nice, was that new?

Another example is halitosis, a disease invented by a marketer.
A perfect example. They took a phenomenon that existed and gave it a name. Now that's brilliant. They packaged it and they promoted it, but they didn't cause people to have bad breath.

Might there be misgivings about attracting women to sports events with primarily male audiences, on the possibility that you might start losing your male audience if you changed the "male" atmosphere?

From my perspective, absolutely not. All it could do is help the sport. If more people watch a sport on television, more people watch commercials; that increases the value of the advertising time and makes the franchises more valuable. Male or female, the more the better. Create a demand for tickets; creating a situation where you can't get a ticket is the best thing you can ever do.

So you don't have to worry that some guys won't want to come to football with kids crying in the stands and women endlessly going off to put on their makeup or do diapers.

That's right. Any facility manager that is worth a darn strictly enforces conduct codes, and the more women that attend events with children, the more these conduct codes will be enforced. They are enforced in our facility. If somebody is swearing and carrying on, we will remove them.

Isn't marketing sports different from marketing many other products? Pittsburgh tried to sell a hockey team for a long time; they could do all the ticket promotions they wanted to, all the advertising, and no one came. However, when they got Mario Lemieux, they didn't have to do promotions. Once the Penguins started to play decent hockey, and had one of the best players in the league, the team sold itself. Isn't that really how most sports marketing is done, rather than by advertising or promotions?

Yes, that's true. A good friend of mine was hired to become the vice-president of marketing for the San Antonio Spurs. That was the year David Robinson was coming out of the Navy. I said to my friend, "You are going to be a genius. Your attendance is going to go up 25 percent if not 50 percent because of David Robinson." Sure enough. Absolutely, winning is everything in the sports business. When you are winning, you market the hell out of your product. When you have something really great to sell, you create a grass-roots following, which is key. In the sports business you are really targeting kids, kids that grow up to be fans.

Can you convert an older person when your team is winning?

The hardest thing for the Devils has been converting Rangers fans. Kids in New Jersey, whose fathers worked in New York and had corporate seats, would always go to Rangers games. It's hard to convert them. But now, after about ten or eleven years, the kids are old enough to buy tickets themselves.

That's the kind of longevity you want. That's why you see teams like the Whalers sponsoring hockey games, or Devils players showing up at schools and doing talks on drug abuse. It's an effort to build a grass-roots following at a very young age.

Isn't an awful lot of sports marketing done gratis by newspapers? In Pittsburgh the Pirates lost an enormous amount of attendance this summer because of a newspaper strike — at least that is the theory.
Yes. There is no question. The media can make a team or they can break it at the gate.

I wanted to ask about differences or similarities between sporting events and concerts. I was interested in what you said about affiliation. It seems to me that is a very important appeal of live music as well, or any event that brings together such a large crowd.
Absolutely.

I was wondering about the demographics. In Britain, where I have been researching, men are twice as likely to go to live music events as women. So maybe there are more similarities than one might at first think between the sporting event and the live music concert. Also, could you compare the two audiences with respect to income?
Audiences for mainline rock are much younger, and the kids come from more up-scale homes. But music is marketed very differently from sports. The live concert business is nothing more than a vehicle to promote albums. It's no coincidence that some world tour takes place a month or two after the record is released, or prior to, or during. Live music is secondary to the selling of albums. But putting on an event itself is not that different, whether it's a game or a concert.

What about the profit structure for you? Do you make more money from merchandising than from tickets for concerts?
Every deal is different. The Grateful Dead control everything. They sell their own merchandise. They are a little industry unto themselves. Other events, we get a flat fee, plus a percentage of the gross. We keep parking, we keep concessions, and we get a percentage of the novelty sales. Concerts are much more profitable than sporting events. It is not even close. That is really why the stadium, which holds about sixty shows a year, is substantially more profitable than the arena, which does over two hundred.

*About affiliation and masculinity: there is an interesting commercial running
with the World Series. It promotes watching football this Sunday. An older guy,
sort of heavy, is sitting in a chair and talking in an animated way about how the
Eagles came into Washington last weekend. Meanwhile, behind him is a little
screen showing some spectacular plays from the Redskins-Eagles game. There you
see him, visibly different in his masculinity from the football players in theirs.*
They are trying to show someone who is overweight, not athletic, who
wants to be affiliated with being an athlete. Everyone has a fantasy, and I
think those kinds of commercials appeal to that.

*But this one says in effect, it is a fantasy. It acknowledges the lack of vigorous
youthful masculinity on the part of the viewer and shows him fantasizing with the
help of the TV screen. What kind of masculinity is stirred in male fans who
affiliate this way?*
Again, I think every generation defines masculinity differently. Take the old
idea of the male as hunter, provider, warrior, protector. Is that what today's
male is? Some of us may feel a bit like that, but now we have the nurturing
male, the involved father, versus the father who is detached from his kids.
The old masculine ideal is, to me, out the window.

*I haven't seen that ad, but from the way you describe it, it doesn't describe a
fantasy identification, but a real bond between men that transcends generation
and physique; there is this essential connection — one plays, the other loves it.*

*What will partly determine how sport changes is how many women are in
positions like yours in sports organizations! Do men sit around asking, "What do
women want?" Or are there women sitting around asking it?*
No good marketer, male or female, is going to throw away a potential
market that can make money. The culture of an organization makes some
difference, but you don't do marketing research on yourself: "This appeals
to me, therefore it is going to appeal to everyone in America."

What is the culture of the front office — the business end?
There is no question that it has been a male-dominated industry, and a
white one, too, in the higher ranks. But that is changing. Let's talk about
race and then back to gender.

It wasn't until the early seventies that many large, Division I universities
had a black player on their football team. It was only twenty-five years ago
that blacks really came on the scene. They are not coming up the ranks as
rapidly as people would like to see. There are not a lot of black managers

and coaches but that's changing. Willis Reed, with the Nets, Wes Unseld, Dennis Greene: all these guys are doing a great job, have great respect among owners and players and managers. I think as more and more African Americans participate, graduate, go into the industry, and gain experience at different levels, success will naturally follow. It is a little more difficult for women. Let's take football: women seldom play the game, so for them to go into coaching that sport is unlikely. Jody Conradt, University of Texas basketball coach, could probably coach as well as any male coach in this country. As far as being able to coach the game, she's incredible. But I think you are seeing more and more women move into top spots in collegiate athletics. Judith Sweet is a Division III athletic director, and president of the NCAA.

That is one of the ironies of the funding of women's teams in colleges: a lot of the coaching jobs, the more important jobs, are going to men. Isn't that the case, if you have a situation where men are competing for coaching jobs with women?
I think that's an overstatement. In fact, I think it's the opposite. Women's athletics, women's basketball for instance, is becoming a very big-time sport in Division I with the final four on television, recruiting, big budgets, and they are selling a lot of tickets. You hire the best person that is available for that job, male or female. Now if I had a male and a female equally qualified for a women's coaching job, I'd hire the woman.

One reason we have been asking questions about race and gender is because sport promotes certain kinds of identities, certain ways of thinking about ourselves. You said earlier that the sports complex did something for New Jersey's identity. What do you think that was?
It is related to the pride you take in where you live — your community, your state, your country. The complex gave people a sense that New Jersey wasn't second class to New York; in fact, we have something to be proud of. It makes tangible differences, too — attracting businesses, for example. There are more international headquarters in New Jersey than almost any state in the country, and that has a lot to do with the international reputation of New Jersey as a port, but also its entertainment and cultural activities. Companies think all these things important.

What is the racial makeup of the audience for a football game, a hockey game, a basketball game? The hockey team is mostly white, the basketball and football teams are mostly black . . .

Well, football is probably close to 50–50. We do demographic surveys: we know the racial makeup of the audience, but actual attendance is related to socioeconomic status. The interest is obviously there: black people are fans and watch television. But attendance at events has gotten to be very expensive; attendance is limited by income.

I just want to leave you with this. The reason I feel so strongly about the industry, even more so about participation, is I think sports is the great equalizer among people. Whether you are black or white, big or small, it doesn't matter. You put somebody on the playing field, you set the rules, and then you let them go. And you know what? The best one wins. Regardless of size and color. That is the beauty of the whole thing. I just wish that more people could experience what it is like to work with and fight for people from different socioeconomic backgrounds, different racial histories, and so forth. What you find is that you gain a tremendous acceptance for people for who they are. That is the great benefit of participation.

Douglas Bennet National Public Radio

November 12, 1992

. . . .

*Douglas J. Bennet is president of Wesleyan University. Prior to joining
Wesleyan, Mr. Bennet was assistant secretary of state for international
organization affairs. He is best known for his decade as chief executive officer
and president of National Public Radio. Well versed in foreign affairs, Mr.
Bennet was head of the Agency for International Development, served as
assistant secretary of congressional relations, Department of State, and was
special assistant to the U.S. Ambassador to India Chester Bowles. On the
domestic side, he served as the first staff director of the Senate Budget
Committee, and was assistant to Vice-President Hubert H. Humphrey,
Senator Thomas F. Eagleton, and Senator Abraham Ribicoff. He also served
as the first president of the Roosevelt Center for American Policy Studies in
Washington, D.C. A graduate of Wesleyan, he received a master's degree
from the University of California at Berkeley and a doctorate in history from
Harvard University.*

The question, to what extent is National Public Radio a business?, is one of the main things we will be discussing. I sent you some
materials that were purposely hyped. What they say is all true, but that
packet is the lead that we send potential underwriters. I read it again coming up on the plane and I think it is pretty good; it is as close as we come to
looking like a business. I think, however, that the way we survive, and
indeed the way we prosper, is as an antithesis to business. Commercial
broadcasting is not selling program, it is selling products. We sell programming. Commercial broadcasting works top down, the networks paying to
have their programs carried. But our stations pay us. We are succeeding as a
business where radio networks are failing because we are doing something
that they won't do. We are starting with our product as programming.

I can say a few words about our funding. I guess I ought to go back and say
one thing about the origin of NPR because it is a very important part of the
lesson. It was first funded by the Corporation for Public Broadcasting. It
was created by public largesse and organized contributions that sustained it
for many years. About three years after the financial crises that NPR had in
1983, we cut off from federal funding altogether and NPR is now self-
sustaining. Public radio stations get about 15 percent of their money from

the federal government and another 35 percent from state and local sources. Public radio never would have been there if it hadn't had the initial public support; it never could have thrived if we hadn't cut it off. National Public Radio currently receives two-thirds or a little more of its income from stations and one-third from underwriters and foundations and corporations.

How are we different from a private corporation? We are a membership organization. The board is seventeen. I'm one. Ten members are elected by station managers, and they are my boss. It is the reverse of what you would expect. We operate totally in the sunshine. Only sensitive personnel issues are dealt with secretly. Otherwise it is a completely open operation. The funding and the legitimacy of the operation originate at the grass roots, not at the advertising agency. People make voluntary contributions to support something that they can listen to for free. So it is just upside down completely in terms of any sort of commercial model. That is not to say though that we don't compete for audience. It is not to say, obviously, that we can operate at a deficit — we can't. We have just completed our fiscal year. The part of the business that does programming, everything but the technical satellite part of it, is about a $30 million a year operation. We just had one of our best years ever. We had a surplus of $150,000 at the end. In other words, it is a tiny, tiny, whisker-thin surplus.

"Other income" includes interest and earnings on ancillary activities like selling cups. Most of it is the revenue for the satellite system that we run for public radio stations which is about a $10 million a year operation.

"Other grants": that's foundations and corporations?
That is all foundations and corporations and there is a tiny, little bit of Corporation for Public Broadcasting money that we still get in the form of competitive grants.

How do you think about NPR's product? And what do you think of as your main competition? Those are closely related questions.
There are three product areas, but let me not discuss two of them. One is the satellite services. We lease a couple of transponders and up-link our own programming and programming for everybody else in public broadcasting. We have some surplus capacity, which we sell. Second, we are a trade association for public radio stations — the members. We lobby for them and represent them before the FCC and so forth.

The largest part of our activity — the largest product — is the programming. That consists of not only "All Things Considered" and "Morning

Edition," but a lot of other public affairs stuff in addition to these, including a new two-hour daily program called "Talk of the Nation," an afternoon call-in show.

We have changed the cultural program offering to try to produce a more multicultural service for the stations. In terms of audience growth, that is our fastest growing area at this point. The news magazines, "Morning Edition" and "All Things Considered," are carried by almost all NPR stations. The reason for that is partly historical. In the old days when CPB was funding us, that was funding to produce those programs and they were essentially a free good for the stations. By 1987 that changed. The stations had to start paying for the programs. By that time they were very well established. They cost the stations a lot. Our NPR dues are 10 to 12 percent of a station's revenue, which is a big slug of money. You couldn't have started those programs if you had gone out to sell them to entities positioned the way public radio stations are positioned in the United States.

There is also an intangible product that I think is worth mentioning. It is credibility. It gives the stations a certain amount of credibility to be associated with NPR.

When we offer underwriting opportunities to businesses, we are saying, "What we are doing is worthwhile, we are well recognized; by associating yourself with us and by being recognized on the air, you will be well regarded by lots of listeners who contribute to stations. They will think you are on the same side of the table." That is different from an advertising buy where you are trying to persuade people, through whatever means, to buy your product. Ours is a very hard message to get through. Corporate cultures reject it, advertising agencies hate it, it is high risk for anybody but the CEO of a corporation: who knows, NPR might report critically on the company. In one case what we said about a product represented by a trade association that was one of our underwriters was not favorable, and the money went away.

The fact is that underwriting from corporations and business interests is the smallest part of our grants income. Most of that is foundation money. We have not known whether we could keep that growing or not, but it looks at this point as if we will.

How does the underwriting at the local stations come to bear on this? Some of them have a lot of corporate sponsors. Does that figure into this story?
The stations pay in proportion to their revenues. I've tried very hard to get them to think about their total revenue. The money that we used to get from the Corporation for Public Broadcasting went to the stations after

1987, so there was a natural tendency in the stations to say, we'd like to keep as much of it as we can. By now the stations have begun to think about their NPR payments in terms of their total revenues. In fact, that makes more sense, because their revenues — especially a lot of their underwriting revenues — they earn by providing the NPR services. I mean, our services are what earn them the most underwriting revenue. Let me put it differently. We think on the basis of anecdotal evidence that 50 percent of all the underwriting and about 33 percent of all the listener money is attributable to the two NPR news magazines.

In the "other income" category, is there a catalog for friends of public radio that includes coffee cups, books, tapes, posters, and so on? Here you do get into a very direct kind of product marketing, into mailing lists and zip codes and credit cards and all of that.

Some public broadcasting entities, not NPR I hasten to say, have created for-profit subsidiaries that do that sort of marketing. I have very strong reservations about it and I make everybody in public broadcasting mad when I say that. People are trying to do it because they don't have enough money to make good programming and they wish they had more. It is one of those areas where the not-for-profit sector and the commercial sector rub up against each other. I think it is important that that continue to happen. But when you get a catalogue that is from a commercial company, with a not-for-profit stamp on it, that raises some questions. The money goes to the for-profit company; that company pays salaries to people who send out the yuppie goods; and then the residual goes to support the broadcasting entity. In the public radio world, the primary example is something called Rivertown Trading, which is a subsidiary of American Public Radio, or Minnesota Public Radio. Their 800 telephone number is on the Garrison Keillor show and I don't think it's right. It is a $100 million a year gross operation, but it is not connected to NPR. It came up in the senior staff meeting at NPR the other day. If they are doing it why aren't we doing it? Maybe we could pull off $4 or $5 million in T-shirt sales. That would help this process a lot.

So is that in your future?
Not while I am there.

Why not?
I just think it conflicts with our public mission. I think it confuses people. We are not an advertising medium. We have to invent ways to survive as

what we are and I think that we are doing that very well now. It is unusual in a time of recession for an enterprise to be chugging along as well as this one is.

About station revenues: what percentage is listener support, what percent comes from the Corporation, and what percentage is from other sources? Is there a general pattern here?
The smaller the station, the larger the percentage of its support from the Corporation for Public Broadcasting. There is a complicated formula by which that money is allocated. A very small station might get 25 percent of its revenue from CPB and a very large station might get 12 percent. Their NPR dues follow the same formula. So they immediately pay out two-thirds of their income from CPB. The other portions vary widely. Some stations have as much as 70 or 80 percent of their revenue from listener contributions alone. There are stations that do very well with underwriting, though I don't think underwriting is ever more than 25 percent of revenue, and it's zero in lots of places.

My sense is that when you get right down to it, what you are doing is selling audiences to those local stations. They know that your programming is going to deliver certain types of people as their local audience. And when you get corporate underwriting you also deliver a particular kind of audience with a particular kind of profile — it is apparent from the sort of underwriters that underwrite NPR that these are the sorts of companies that somehow match the profile of your listeners. Even though there is your public service mission, the product itself that you are actually selling is not so much the programming as it is these audiences.
Let's separate the kinds of revenue. Half of the quarter of a billion dollars a year that keeps whole public radio system going is from public sources, tax sources of some kind. It may go through a state university, but half of it is public investment. Another quarter comes from listeners. And that is a very sensitive issue in this discussion. One of the things the listeners say about public radio is that they are listening because they don't like ads. All of these factors tend to constrain dependence on underwriting. I don't think the stations use our programs to attract a specific kind of audience. They use our programs to attract a substantial audience, and that audience has certain characteristics that are pretty much laid out in the material I sent you. The result of having that kind of an audience is that they are more likely to get listener contributions, and to attract the kinds of businesses that you are talking about. We don't program the way we do to attract underwriters or

audience. That is not a consideration. We program the way we do because we can see ourselves serving a curious audience. I think the unifying characteristic of the audience is curiosity. Ours is truly a very different motivation from somebody who wants to sell soap.

This brings us to another area that is part of the debate about public funding for NPR. On the one hand, NPR is trying to argue that it is providing a public service, and on the other hand, somehow it has to produce programming to keep that very sensitive demographic profile. Why should this up-scale audience have its particular tastes subsidized at public expense?
I think the answer is what I call the museum answer: society needs to provide itself with certain "goods." Museums are that kind of a good; NPR is that kind of a good. What NPR provides never would have existed if it hadn't had public subvention. Now that subvention isn't so much any more.

The profile of the audience in terms of gender and race and so forth is broad. Its unifying characteristic is that it is very highly educated. Everything else flows from that. The income levels flows from that. And the curiosity I think flows from it. That is what pulls the audience together. If the question is whether we should be reaching a broader audience, the answer is that it would be nice, but it is not important enough to change the programming.

A second question is, could you imagine different kinds of services that would reach different kinds of people with different kinds of needs? The answer is by all means yes, and I think it is a tragedy that we are not doing that now. English as a second language, readings for the blind—there are all sorts of possibilities you can imagine using radio for, but they are going to have to be at least kicked off and maybe sustained by a public investment greater than at present.

If you were to find that new types of programming shifted the demographics of your audience down-scale, would that bother you?
We have tried to *do* that. We are into things like "Afro-Pop Worldwide" and other cultural offerings specifically designed to broaden the audience, and they in fact do. It is a plus, not a minus. Whereas, if I were trying to sell advertising time all it would do is confuse demographics—not what you want.

If your audience went down-scale, you wouldn't be able to appeal to corporate underwriters in the same ways.

DOUGLAS BENNET *National Public Radio* [167

I don't think that's right. In the first place, I'm not sure I'm comfortable with the terms "down-scale" and "up-scale." I'm more comfortable with "broad" and "narrow," and the broader it is, the greater the appeal. I think it's very important to get hold of how small a consideration corporate support is. It's not that it's negligible but . . . For example, we have self-imposed limitations on what NPR will put on the air about a corporation. Our limitations are much tighter than the FCC's limitations. There are rules governing what we allow ourselves to say about underwriters. You can't use superlatives but you can use adjectives.

The main point is, we have a broad audience, and that gives us access to a diversity of funding sources not available to commercial broadcasters. Only the need for audience homogeneity could produce a profile of radio broadcasting that looks like what we have in the United States. Clearly that need is driving commercial broadcasting. It is an incredible waste of a resource. Whatever it is that we have done in this country to produce this outcome—this incredible narrowness of the use of the radio broadcast spectrum—represents an incredible failure. I think it goes back to the very early days when broadcasting was converted into a commercial enterprise. Think about the other kinds of services you could have, if you could just take a few of those stations and use them for something else. But in order for that to happen somebody has to make a regulatory decision, someone has to make an investment.

Can you describe for us a situation where you specifically decided that in order to increase the diversity of your audience—racially, by gender, by income bracket— you would develop a program format that you thought would bring in a new group of listeners?
Yes, we scrapped NPR's whole cultural offering about five years ago, and started building up this multicultural service. And the change was total. The guy who was in charge of cultural programming left and I had an opportunity to recruit somebody else. I spent two years trying to find somebody to do what we are talking about, and I found somebody outside radio who was able to.

One of the conscious things we've done on the news services is to have a lot more minorities on the air. I mean Richard Gonzales covering the White House sends out a very big signal to Hispanic listeners everywhere.

Here is another example. John Hockenberry did a show that was proposed for production by an independent radio producer in New York. It was an evening two-hour show with a call-in dimension, aimed at current cultural issues, topics, interests. The purpose of it was to reach a more diverse and younger audience. We never had a chance to measure its audience because we were not able to sustain the program financially. The thing that is wrong with the whole structure, incidentally, is that we don't have enough resources for innovation. I keep trying to get foundations to give us blocks of money for innovation and we have been fairly successful in doing that. We have some internally generated resources, but in this case the program was costing—I suppose the budget was one million three, maybe one million eight—and I saw clearly after six months that we simply were not getting the underwriting that we needed to sustain it, and we killed it.

According to your figures, almost half again as many NPR listeners are men as women. It's close to 60 percent male and just a bit over 40 percent female. How do you decide what gender issues to address and in what ways? Are women and men involved more or less equally in production and in basic decisions?
I never thought about it the way you've asked it. I've been aware that the audience is slightly more male than female, but I'd guess that this relates to the numbers of men and women who have completed college.

On the question of how we decide what to cover, I don't think that our cultural programming ever has to make a gender-related choice, but the news department does all the time. As with all editorial choices, this one is delegated to the news department. It is extremely important in any cultural institution or news institution that you have a balance of gender and race in leadership roles. In my experience it's the only way you are going to get any kind of sensible balance in coverage. NPR has always been a hospitable place for women. Susan Stamberg was host of "All Things Considered" at a time when it was widely believed that the screechy voices of women would never be tolerated on the air, and Irving R. Levine was the thing to have. We have women at all decision-making ranks in the company, and that works very well. I think the editorial meeting has probably slightly more women than men. On race: we've had in recent years a very aggressive affirmative action effort, which I am very proud of personally and which has changed the way the company works. It's changed what it's like as a workplace; it's changed access for minorities. The multiculturalism of our cultural programming wouldn't be possible if we didn't have a very diverse staff.

You said you didn't think that a shift in the composition of your audience would affect you financially because corporate underwriting is such a small part of the whole pie, and listener contributions are a very big part. Do you think that if there was a shift in the composition of the audience it would be as likely that you'd be able to generate as much in contributions? Are people with larger discretionary incomes more likely to respond to a pitch on the radio to do something good?

The data on charitable giving don't support that in general. There is an inverse relationship between income and propensity to give. The contributions that we depend on average $50 or $55 across the country. I think that we have a very long way to go before we start to hit any kind of resistance because of poverty. I think our audience will continue to grow. I think it will continue to get more diverse, and I think audience revenues will continue to grow faster than any of our other revenue flows. (I wonder if this is a peculiarly American phenomenon. Every time I'm visited by an Eastern European newly freed potential broadcaster who wants to save democracy in his country through radio I wonder whether this is a transferable model.)

In a sense, you are the last general radio source left, as commercial radio stations become more and more niche operations. You are trying to remain a national service.

And to generalize, to broaden. One of the things I ran into when I got to NPR was derivative, commercial broadcast research that said, you've got these classical music listeners who never want anything else. You've got news listeners and they will never want anything else. The evidence was clearly the opposite. The evidence in our audience anyway was, if you can think of ways to surprise people or entertain them — give them a "Car Talk" or put "Afro-Pop Worldwide" into a classical format station — guess what: the audience goes up. Radio stations are homogeneously devoted to these formats, and it is just stupid. It is a failing business.

I'm interested in the music in particular. What percentage of NPR stations are playing classical music, and does that guarantee certain demographics, in class, race, and gender?

The stations on the lower frequencies, long before NPR was there, were mostly associated with educational institutions, and I think that the predominance of the classical music format came out of that association, for whatever reason: reasons of audience, or the taste of the dean or whatever, the availability of old records, I don't know. There are very few commercial classical stations. There are something like twenty-two markets in the country now where there is a commercial classical station. Most public radio stations play some classical music still. One of NPR's services is "Performance Today," a two-hour daily classical music service, about classical music performance in the United States. I don't know if you ever hear it or not, but it has gotten to be a very nice show. My point is not to give up European classical music; it is not to be so Eurocentric about it. I'm going to offer the same people who like that some other things too. I never could understand jazz, until I started to listen to Marian McPartland. I began to get it. And I am very glad I did.

A station here in Connecticut defines itself as classical music and news, and states on the air that it is a unique service. How does that fit in with the mission of NPR? How does a station qualify to join NPR? Can you pay your money and get in?

You have to meet certain criteria. You have to be on the air for nineteen hours a day at least and you have to have a staff of a certain number and a budget above a certain amount and be a not-for-profit, secular station. Any station can join once it meets those criteria. The missions of the stations are varied. What I have been telling you about is NPR's mission; I would have to say it reflects my own views to a considerable degree. The stations are totally independent. They are licensed by the FCC and they are responsible for what they put on the air. They contract with us to put our NPR programming on the air but are totally free to do whatever they want to do.

In the discussion that goes on with Hartford, for example, we say, "Why don't you use all of 'Morning Edition'? You are killing your audience." And we are immediately rebuffed. "You don't understand the Hartford market, and please leave me alone." We say, "Look at what's happening here with 'Car Talk,'" which they just took off the air. We have a marketing division that worries about things like this. They had it on at a time slot when there was no audience, and it is a very expensive program. The thing to do was to put it on on Saturday morning the way everybody else does, backed up against "Weekend Edition," the morning program on Saturday. It is a gold mine. Once you have anything on the air, assuming that anybody is listening, they are listening because they like it. That is one of the nice things about radio. The number of people who listen but hate what you are doing is minuscule — they can always go do something else.

Does NPR have no leverage at all?

No, we have no leverage at all, and I wouldn't try to exercise any. We are at least providing a much broader selection for stations that want it. What we expect is not that they all use all the breadth, but that stations in specific situations will have more to choose from, and that we will give legitimacy to the idea that it is possible to succeed as a public radio station doing something other than classical music.

Anybody who listens to NPR knows that the most frequent complaint about it is that it's supposedly left wing. What impact do those sorts of persistent complaints have, if any? Do you have a sense of your own product, your own news, having a bias of any kind?

We struggle not to have bias. We struggle for objectivity, we struggle for breadth. My own view of the bias issue — and this is supported by the *Los Angeles Times* polls about media in general — is that people view media as inherently prone to bias, unless its C-SPAN or something, because they are intermediaries. Who knows what the intermediary may have in mind? Who knows whether that reporter is interpreting the event properly? So you start out with a degree of skepticism. Second, I think that this is a very unsettled time. A lot of favored beliefs are turning out to not work very well, whether about families or Israel or whatever. It makes people very nervous. They think their anchors are slipping. Then you give them a long-form treatment of a subject, hopefully not just Republican or Democrat, but eight different dimensions of a fairly complicated issue. And then add in the possibility that you are talking about something that is a novelty like AIDS. We took an incredible beating because of our early coverage of AIDS. The charge of bias was the charge of agenda-setting. "I don't care about this, I don't want to hear about it. And these guys are on there day after day talking about it. They must have their own agenda. They must have a bias." That's what I think it is. The response that you get when you say that to people is amazingly receptive. I do an awful lot of talking around the country with different kinds of audiences. An awful lot of people say, "Jesus, maybe that's right." I don't know that when they go out to their car and listen to the next radio broadcast they remember.

Do we feel political pressure that is couched in terms of bias? It's there but it's ineffective. One of the reasons we did what we did in 1987 was to be less vulnerable than we might have been. We just have been through a reauthorization fight. It was, I think, the tag end of the Jesse Helms, social issues attack that had worked all right with NEA [National Endowment for the Arts]. But by the time you got to public broadcasting using the same arguments, it didn't wash. The reason it didn't wash is because the whole public can listen to public broadcasting. You can turn this thing on if you care about it. You can turn it on and hear whether you think it is biased or not. The result of that fight was that we won a smashing victory on re-authorization. And we have continued to have federal appropriations that have increased ahead of inflation. So I don't feel vulnerable to this attack at all. It has no impact on our news department at all. What does have an impact, and a profound impact, is grass-roots listener communications. When somebody says that we have failed to treat a subject fairly, we take it very seriously. We go back over it and try to find out whether we did or not. And you never get it exactly right. It comes with the territory. We are grass-roots oriented and grass-roots based and not just coming out of some advertising agency focus group someplace. We are more balanced. We do better reflect a sense of what is going on in the public mind. There is no broadcast organization in this country that has the kind of contact with its listeners that we have.

You say, "We are not biased." Obviously, you are biased. You have a bias in favor of liberal, secular humanism as opposed to Pat Robertson, right-wing Christianity. He's the one with the bias.

You have a bias in favor of liberal policy regarding race, gender, et cetera. That's going to be reflected in your audience.
My answer is, if those are biases, then I'm very happy to acknowledge them. We are secular. On the question of the diversity of society, that is not a question of policy, it is merely a recognition of a reality. There are some of us who greet it as desirable, and it goes along with a lot of federal legisla-tion. I think if you are going to get tax money for anything that you have an obligation to reflect the society in your hiring practices.

What about David Duke's point of view? You are not going to have commentators who reflect David Duke's ideology. Is it rhetorically effective to take the position that you are not biased or to take the position that you are taking now: we have certain biases and we stand by them?
I would hope that David Duke would be covered no less sympathetically than any other candidate for public office. We struggle very hard to be sure that is true. You've heard more non-primary-party candidates on our air — and they got their say, even if they didn't get covered as much as the major candidates. I would be very alarmed if we had not recorded David Duke as a real event of American politics, and I think we probably did do a pretty

good job of getting across what he thought, what he was saying, how people were reacting to him.

If you were to interview David Duke, the kinds of questions he would get would reflect a certain critical relation to him, a political edge, why deny it?
I don't deny it, because I don't know what the evidence is. For you to make the point you've got to show the evidence. I'm hearing you, but it is an elusive thing. We've had content analysts who get nowhere, and people who want to look at the age, sex, and state of birth of our commentators: it doesn't prove much that Bob Edwards actually isn't from Washington, D.C. What you get down to is the ear of the beholder, the perception of the individual listener. I don't know that the world we are portraying is different from the world that is really there. We are portraying it — there is some shorthand involved in that — but if we are doing what you are saying, we are not succeeding.

We had people here from the magazine industry, the hotel industry, from television and film. Almost uniformly they have said in one way or another: "We don't really have a mission. We respond to a market, we respond to our investors, we are looking to serve a particular audience, we will cater to that audience's needs." Obviously you are in a very different position. Could you give us a sense of what the mission of NPR is?
The essential mission has to do with informing, with editorial integrity, with achieving the greatest degree of objectivity we can. There are other dimensions, about affirmative action and so forth. They are all things that you would not find in the mission statement of a hotel chain.

Where did your mission derive from, if not from what the audience wants you to do?
I think the model is very close to an academic one. You don't teach to an empty classroom. But you don't base your curriculum solely on what the market demands — even *primarily* on what the market demands — if you are a serious educational institution. The question to ask is, what is it that people are selling? Commercial broadcasters — the programming is incidental, right? What is important is the product that they are selling. That is not true of an educational institution. Our mission is much more akin to an educational institution's mission.

Is it like Matthew Arnold's notion of the best that has been thought and said?
Yes, I'd have to say yes.

Other people are saying their mission derives from what they think their audience wants them to do. You are saying your mission derives from the principle you enunciate in your mission statement.

Obviously that is not sufficient: the mission statement has to come from someplace. The notion of differentiation was very important early in the funding of public broadcasting. The idea was to provide something different from commercial broadcasting. If so, it was still audience driven in a kind of perverse way.

Other media people say, "We don't want to do anything to our audience. We just want to find out what they want and give it to them. We don't want to transform the audience."

I do. I do want to transform them. But hear how: the point is to inform them better than they are now informed. That's all.

And to entertain them more broadly, you are saying.

We do do things that are entertaining and we do them for a variety of reasons. They are not really central, I don't think. My sense of what we are trying to do is opening doors and opening perspectives. To the degree that we are looking for a transformation, that is what it is. Whereas, I would argue, that is the last thing that a commercial broadcaster cares about. What they want is a bunch of happy campers who will buy whatever it is that is paying for the program. Our plan is a lot more fun than theirs.

Could you talk a little bit about finding and managing and shaping creativity? I don't just mean in the arts, but also in news and public affairs.

It is a complicated thing. Again, I think that it is a sort of bottom-up operation. There is some training that goes with radio, which is not very complicated. There is very complicated training — or learning — that goes with good journalism. We just try to hire very good people and create an environment in which they can operate. We also use a lot of people around the country who have had experience producing for radio and whom the editors have confidence in. There is a very stringent editorial process. There are at least two layers of editorial control before anything gets on the air, which the reporters would argue destroys their creativity completely. I think the institution, through the editorial process, has a major role in deciding what goes on the air, just as there are editors on newspapers who decide what is going in the newspaper. Our news operation is very much akin to print journalism, almost more than to television.

On the question of whether intuition counts, I hope that it counts a lot. Let me give you a recent example. We had an opening for a host. Someone in our research department came in and said, by the way, if you don't mind, we'd like to test these hosts in one of these electronic situations of the kind that ABC used the other night in the presidential debates. I said forget it. We're not going to hire people that way around here. We value intuition, and that carries with it the danger of bias.

Could you talk specifically about some decision — maybe the one to include "Car Talk," for example? How was it made? Who had a role in making it?
"Car Talk" started as a local program on WBUR in Boston. They had a talk show and they happened to have these two people come one day and do it, and it worked pretty well. The person that was going to do it the next week was sick or something and that was the beginning of the show. Well, we had a Sunday morning show with Susan Stamberg. Somehow she became aware of "Car Talk," and started using excerpts; her show was a magazine that had room for different kinds of material.

So it was her decision?
No, it would have been the producer's decision. The excerpts were successful, and it seemed that "Car Talk" might work nationally. So we started distributing it. The way the arrangement worked then was that WBUR had the rights to the show and we paid them and charged the stations for it. Now we have an arrangement with the Magliazzi brothers. Most of what we distribute in our cultural programming we don't produce ourselves.

So that wasn't really a big decision at any one point, but a kind of staged decision by a number of different people along the way?
Yes. And that is fairly typical. We, unfortunately, can't afford to make big mistakes. That creates a certain amount of incrementalism. "Car Talk" is good radio. I think that's the answer. It's legitimate humor, it's spontaneous, that is the only justification for it.

We have been giving consultants a chance to jump in at the end with anything that they felt we skipped, or any final comments.
Well, I appreciate the enormous amount that you all know about what we do.

We are your niche audience.

Well, look at you. You ought to be ashamed.

I am obviously a partisan of this enterprise now. I'm not from a radio background, not a news background. I'm very much engaged in it now, but I remain sort of curious about whether it's going to work or not. And when it does, I wonder if it is not a model for a lot of other things. Radio is so cheap, and it was so betrayed as a medium, the uses of it are generally so narrow and so unimaginative; you have to ask yourself whether, if you are willing to make a new investment, you couldn't have lots of other kinds of services. The digital technologies that are coming offer an opportunity to transform radio totally in two ways. One is that the technology makes possible a lot more frequencies. You can do a lot more with your radio dial. The other is that you can do direct satellite, to receive or broadcast. You can get a signal from someplace to the satellite, to receivers all over the United States. That makes it possible to do narrow-casting in a way that has never been possible in radio before. A local station has to be doing something that will appeal to large enough segment of the local population to make sense. And that leaves out all sorts of things. I mentioned some of them. Children's programming is not working on radio, not at all. I think there are all sorts of cultural things that would be a hell of a lot of fun on the radio. There's very little radio drama. Radio drama can be very very compelling. It costs enough to do so that we do very little of it now.

The suggestion I would leave you with is that the pattern you're studying doesn't have to be this way. This is one outcome. There are lots of other possible outcomes. As we make the regulatory decisions and financial decisions that go with this new technology, I would just step back and do it differently. Commercial interests aren't going to come through. No way. But *we* are going to capitalize on the additional radio spectrum to do a whole bunch of things. It's going to cost something.

I gave this speech somewhat more eloquently in a congressional committee the other day, and the chairman at the end said, "What are we talking about for cost?" I said, "I don't know, but I bet it's a billion dollars." He threw up his hands in despair. But you can buy a lot of museums for that.

Essays

Michael Curtin **On Edge**

Culture Industries in the Neo-Network Era

. . . .

*Michael Curtin teaches in the Department of Telecommunications and is
director of the Cultural Studies program at Indiana University. He is the
author of* Redeeming the Wasteland: Television Documentary and
Cold War Politics *and is coeditor with Lynn Spigel of* The Revolution
Wasn't Televised: Sixties Television and Social Conflict. *His current
work focuses on the extranational implications of the electronic media age.*

The general-circulation magazine — *Time, Newsweek, Life, Look*
— provided a site of popular discourse and imagination throughout the
Great Depression, World War II, and the postwar period. These mass
magazines were symptomatic of a distinctive moment of national unity,
according to publishing executive Mark Edmiston: "We had in this country
at that time a sense of shared experience" (136).[1] Yet in the 1950s, these
popular publications would find their status challenged by the rise of television and the fragmentation of the magazine market. Television would
then prevail as the primary mediator of national consciousness until the end
of the 1970s, only to succumb to its own period of audience fragmentation
and industry turmoil. Even worse, says Edmiston, no single medium has
emerged as television's successor. "When I put on my citizen hat, I get very
worried," he muses. "I think there is clearly a breaking down of any consensus in the country" (141).

Edmiston's concerns are shared by many others, perhaps most notably
by author Ken Auletta, whose best-selling book, *Three Blind Mice*, chroni-
cles the decline of the major television networks.[2] Auletta contends that
despite their shortcomings, the three majors provided a common hearth
where the American people gathered both to be warmed by popular entertainment and to reflect upon the most pressing issues of the day. The fire in
this common hearth now appears to be burning low, and many participants
in the culture industries see the current era as particularly volatile, marked
by contradiction and uncertainty. Of particular concern are the changing
technologies of communication, all of which promise to subdivide the national audience and splinter the body politic.

Such dire forebodings about changes in mediated communication are
not historically unique. Similar concerns about social coherence and sta-

bility have accompanied the introduction of new media technologies in earlier times. Indeed, historian Warren Susman argues that every era of technological innovation has generated dialectic tensions between utopian and dystopian representations of new media.[3] This dialectic is more than a reflection of human ambivalence, however, for it is also an expression of the multiple and conflicting tendencies that arise at any such moment of change.

Perched as we are on the edge of a new era, it is useful to consider the disparate forces that are shaping our cultural environment and to speculate about their impact on public life. A brief analysis of historical trends will not only reveal how the culture industries have sought to organize collective experience through the postwar era but also help us understand the seeming chaos that now confronts media practitioners. I hope to show that the national mass audience is an exceptional blip in the history of humankind and its passing does not mark a decline in societal consensus, much less the demise of the nation. General-circulation magazines and network television were intimately connected to a Fordist era of mass production and mass consumption. Our "shared sense of experience" was less a matter of consensus than it was a manifestation of a particular set of social relations. Changes in the national and global economies over the past two decades help to explain the fragmentation of the national audience and the reorganization of the culture industries. This current period is in fact tied to a set of historical patterns that are fairly coherent, despite a dialectical tension between globalization and fragmentation. By comparing the organization of the culture industries during the Fordist and neo-Fordist eras we can begin to understand some of the shifting forces confronting practitioners in the fields of information and entertainment.

Network TV and National Consciousness

The high network era was in large part a product of explicit government policy that began during television's infancy, the late 1940s and early 1950s, when major corporations in the entertainment and electronics industries wrestled among themselves for control of broadcast licenses and struggled over the technical standards that would guide equipment manufacture. The outcome was a fairly reliable technology based on VHF (very high frequency) transmission. Yet it became clear early on that UHF (ultra high frequency) offered an alternative that promised many more channels, and hence a greater range of choice for the viewer. Rather than encourage this alternative, however, the Federal Communications Commission endorsed the standards promoted by a powerful industry lobby headed by the Radio Corporation of America (RCA), a major electronics manufacturer and owner of the National Broadcasting Company (NBC). The final outcome of the policy process was a "mixed system" that privileged a limited number of VHF stations and created a second-class tier of UHF stations. RCA benefited tremendously from this arrangement since it already was heavily invested in VHF technology and, through its subsidiary NBC, had negotiated affiliation contracts with key VHF stations across the country. Consequently, FCC policy not only anointed RCA's leadership in manufacturing, it also limited the number of stations that might be able to mount a competitive national network.

The FCC's actions were partially motivated by a postwar backlash against New Deal regulators who had tried to rein in RCA's dominance in radio broadcasting during the late 1930s and early 1940s. This postwar favoritism toward powerful broadcast corporations was sustained throughout the fifties by a series of Eisenhower appointees whose predispositions brought about such a cozy period of government-industry cooperation that one former commissioner referred to it as the "whorehouse era" of the FCC.[4] The product of this collaboration was a television system with two-and-a-half national networks: NBC and CBS had affiliates in every market, while ABC could reach viewers in major cities but enjoyed only spotty coverage in smaller markets. Consequently, it would be folly to construe the high network era as an inherent outcome of the technology or primarily as a manifestation of national consensus. It was instead the product of systematic favoritism that allowed powerful elements within the radio industry to limit the development of the technology so as to seal out aspiring competitors from the motion picture, newspaper, and magazine industries.[5]

The network system also was the outcome of a policy process that favored national interests over local interests. During the early years of television, the FCC allowed NBC, CBS, and ABC to own and control stations in five local markets and to seek affiliates in other cities across the nation.[6] All three networks snatched up stations in major urban centers — New York, Chicago, Philadelphia, Los Angeles — hoping to secure control of the largest markets, and then turned their attention to rallying affiliates in other locales. Once they consolidated these alliances across the country, the networks began to pressure local stations to turn over increasing portions of their broadcast day to national programming. Although purportedly owned by local interests, many small stations were only too happy to turn over creative responsibilities so as to lower their own costs and raise their profits. Yet some larger stations, such as those in Chicago, struggled to sustain local television production so as to nurture local interests and to promote the city's sense of identity. In fact, the "Chicago School" of television was so successful during the early years of the medium that many of its programs were also carried regionally and even nationally, thereby competing with producers in New York and Hollywood.[7]

To some extent, this was a replication of the radio era when Chicago was a major center of regional and national program production. Two of the most durable genres of broadcast programming — the soap opera and the domestic comedy — first evolved in Chicago, and *Amos 'n Andy*, the most popular radio program of all time, emerged out of this milieu as well. Nevertheless, Chicago radio lived a conflicted existence throughout its history. Despite the creativity of Chicago producers, they were usually underfunded and often prodded to produce programming that erased the traces of local origin in favor of a more national sound, one closely associated with the networks.[8]

During the television era the same pattern would reemerge. As a result, most of the revenues generated by the Chicago School were skimmed off by the networks rather than reinvested in local production. By the mid-fifties, Chicago TV began to wane as the networks consolidated their operations and began to forge alliances with the creative community in Hollywood.[9] In what was then referred to as a streamlining maneuver, the networks systematically disassembled Chicago television by the end of the decade despite a government regulatory structure explicitly premised on the principle of localism.[10]

Favoritism toward national television was further reinforced by spatial biases in the advertising and consumer products industries as well. As productivity in the civilian economy mushroomed throughout the 1950s, huge corporations pursued the largest possible domestic markets with the enthusiastic encouragement of advertising executives and social scientists. Of the latter, Frank Stanton, who became president of CBS, and A. C. Nielsen, whose firm became synonymous with TV ratings, both portrayed the television audience as a national entity that displayed relatively homogeneous preferences and aspirations. Even on those rare occasions when advertisers reflected on the distinctive motivations of, say, African-American consumers, their rhetoric focused largely on those characteristics that black and white viewers shared.[11] Advertisers saw national television as the greater leveler, smoothing out disparities in life-style and income, making all homes accessible to their products.

The tendencies just outlined bear the unmistakable marks of a Fordist economy in which mass consumption interlocks with systems of mass production, mass marketing, and national regulation.[12] The network television era should therefore be seen less as a product of popular consensus than as a symptomatic expression of a social order built upon a historically specific form of capitalism. By the mid-1950s, when some 60 percent of American families owned a receiver, network television displaced the general-circulation magazine as the preeminent national advertising medium. By the beginning of the following decade, close to 90 percent of American homes owned a television, bringing presidential politics, space exploration, and the antics of Jethro and Granny into the living rooms of almost every American family.

Yet despite this consolidation in the culture industries, the sixties was not necessarily an era of consensus, for television viewing became both a shared experience and an object of sustained social conflict.[13] On some level, almost every major issue of the sixties revolved around questions of televisual representation. Americans watched and argued about what was on; even if they weren't watching, they were arguing about what was on, or what wasn't.

The intensity of the struggle grew so powerful that presidents and vice-presidents lavished tremendous attention on television, perhaps believing that their political fortunes were somehow bound up with those "wires and lights in a box." Reputedly, the medium delivered the presidency into the hands of John Kennedy, while snatching it from the grasp of a less telegenic Richard Nixon. Kennedy's successor, Lyndon Johnson, contended that television also played a significant role in his political fortunes, ultimately driving him from office at the height of the Vietnam War. He was succeeded, of course, by a rehabilitated Richard Nixon who relied on the media savvy of Roger Ailes to help reinvent his public image for the age of television.

But even a more telegenic Nixon never lost his disdain for the small circle of network insiders who controlled access to the national airwaves. This continuing mistrust encouraged the administration to begin promoting cable television as an alternative mode of distribution that promised to undermine the power of network oligarchs and to promote the interests of the so-called silent majority.[14] Nixon was not the only one frustrated with the major networks, however. Enthusiasm for cable television was growing in many quarters, with promoters promising a technological utopia of media plenitude, a "wired nation," which would bypass the centralized circuits of network power. Ironically, Nixon's mistrust of network power was discursively articulated to the utopian aspirations of progressive reformers who also sought an alternative to media oligopoly, one rooted in grass-roots community television.

Yet it would take almost another decade before cable became a commercially profitable technology and began to challenge the concentrated power of the national networks. Neither government policymaking nor technological innovation alone could displace the network oligopoly.[15] Rather, increasing corporate competition among the media industries contributed the final impetus toward change. Cable television would begin to grow in the late 1970s with the emergence of satellite program providers such as Home Box Office (owned by Time-Life), Music Television (owned by Viacom), and Turner Broadcasting. These new services represented the very groups that had been locked out by the FCC in the early days of television regulation — publishers, Hollywood studios, independent program syndicators, and regionally based broadcasters. The software they provided became the core around which new viewer loyalties would be built. In 1980, the prime-time audiences of the three major networks began diminishing by fits and starts, dropping from more than 90 percent of viewers to roughly 50 percent today. As the audience began to fragment, network executives were joined by numerous social critics who made dire predictions about the impact this would have on national consciousness.

Neo-Fordism and the Culture Industries

The temporal pacing of these developments in popular media coincided with profound changes in global capitalism as it moved into a period of crisis during the 1970s and 1980s. Faced with increasing competition and falling rates of productivity, major corporations began to reorganize their operations so as to become more flexible in manufacturing and more responsive to local markets. Although this transition has been described a number of different ways, I refer to it here as neo-Fordism in order to connote a period in which Fordist principles of mass production, mass marketing, and mass consumption exist side-by-side with emerging forms of flexible accumulation.

David Harvey distinguishes four types of flexibility as characteristic of this new era. The first type involves physical reorganization of the workplace designed to speed up labor processes and enhance productivity. The second level is to be found in labor markets, which are now characterized by the proliferation of subcontracting, part-time employment, and other forms of casual labor. New modes of flexibility also mark a third level, the arena of state policy. For the past two decades, deregulation and/or privatization have been driving the policymaking process in nations around the globe. Besides allowing firms to jettison social responsibilities, this trend has facilitated gigantic corporate mergers and acquisitions. The fourth type of flexibility is the increasing geographic mobility of financial capital, production processes, and people. To these I would add a fifth level of flexibility, one that emphasizes new modes of marketing and distribution, and specifically draws attention to the contested terrain of popular culture. Harvey argues that even though these types of flexibility are not entirely new, they have become central tenets of capitalist strategies since the 1970s.

Such an analysis points to the dialectic relationship between processes of globalization and fragmentation. Rather than a chaotic collapse of national communities and mass consumer markets, Harvey describes this period of transition as marked by the strategic advantages of emerging neo-Fordist principles: "Flexibility has little or nothing to do with decentralizing either political or economic power and everything to do with maintaining highly centralized control *through decentralizing tactics.*"[16] Corporations no longer concentrate their production operations at centralized facilities and they no longer focus their marketing campaigns on a single national audience. Instead, companies like Coca-Cola emphasize a flexible strategy that cultivates indigenous franchise operations around the world. Although the headquarters remain in Atlanta, Ira Herbert is quick to point to the multinational composition of the executive workforce (5). Furthermore, he directs our attention to pattern advertising in which a single concept is spun out in local contexts around the globe. Coca-Cola emphasizes flexibility in its corporate operations and multiplicity in the ways that messages about the product are circulated, both within nations and across national borders. He tells us that each consumer group "should be communicated to in their own way with their own message, with their own sound, with their own visualization. Just as an example, two years ago brand Coca-Cola would create a dozen commercials for the year in North America. [This year] we have just finished producing twenty-six and it is only April" (7). According to Herbert, the ideal outcome of this flexible strategy is for consumers to see Coca-Cola as woven into their local context, an integral part of their everyday world. Yet at the same time, it remains a singular product marketed by a multinational executive workforce that speaks English and is based in Atlanta.[17]

Reorganizing the Culture Industries

This same globalization/fragmentation dialectic is at work throughout the culture industries, and in part it can be attributed to new modes of electronic communication. Since the 1970s, national network broadcasting has been challenged by numerous competitors: satellite, cable, cassette, CD-ROM, Internet, etc. The modes of distribution have become not only more flexible but also less consequential. Broadcasting a program or advertisement in television prime time no longer guarantees broad national exposure. Cultural products now circulate in a variety of media throughout the world, almost regardless of government communications policy, copyright law, or corporate monopoly. The blockbuster film *Waterworld* was, for example, circulated on bootlegged videotapes in the Soviet Union *before* the feature film was officially released to theaters in the United States and more than a year before it would reach network television.

Not only do Hollywood studios have less control over the subterranean circulation of their products but they also recognize that they no longer can dependably construct mass audiences by controlling technology, government regulation, or market economics. Whereas in the past viewers would choose the least offensive program from among the offerings of the three national networks, they now are hailed by a plenitude of choices in a variety of formats. The emergence of "software" as an industry buzzword conveys the recent shift in emphasis away from a few highly regulated channels of exhibition toward multiple circuits of distribution that transcend national borders. In this new environment, audiences will cluster around a product because it meets their distinctive needs or tastes. In other words, the national/industrial infrastructure that played a crucial role in fostering the high network era of television is becoming less influential, and consequently future audiences/users are more likely to be produced by the cultural forms themselves. In response to these trends and in response to the growing importance of extranational audiences, media conglomerates are developing more flexible strategies that take into account the globalization/fragmentation dialectic.[18]

We can see this new logic at work in the culture industries first by turning our attention to recent developments in television. Both Paramount and Warner Bros. recently launched networks whose viability will primarily hinge on the quality of the programming, according to most industry observers.[19] To some extent these new networks are disadvantaged by their lack of powerful broadcast affiliates in the top one hundred markets, but cable and direct broadcast satellite technology make it possible for them to reach more than 80 percent of U.S. viewers and an even larger percentage of the most affluent households in the nation. Government regulation no longer hampers their ability to address a significant audience across the North American continent, and the reach of their programming is no longer constrained by the geographic diffusion patterns of terrestrial broadcast transmission towers.[20] Just as importantly, ratings data are no longer as reliant on mass circulation figures. Unlike the 1960s, researchers now gather and sell information about demographically defined subsets of the national audience, and advertising agencies now commonly advise their clients that particular groups of viewers are often more important than synchronic national exposure.

Warner Bros. and Paramount therefore hope to follow the example set by the Fox Network, which based its rise to prominence on programming tailored to a young, urban audience.[21] Drawing on some of Hollywood's most talented producers, Fox attracted these viewers with irreverent programs such as *Married with Children*, *The Simpsons*, and *In Living Color.* These are the programs that television producer David Kendall refers to as having an "edge" (62). They work against Kendall's general principle that television at its best (i.e., most profitable) produces shows with universal values. While it is true that the most powerful networks still rely on mass-appeal programming, new modes of distribution are challenging the axiomatic status of Kendall's assertion. Networks used to focus on maximizing national audiences largely because their competition was limited to one or two other networks that were similarly aiming at mass circulation. Now, however, the major networks find themselves trying to hold together a national audience that is being hailed by a growing variety of niche programmers whose success rides almost exclusively on their appeal to distinctive subsets of viewers.

Here is where we come to a paradox that is peculiar to the current situation. Historically, the popularity of cultural forms has been notoriously difficult to predict. Consequently, large corporations focused most of their efforts on controlling the channels of distribution rather than the creative process itelf. They did this through oligopoly, federal regulation, and control over technological development. In the current era, many major media corporations are still trying to operate according to this logic. It therefore makes a lot of sense that huge telephone, cable, computer, and broadcasting firms are now scrambling for partnerships that offer the prospect of controlling future distribution channels. The irony is that these consolidations may prove no more effective than the dominant organizational posture IBM once enjoyed in the computer world. If current economic, political, and technological trends continue, it will become increasingly difficult for large corporations to control the distribution of cultural forms.[22] Thus, like the computer industry, we may be witnessing a shift away from an emphasis upon hardware and limited channels of distribution toward software and flexible corporate conglomerates. Rather than a centralized network structure anchored by New York finance, Hollywood studios, and state-regulated technology, the neo-network era features elaborate circuits of cultural production and reception.

This transformation is not a radical break with the past; rather, it is a transitional phase in which Fordist and neo-Fordist principles exist side by side. For example, studio chieftain Strauss Zelnick claims that the mass market is still at the heart of Fox's movie business. "You make your real money when you have the broadest possible market," says Zelnick. "And you get the broadest possible market by making movies that are great stories" (23). David Kendall agrees with Zelnick by pointing to the fact that the major networks are still looking for series that focus on universal values and concerns. On the other hand, as we have noted, many of the great success stories in television have recently tended to come from niche operators like MTV, Turner, and Fox Television. A similar principle seems to be at work in the radio industry, where Broadcasting Partners regularly outperforms national networks. "Usually, if you have a locally programmed equivalent, it will beat the [national] satellite service," says CFO Nathan Pearson (122). Mark Edmiston also directs our attention to micro markets and the "zine" phenomenon. "As you get narrower in interest," he notes, "you tend to have more intensity of interest [and] the person is more likely to pay the extra money" (137). Thus, success in the magazine business no longer rides on the publication of a general-circulation magazine, but instead relies on the ownership of a collection of specialty publications that profitably manage the relationship between market size and the intensity of consumer interest.

Such an approach engenders a constant search for narrowly defined and underserved markets. Race, gender, and ethnicity have now joined socioeconomic status as potentially marketable boundaries of difference. Edmiston explains, for example, that magazine publishers are currently investigating whether women skiers share a set of needs and interests that are distinctive enough to constitute a commercially viable subscriber base. Similarly, Pearson's Broadcasting Partners fashioned a successful niche by subdividing the African-American radio audience, targeting adults with a pronounced aversion to rap music. In neither case are these niche marketers basing their decisions on allegiances to particular groups at the margins of mass culture; rather, they simply are following a neo-Fordist marketing strategy, one they characterize as strictly capitalistic and generally disinterested in content issues.

The same could be said about Time-Warner, whose music subsidiary Death Row Records specializes in rap music by such popular but controversial artists as Snoop Doggy Dogg, Dr. Dre, and Tupac Shakur.[23] Time-Warner's pursuit of this fragmentary market is complemented, however, by Warner Television, which is trying to market programs to the major national networks and to international syndicators by employing writers like David Kendall who repeatedly disavow any knowledge of, or concern for, specific subsets of viewers. Indeed, Kendall tells us that the market data he has seen tends to lump Hispanics with other minorities, to ignore differences among international markets, and to turn a blind eye to gay and lesbian viewers. The point for him is to focus on "universals" that will translate to most social contexts. Within the Time-Warner empire itself we therefore can observe a double movement between the global and the local, between the mass market and the niche market.

Similar patterns seem to be operating in the hotel industry, where niche marketer Peter Sonnabend notes, "Our hotels, we like to think, are a special collection — unique properties in unique locations — and those hotels have done pretty well, even in these very tough times" (36). Their successful formula is based on distinguishing the Sonesta experience from the "cookie-cutter" accommodations provided by Marriott, Hilton, and Sheraton. Original artwork, local flavor, and distinctive architecture are all aimed at a specific up-scale clientele that wishes to distinguish its tastes from the mass market and is willing to pay a premium in order to do so. Thus, the hotel industry seems headed in two directions at once: toward consolidation among a handful of megafirms, and toward niche operations that cater to particular tastes.

This trend should not, however, be confused with the emergence of a dual economy. The megafirms are also quite active in niche markets, with firms like Marriott setting up specialty subsidiaries such as Marriott Courtyards and Residence Inns (48). Furthermore, small independent hoteliers like Sonesta do not necessarily travel their route alone. They develop properties in Cambridgeside (next to a major shopping mall development near the heart of Boston) and near Disney World (among the endless clutter of leisure enterprises feeding off the Disney mainstream) (42). Sonesta's very success is based on its relationship to and its distinction from cookie-cutter hotels and mass entertainment sites. The Sonesta experience is not marked by the fact that it offers something intrinsically local or "authentic," but rather by the ways in which it is distinguished from the competition at each particular site as more local, more authentic, or more tasteful.

This relationship between niche and mass markets directs our attention back to the new modes of corporate organization within the culture industries. Notice that David Kendall works for Warner Bros. Television, which is a relatively autonomous part of the Time-Warner empire, a firm with extensive holdings in film, cable, broadcasting, music, and publishing. The corporation reportedly has been careful to avoid steering its diverse units toward creativity that narrowly conforms to a synergistic imperative. Nevertheless, it has strategically positioned itself to reap the benefits of creative work carried out in a variety of contexts: large-scale, highly integrated enterprises (*Time Magazine*), boutique production operations (TV sitcoms), and seemingly autonomous niche venues (Death Row Records). Note also that each operation targets a different market: the middle-class, college-educated magazine reader; the mass television audience; and the trendy, urban youth culture. Creative synergies are not explicitly mandated between these various operations, but the circulation of creative content among these and the many other divisions of Time-Warner is managed so as to maximize profitability. Rap music, which began as a niche phenomenon, for example, has been leveraged throughout the many distribution circuits of the corporate conglomerate.

Scott Sassa — who is often credited with writing the original business plan for the Fox TV network and is now president of the Turner Entertainment Group — operates in a similar corporate environment.[24] He is responsible for maximizing the "value chain" among Turner Broadcasting, TBS Superstation, TNT, Castle Rock Entertainment, New Line Cinema, Turner Pictures Worldwide, the Cartoon Network, Hanna-Barbera Productions, TNT Latin America, Turner Home Video, Turner Publishing, and Turner Licensing and Merchandising. Sassa says there are two aspects to his job. One is to encourage the creation of popular copyrighted material. The second is to develop a system that leverages content "further, higher, faster than anybody else."[25] The point is to spin out the profitability of all copyrighted material at as many levels as possible. These can be new blockbuster copyrights, such as "Seinfeld" or *Forrest Gump*, or they can be libraries of earlier materials, such as "I Love Lucy" or *Gone with the Wind*. Large entertainment conglomerates also leverage niche products such as "Johnny Quest" and "Saved by the Bell," which can be very profitable if marketed through the appropriate channels. This includes not only film, television, cable, music, publishing, and computer software but also ancillary merchandise, franchise agreements, and overseas marketing. "Every copyright that starts out anywhere in the system gets leveraged every which way imaginable," says Sassa.[26] The key to profitability is still distribution, but the distribution system is more diverse and decentered. It also remains highly volatile, given the unpredictable nature of popular responses to new cultural forms. Huge entertainment conglomerates therefore attempt to leverage the profitability of existing products, to counterbalance losses from their many unsuccessful ventures, and to secure copyrights to marginal cultural forms that may prove profitable in the future.

They also try to externalize the risks inherent in the creative aspects of the industry. Movie executive Strauss Zelnick provides useful insights as to how megafirms manage creativity. Zelnick devotes almost all his time to the distribution of cultural products that are produced by a casual labor force that is signed on for each specific film project. Only a handful of the twelve hundred employees at Twentieth Century Fox Film Corporation are directly involved in making motion pictures.[27] The rest come and go, many represented in their contractual negotiations by agencies such as Victoria Traube's firm, International Creative Management. Zelnick describes the creative process as one that is relatively free from corporate calculations. Good stories cannot be churned out by the numbers, we are told. And yet the folklore of the industry unconsciously sets creative boundaries: what themes are hot this season, which audiences use which media, what translates well in overseas markets. It is folklore that members of the casual workforce ignore at their own peril. The informal maxims that circulate at meetings and social gatherings structure the process of seemingly autonomous creative activity.

A similar dynamic is at work in the advertising industry, and Stephen Oakes is the quintessential independent whose creative work is linked to the needs of major corporations through the mediation of a community of animators, producers, and advertising representatives. Many ad agencies, which over the past decade have themselves gone through a period of merger and conglomeration, have cut back their creative staffs and now contract out much of this labor. They set the boundaries for creative labor through a network of personal interactions. Note that Oakes—like Kendall, Zelnick, and Traube—places tremendous significance not on the audience but on the internal networking and communication within this community. It is a site where perceptions of audience tastes are constructed and where creative practitioners strive to bring their distinctive abilities to the attention of other practitioners. "It is very competitive to do the work that we do," says Oakes. "It takes a lot of cold calls and little cliques and friendships to get these prizes because handing out the assignment to do a [television] commercial is a really guarded moment when the creative team at an ad agency is really displaying [its] sense of taste and control of who is going to do these things" (73; also see Oakes: 81, Traube: 95, Kendall: 56, and Kendall: 62). Although not career employees of the same firm, this casual workforce is concentrated in specific creative locales, New York City and Hollywood being the most prominent. Interestingly, many of the most crucial aspects of success revolve around what Anthony Giddens and Erving Goffman have referred to as "facework," those forms of personal interaction that sustain trust between institutional actors.[28] Thus proximity and social interactions are keys to organizing a casual workforce via what David Kendall refers to as the fiction of the industry.

Yet these concentrated creative communities may be undergoing a process of dispersion themselves. In part, this is attributable to the growing phenomenon of telecommuting, something especially popular among those who work in the culture industries. Even more significant may be the emergence of new creative locales: Silicon Valley, the Microsoft campus in Seattle, the South Park neighborhood of San Francisco, the Spokane garage of "Myst" creators Rand and Robyn Miller, and the research institute in Champaign, Illinois, where computer whizzes fashioned the Mosaic software template that now dominates navigation of the World Wide Web.[29] In the past, many culture industries were concentrated around capital-intensive resources in New York City and Hollywood, while less capital-intensive forms — such as music and print fiction — developed multiple and dispersed centers of creative activity.[30] As the costs of film, television, and multimedia production continue to fall, will a similar process of dispersion take place? Can this mean the emergence of new creative locales? During the 1950s or 1960s, it would have been a foregone conclusion that New York and Los Angeles would continue to dominate the national cultural landscape. Yet neo-Fordist principles are reshaping the current geography of social relations at many levels, and much of this change is facilitated by new technologies.

New Locales, New Affinities, New Migrations of Talent

Looked at more broadly, electronic media may be reshaping the cultural landscape in other ways as well. Historically, the telegraph and telephone enabled the geographic separation of blue-collar and white-collar labor during the Fordist era of vertical integration. Headquartered in one location, major corporations knitted together a network of operations throughout the nation as marketing, finance, and planning were increasingly separated from manufacturing operations. Specific cities became renowned for their concentration of corporate headquarters where white-collar workers collaborated not only within their own firms but also with counterparts in related organizations. New communications technologies (computer, fax, teleconference, etc.) are now enabling further dispersal of the corporate workforce as "back office" operations are being moved outside major cities to locations such as New Jersey, while city centers like Manhattan remain the site for "facework" occupations such as corporate law, advertising, and finance.[31]

As part of this transition, local governments are forging cultural policies to enhance the attractiveness and to solidify the distinctive identities of these growing suburban enclaves. As Meadowlands sports promoter Dennis Robinson explains, New Jersey is competing with New York City both through its land development policies and through efforts to position itself as a prominent part of the national and global circuits of entertainment and spectacle. New Jersey wants to stage major performances that used to be almost exclusively available in urban centers. This growing competition for cultural events is inextricably tied to a competition over the value of local real estate. As Dennis Robinson puts it, "Who ever thought about New Jersey as an entertainment center — internationally, regionally, or nationally — before the existence of the [Meadowlands] sports complex?" (152). Now, however, northern New Jersey is promoting itself as a location to be valued on a par with the Big Apple.

This growing competition between places furthermore registers in Robinson's account of New Jersey's attempt to court the Yankees baseball team, an effort that drew a swift and furious response from corporate leaders in the city. The Rockefellers, who are heavily invested in Manhattan real estate, led the counterattack, no doubt because they understood the economic logic of losing the Yankees to a competitor across the Hudson River. This rivalry over major cultural events revolves around both the immediate economic gains from the events themselves and the long-term value of local real estate, a value determined by the recognizable differences between places.

The spatial objectives of New Jersey's aggressive cultural policies are being complemented by a temporal component as well. The state is trying to promote allegiances to its sports teams as part of a conscious effort to tap youthful enthusiasms that might carry over into the future. New Jersey planners see local sports events as an active form of spectatorship that promotes place-bound affinities across the generations. "In the sports business," says Robinson, "you are really targeting kids, kids that grow up to be fans" (157). These allegiances not only have a tremendous influence on those who grow up and remain in the same area, but as we have seen with championship rounds of major sports events, these allegiances may transcend the local and play a significant role in national and even global impressions of particular places.

The ambitions of New Jersey policymakers are indicative of shifting relationships within the New York metropolitan area, a decentering process that has been described by a number of geographers such as Edward Soja.[32] It also has to do with shifts in the relative power between urban areas across the nation. Thus Charlotte and Phoenix now have NBA basketball teams; Tampa and Denver have NFL football franchises. All four of these cities have emerged as powerful urban centers over the past two decades and are beginning to challenge the economic and cultural dominance of cities like New York. This shifting balance of power helps us understand how migrations of talent may be changing in the neo-network era. As government policymakers and corporate managers develop more flexible, decentralized operations, the geographic allocation of talent must be transformed as well. During the past century, high performance on the job was usually rewarded by a transfer to the corporate headquarters in a major metropolitan locale. But this appears to be changing. Peter Sonnabend and Nathan Pearson work hard to find dynamic staff members to serve their local operations and then have to work even harder to keep them in place (Sonnabend: 52; Pearson: 126). As major corporations become more decentered, and as communications technologies continue to evolve, we may witness a greater dispersal of talent in both the corporate and cultural domains.

The Neo-Network Era

The national audience was the primary target of culture industries throughout the Fordist era. Companies focused on what David Kendall refers to as the universals of family and workplace, not because these were inherently national constructs but because they proved compatible with the economic, political, institutional, and legal relations that favored national mass markets. Now, new technologies, deregulation, and relentless competition are undermining these national frameworks and reconfiguring the cultural landscape. Although mass markets continue to attract corporate attention and blockbuster copyrights are still a priority, the mass audience no longer refers to one simultaneous experience so much as a shared, asynchronous cultural milieu.[33] That is, culture industries enjoy less control over the daily scheduling of popular entertainments and strive instead for broad exposure through multiple circuits of information and expression. They also seek less to homogenize popular culture than to organize and exploit diverse forms of creativity toward profitable ends. Flexible corporate frameworks connect mass market operations with more localized initiatives.

Therefore, two tendencies are now at work in the culture industries. One focuses on mass cultural forms aimed at broad national or global markets that demand low involvement and are relatively apolitical. Firms that deal in this arena are cautious about the prospect of intense audience responses either for or against the product they are marketing. By comparison, those forms targeted at niche audiences actively pursue intensity. They seek out audiences that are more likely to be highly invested in a particular form of cultural expression. These firms aim not to change niche groups, but to situate products within them. We are therefore witnessing the organization of huge media conglomerates around the so-called synergies that exploit these two movements. MTV identifies itself as hip, young, and alternative, while also conforming to the imperatives of Viacom, a multifaceted corporate parent whose holdings include Paramount studios, United Paramount television network, Blockbuster Video, and Simon & Schuster.[34] The Fox network pursues a similar strategy in its relations with the Wayans family. Their searing critiques of race relations in American society and their risqué sexual humor are ultimately folded into the agenda of the politically conservative Murdoch media empire.

One of the consequences of this new environment is that groups that were at one time oppositional or outside the mainstream have become increasingly attractive to media conglomerates with deep pockets, ambitious growth objectives, and flexible corporate structures. As the channels of distribution have grown more diverse, the oppositional has become more commercially viable and, in some measure, more closely tied to the mainstream. The voracious appetite for innovation in the culture industries means that niche markets are constantly serving as testing and recruiting grounds for new cultural forms. Flexible corporate structures have made it possible to quickly leverage niche artists into major mass phenomena when executives sense a growing audience interest. We have witnessed this pattern with grunge music groups, African-American film directors, and obscure computer software developers. In many ways their work has become mainstream, part of our shared experience. And perhaps they have lost some of their edge. Yet even those niche artists whose work is not leveraged into a mass phenomenon can be profitable if properly exploited through the "value chain" of the conglomerate. They remain outside of the mainstream and yet they have become part of a global/local dialectic that maintains centralized control through decentralizing tactics. Therefore it is not surprising to read socialist Barbara Ehrenreich's regular commentaries in the pages of *Time* magazine or to learn that some of the most controversial rap singers are signed to "independent" record labels controlled by Time-Warner enterprises. What is surprising perhaps is to hear executives in the culture industries spontaneously disavow their ability to control the creative process and the distribution of popular cultural forms in the neo-network era of post national media.

Notes

1 Page numbers in parentheses reference the interviews in this volume. Although Edmiston doesn't mention them, radio and Hollywood film also were major contributors to mass culture during this period. In fact, general-circulation magazines such as *Time* were actually targeted at an educated middle-class reader, whereas film and radio during the height of their popularity tended to address much more diverse audiences.

2 Ken Auletta, *Three Blind Mice: How the TV Networks Lost Their Way* (New York: Random House, 1991). Also see his reflections on the fortunes of television news, "Look What They've Done to the News," *TV Guide*, 9 November 1991, pp. 4–7.

3 Warren I. Susman, *Culture as History: The Transformation of American Society in the Twentieth Century* (New York: Pantheon, 1984).

4 James L. Baughman, *Television's Guardians: The FCC and the Politics of Programming, 1958–1967* (Knoxville: University of Tennessee Press, 1985), p. 13.

5 Among the firms that were frustrated in their attempts to forge competitive regional and national networks were Paramount Pictures, Time-Life, and the *Chicago Tribune*.

6 The networks could own five VHF and two UHF stations, but given the second-class status of the latter, few exercised this option.

7 Joel Sternberg, "Television Town," *Chicago History* 4, no. 2 (Summer 1975): 108–117, and Christopher Anderson and Michael Curtin, "Mapping the Eth-

ereal City: Chicago Television, the FCC, and the Politics of Place," *Quarterly Review of Film and Video*, forthcoming.

8 Les Brown, "When Chi Radio Was in Bloom," *Variety*, 28 March 1962, pp. 61–62; Melvin Patrick Ely, *The Adventures of Amos 'n' Andy: A Social History of an American Phenomenon* (New York: Basic Books, 1991); Robert C. Allen, *Speaking of Soap Operas* (Chapel Hill: University of North Carolina Press, 1985), pp. 101–121; Lester A. Weinrott, "Chicago Radio: The Glory Days," *Chicago History* 3, no. 1 (Spring–Summer 1974):14–22; and Sarajane Wells, "Looking Backward: My Life in Radio," *Chicago History* 7, no. 3 (Fall 1978):179–182.

9 Christopher Anderson, *Hollywood TV: The Studio System in the Fifties* (Austin: University of Texas Press, 1994); Tino Balio, ed., *Hollywood in the Age of Television* (Boston: Unwin Hyman, 1990); and William Boddy, *Fifties Television: The Industry and Its Critics* (Urbana and Chicago: University of Illinois Press, 1990).

10 Throughout the history of the FCC recurrent tensions have existed between the policy discourse of localism — which nostalgically characterizes broadcasting as a surrogate for the New England town meeting or the village green — and the economic realities of commercial network broadcasting. See Anderson and Curtin, "Mapping the Ethereal City."

11 Dwight Brooks, "In Their Own Words: Advertisers' Construction of an African American Consumer Market," *Howard Journal of Communication* 6, no. 2 (October 1995).

12 My use of the term Fordist is not meant to imply the total domination of all aspects of the economy by these modes of operation. Capitalism has always been characterized by internal contradictions and patterns of uneven development. Chicago's regional broadcast operations are a good example of some of the tensions at work in this era. Nevertheless, Fordist principles were at the heart of corporate behavior among the most central actors in the national and global economies during most of this century.

13 Lynn Spigel and Michael Curtin, eds., *The Revolution Wasn't Televised: Sixties Television and Social Conflict* (New York: Routledge, 1996).

14 William E. Porter, *Assault on the Media: The Nixon Years* (Ann Arbor: University of Michigan Press, 1976).

15 Indeed, cable technology has been around since the 1940s and failed to "revolutionize" television until it became the focus of policy debates in the 1970s. See Thomas Streeter, "Blue Skies and Strange Bedfellows," in Lynn Spigel and Michael Curtin, eds., *The Revolution Wasn't Televised*.

16 David Harvey, "Flexibility: Threat or Opportunity?" *Socialist Review* 21 (January 1991):73. Harvey's analysis is most thoroughly detailed in *The Condition of Postmodernity: An Inquiry into the Origins of Cultural Change* (Cambridge, Mass.:

Basil Blackwell, 1989). For another take on this transition see Alain Lipietz, *Mirages and Miracles: The Crises of Global Fordism* (London: Verso, 1987).

17 This kind of thinking is applied to a variety of industries by Kenichi Ohmae's best-seller, *The Borderless World: Power and Strategy in the Interlinked Economy* (New York: Harper Business, 1990). Ohmae is a managing director of McKinsey and Company, one of the world's largest and most influential corporate consulting firms.

18 I use the term extranational to connote social phenomena that are either more local (subnational) or more global (transnational) than those that have dominated the modern era.

19 *Electronic Media*, 2 January 1995, pp. 34–39, and *Variety*, 15 January 1996, pp. 39, 42.

20 The same is true transnationally. Rupert Murdoch's Sky Channel in Europe and Star TV in Asia are reaching vast and growing audiences despite the concerns often articulated by national regulators. The same is true with CNN, whose satellite networks have proven so successful that they have invited competitors. CNN is now locked in a fierce struggle with Televisa, NBC, Reuters, and BBC, each of them vying for the attention of Hispanic-speaking viewers throughout the Western Hemisphere.

21 Interestingly, Fox recently rose from a niche operator to a major network competitor by successfully outbidding CBS for the rights to broadcast National Football League games. This has not only encouraged some CBS affiliates to defect to Fox but also altered the network's attractiveness to Hollywood producers who are shopping around ideas for new programs. Thus, the deep pockets of Fox's corporate parent (Murdoch News Corp.) have allowed the network to pursue a growth strategy primarily based on a heavy investment in programming.

22 The exception here is high-tech, capital-intensive spectacles such as the Superbowl, the Olympics, and the presidential elections. In these cases, licensing agreements or logistical requirements favor major operators like ABC. But many spectacles, such as the Brown/Simpson tragedy, are remarkable because of their unruliness. During the Simpson trial, the major television networks struggled desperately to compete against each other and against niche services such as Court TV, CNN, and *Hardcopy*.

23 Nisid Hajari, "Looking for Rapprochement," *Entertainment Weekly*, 9 June 1995, pp. 16–17, and Richard Zoglin, "A Company Under Fire," *Time*, 12 June 1995, pp. 37–39. At the time this was written, 1995, Time-Warner still had significant ties to Death Row Records. Due to both internal and external controversies, as well as the continuing success of its music releases, the small record label has gone through a series of ownership and managerial changes too complicated to detail here. Interestingly, however, two of the firms angling for a role in the future

of Death Row are Sony and MCA (now owned by Seagram and Matsushita). See Adam Sandler, "Death Row Slapped with $75 Mil Lawsuit," *Variety*, 15 January 1996, p. 38, and "Spirit of Seagram Spreading through MCA," *Variety*, 22 January 1996, p. 8.

24 Indeed, so similar that the two firms seem headed for a megamerger. In this essay, however, I refer to Time-Warner and Turner as separate entities even though they have announced their intentions. I do this because, as of February 1996, the merger has not yet been finalized and Ted Turner has been quoted in the trade press as expressing reservations about going through with the deal. Furthermore, federal regulators have not yet given the go-ahead. As with the proposed Bell Atlantic-TCI deal two years ago, mergers of huge, multifaceted corporate entities can go awry before they are consummated. Nevertheless, the fate of the TWT deal is of little consequence as far as my argument goes. Whether operating as one or two corporate entities, these firms will continue to pursue the strategies discussed in this essay.

25 Interview in *Wired* (March 1995):112.

26 Ibid. Sassa's use of the term "copyright" to refer to cultural forms points to the increasing emphasis on intellectual property law as a means of controlling distribution in a fragmented and globalized market environment. Rosemary Coombe examines the implications of this strategy so far as oppositional and parodic modes of expression are concerned in *Cultural Appropriations: Authorship, Alterity and the Law* (New York: Routledge, forthcoming).

27 Zelnick: 21. My use of the term casual labor force may seem strange when referring to film stars or popular musicians. Unlike agricultural laborers, temporary office staff, or part-time factory workers, these performers command lavish compensation packages. Yet this top tier of the entertainment industry conceals the far larger pool of creative workers who toil long hours for little pay and no benefits. The key to success for these workers is to convince decision makers in the industry that they understand what it takes to produce hit material. And the key to success for industry executives is to secure an advantageous contract before leveraging a performer's career into the realm of stellar popularity. The success rate on both sides of the equation is extremely low. Nevertheless, the corporate conglomerate can counterbalance its losses, whereas the casual creative worker is particularly vulnerable to market forces. This labor strategy is not entirely new, of course. Postwar antitrust actions, such as the 1948 Paramount case, sparked the trend toward casual labor in the film industry. Other parts of the culture industries were similarly affected. Yet deregulation since the late 1970s has failed to reverse this trend, largely because of the forces described here. These flexible relationships between creative and administrative talent were first described by Paul M. Hirsch, "Processing Fads and Fashions: An

Organization-Set Analysis of Cultural Industry Systems," *American Journal of Sociology* 77 (1972):639–659.

28 Anthony Giddens, *The Consequences of Modernity* (Stanford, Calif.: Stanford University Press, 1990); Erving Goffman, *Behavior in Public Places* (New York: Free Press, 1963).

29 Shortly after Mosaic began to grow in popularity, some of the developers were lured away to join a small entrepreneurial venture called Netscape. By the time of this writing, Netscape had rapidly grown to be the industry standard on the World Wide Web, a matter of intense concern to Microsoft's Bill Gates, who understands the importance of software standards as a way of controlling the distribution of cultural forms. Gates has come up with a competing Web browser, and Netscape is now reportedly looking for a large corporate partner in hopes of bolstering its fortunes in the showdown with Microsoft.

30 Music is an obvious example of dispersed creativity, with the "capitals" of various styles being located in diverse locales: Chicago blues, Nashville country-western, Austin alternative country-western, New Orleans Cajun-pop, Seattle grunge, Athens (Georgia) alternative rock-pop, etc. Entertainment firms are now feverishly in search of new locales and are said to be scouting the garage band scene in such locations as Columbus, Ohio. Ethan Smith and Mike Flaherty, "Local Heroes," *Entertainment Weekly*, 17 March 1995, pp. 28–30.

31 Regarding these changes, see Janet L. Abu-Lughod, *Changing Cities* (New York: Harper Collins, 1991), and Manuel Castells, *The Informational City: Information Technology, Economic Restructuring and the Urban-Regional Process* (Oxford: Basil Blackwell, 1989).

32 Edward W. Soja, *Postmodern Geographies: The Reassertion of Space in Critical Social Theory* (New York: Verso, 1989).

33 National and global media events still pull together huge audiences on an occasional basis, but I am referring here to the more common tendency for large groups of people to share exposure to cultural phenomena in a more temporally diffuse manner. For example, the advertising agency D'Arcy Masius Benton & Bowles conducted a global study of the attitudes and market behaviors of teenagers around the globe in 1994. It argues that a world youth culture does in fact exist based on shared (but not necessarily simultaneous) exposure to specific trends in clothing, media, and popular amusements. "The World's Teenagers," *Sparks!* (A proprietary study from D'Arcy Masius Benton & Bowles, 1994).

34 On MTV, see Andrew Goodwin, *Dancing in the Distraction Factory: Music Television and Popular Culture* (Minneapolis: University of Minnesota Press, 1992).

Gage Averill **Global Imaginings**

· ·

Gage Averill (Ph.D., University of Washington, 1989) is associate professor of music and Latin American studies at Wesleyan University. He is an associate editor and book review editor of the Yearbook of Traditional Music (ICTM), contributing editor and columnist for The Beat *magazine, and author of* A Day for the Hunter, A Day for the Prey: Power and Popular Music in Haiti *(1996, University of Chicago Press). His primary research interests are Haitian popular music and American barbershop harmony.*

We market in more countries than belong
to the United Nations.
— Ira Herbert, former chief marketing
  officer for the Coca-Cola Company

In early 1995, Kellogg's introduced Corn Flakes into Indian markets, where it was previously available only as a specialty item on the black market for $10 a box. Billboards in the country's major cities boasted that Corn Flakes were "changing the way that India eats breakfast." Kellogg's was counting at the start not on the great majority of India's population, few of whom could afford store-bought products, but on a techno-cratic, managerial, and business class with a life-style in rapid flux — a group that can be termed a "comprador elite" or a transnational capitalist class. Even this small portion of the population constitutes a huge market in such a populous country, and it serves as a form of advertising for a consumerist life-style in India. Lest the world get the impression that Kellogg's was banking solely on the "global brand" strategy, the company planned to introduce a new product tailored to the local market: "Basmati Flakes."[1] At the risk of reading too much into Basmati Flakes: Kellogg's would seem to be engaging in an emergent corporate strategy to penetrate resistant for-eign markets: playing to a thin or superficial version of cultural difference as a means of establishing globally uniform habits of consumption. This could be viewed as a kinder, gentler form of transnational capitalism, one less susceptible to the charge of cultural imperialism. Its appeal has been en-hanced by new technologies of flexible production and by the spread of ideologies of local identity that demand products with local specificity, especially from global culture industries.

The world market, as Marx noted prophetically in the *Grundrisse*, has always been the ultimate horizon of capitalism. Developing new markets and incorporating them into global exchange has traditionally helped capitalism to weather treacherous, periodic contractions. Capitalism has sought to annihilate space and time in order to saturate the world market, all the while reducing "turnover time" (the interval between investment of capital and the return on that investment in the form of profit).[2] Capitalism earnestly seeks to clear the playing ground of precapitalist forms of production and exchange. Yet the world's cultural diversity and the precommercial practices that constitute local traditions have served as a source of friction and resistance to commercial incorporation and hegemony. What sometimes passes for generational conflict in the countries of the South (or even for a bland *National Geographic*-style "tradition and modernity" contrast) often masks the confrontation between traditional culture bearers and the proponents of cultural dislocations demanded by ascendent capitalism. A stubborn problematic facing all transnational corporations is the deep chasm between their ideal world (a "frictionless" global market characterized by the free flow of goods and services) and the culturally variegated real world (where cultural differences, precapitalist practices, and cultural nationalism or even cultural protectionism tarnish the allure of commodities and make the game of transnational marketing infinitely more complex and costly).

The discussions with representatives of culture industries that form the basis of this book have reinforced the impression that contemporary industries are extremely conscious of the global dimension of their operations. Many of our interlocutors operate across national boundaries, courting international markets, audiences, and clients. For example, Strauss Zelnick expected Twentieth Century Fox to earn half of its revenues from foreign markets in the near future, and noted that the company has "a huge staff that does nothing but license our pictures in all markets around the world" (21). Victoria Traube speaks of the importance of foreign release ("at the same time as home video") in an overall profit strategy (92) and describes a $13 million deal for worldwide distribution rights to a film. David Kendall explains that budget deficits incurred in producing and airing situation comedies in the United States are counterbalanced by foreign sales (55). Even some of the names of our interlocutors' businesses testify to the profound consciousness of the global business environment: for example, International Creative Management or Sonesta International Hotels (formerly Hotel Corporation of America).

Their pervasive concerns with globalization led me to attempt to pry further into the role that culture industries play in the globalization of culture and the means by which they address the problematic of local culture. Do they view themselves as agents of cultural change on a global scale — as Stuart Ewen has termed them, "Captains of Consciousness"?[3] Or do they see themselves as *dictated to* by global audiences, as *"captives* of consciousness"? How do they take cultural diversity and difference into account in their global activities? The core issue for me was this: How do they imagine the globe in order to do business in it? This would seem to be an extension of questions raised by my fellow contributors concerning how audiences are created and shaped by culture industries.

While our interview base was necessarily small, and while the dialogues were occasionally marked by cultural differences of our own (something like an "eggheads" vs. "fatcats" ideological divide), our consultants provided intriguing testimony about the relationship between strategies emphasizing global brands and those that stress products and texts customized to appeal to local cultural demands (even while the cultures in question are increasingly homogenized at the level of consumption and global interrelatedness). I link the reliance on global brands to a form of capitalist production dubbed "Fordism," characterized by mass production, mass markets, and mass media advertising. Conversely, what I note as a shift toward customized products is connected in my argument to a larger move toward flexible production, consumption, and capital accumulation, which many see as a defining characteristic of the postmodern era.[4] In this essay, I argue that this shift is indeed taking place, however unevenly, and that flexible production seems more capable of coping with a set of challenges — including a rise in asserted cultural differences (cultural essentialism), cultural nationalism, ethnic separatism, religious fundamentalism, and intensified subcultural affiliation — that emerge from crises of legitimacy in the modern world system, and that simultaneously open up profit-making opportunities for transnationally operating culture industries.

Transnational Corporations and the Global System

I begin by sketching some characteristics of globalization. The imperial powers, as Sklair has said, "etched the forms of capitalism onto the global system."[5] At least from the period of colonial expansion, all of the world's peoples have been drawn into a single historical time. The principal agents of this transformation have been transnational corporations — supported by the nation states of the West in which they have been based — working alongside and through sympathetic elites (comprador elites or transna-

tional capitalist classes) in developing nations. These agents, their technologies (from the railroad to fiber-optic cables and communication satel-
lites), and their commercial and industrial processes made the world an
increasingly integrated place, with each part vulnerable to — and dependent
upon — distant forces and events. They helped to export from the industrialized West to the rest of the world a set of features associated with
capitalist modernity (including secular individualism, urbanization, nation-
states, mobile nuclear families, and the notion of popular sovereignty) that
are not necessarily components of capitalist production but that tend to
emerge and travel along with it as part of its cultural baggage. The speed-up
in production and the increasing mobility of capital quickened the pace
of social life around the globe, creating new senses of space and time. Social interactions were distantiated, disembedded from face-to-face encoun-
ters, and enmeshed in impersonal interactions across large distances and
timeframes.[6]

Most importantly, however, transnational corporations exported a belief
that human needs can be satisfied through the purchase of commodities, a
"belief system" that Sklair calls the "culture-ideology of consumption."[7]
These beliefs and the set of practices associated with them have served as the
motor of the entire enterprise, and in this sense, culture has helped to pave
the way for consumption. Global advertising played a major role in stimulat-
ing demand for commodities and in developing frames of meaning for the
consumption of commodities. Describing consumption as "a thoroughly
cultural phenomenon," McCracken[8] argues that the system of goods is
equally a system of meanings. As cultures around the globe were confronted
by a gap between the standard of life-as-lived and the standard of life
portrayed by the media (through so-called "demonstration effects" of advertising), audiences were encouraged to bridge this gap through consumption.
By purchasing commodities, consumers participate in these meanings as a
part of what McCracken has called a "cultural project" of self completion.[9]

Advertisements manufacture demand for products by linking cultural
meaning with goods. Ira Herbert, one of our interlocutors, discussed this
function of advertising: "Our role here at the Coca Cola Company is to
perpetuate and develop a specialness about the brands that we sell, which
take the product above and beyond what is actually in the bottle itself"
(4). This effort was so successful in establishing an image and feel for the
product that consumers in the United States objected to advertising that
didn't reinforce "this icon, this image (the Doris Day, apple pie, rosy cheek,
this-is-America kind of thing)" (7). An advertising agent heavily involved

with the Coca-Cola account spoke of "Coca-Cola situations," "Coca-Cola values," "aura . . . specialness of Coca-Cola or 'Cokeness.'"[10]

In short, I argue that the extraordinary cultural changes wrought on the entire globe by the West in the last few generations have had at their heart the motor of capitalist accumulation and the desperate drive to globalize markets. To this end, transnational corporations have striven to globalize the advertising logic that breeds a desire for consumerist life-styles.

The United States, Global Asymmetries, and Persistent Peripheries

With English as an international language of business; with the triumph of liberal democracy and/or some form of market economy throughout Latin America, Eastern Europe, and even China; with the success of international organizations linked closely to U.S. policy (such as the International Monetary Fund and the World Bank) in dictating the terms of global development; and simply in terms of the continued strength and overall size of the U.S. economy, the United States has been very successful in promoting its own interests, its own transnational corporations, its free-market ideology, and its cultural products. Considering that cultural products are America's second largest export, the United States would seem to have been particularly successful in this arena.[11]

For some decades, Marxist critics attributed this control of the flow of information from the First to the Third World as a project to establish and maintain American hegemony through what was termed cultural imperialism. These theories[12] relied too heavily on the content of cultural flows and placed too much emphasis on the United States rather than on transnational capitalism as the agent of cultural change, and they may seem hopelessly inadequate today in accounting for the many directions of the world's cultural flows. Yet these flows are still extraordinarily asymmetric, and American popular culture, I maintain, retains a somewhat privileged position in the not-so-free flow of images and signifiers. Despite a relative decline in America's preeminence, the United States is still a senior partner in the bloc of capitalist countries promoting transnational capitalism.[13] As Stuart Hall has argued, "The new kind of globalization is not English, it is American. In cultural terms, the new kind of globalization has to do with a new form of global mass culture."[14]

Contemporary cultural flows seem to follow neither the more rigid center-to-periphery model of the kind promoted by Wallerstein in his first major work on the world system (1974),[15] nor the chaotic, decentered, heterogeneous and disjunct flows posited by some other contemporary critics.[16] Appadurai and Buell lean too heavily on emergent and anecdotal evidence to signal the arrival, or even the completion, of a radically "decentered global ecumene."[17] Their "new view of world order . . . a decentered, democratically egalitarian view of world organization,"[18] hints at a dangerous erasure of politics from analysis of the global system and too easily writes off American hegemony in the global political economy.

One result of this brand of scholarship is an exaggeration of the degree to which formerly marginalized peoples have accumulated cultural power in the postcolonial global order. Subaltern peoples have certainly generated powerful cultural discourses: Third World literature, film, music, and dance circulate more freely in global arenas and with greater impact than ever before. These expressive discourses crowd the center, demanding to be recognized as voices of a postmodern, hybrid, and culturally heterogenous future. In addition, the former colonial powers have replicated much of the world's sociocultural diversity within their own boundaries (in the form of immigrant groups, diasporas, and minorities), and this "peripheralization of the core"[19] has forced a crisis of multicultural representation on their nation states, a crisis related to the loss of a relatively homogeneous "public space" and the challenge to national consensus mentioned by one of our interlocutors (Edmiston: 141). None of this, however, fundamentally restructures the asymmetries of global wealth and power, although it may mask or blur these distinctions. The asymmetries of access and accumulation are still deeply implicated in the directional arrows of human population movements and diaspora formations, despite efforts to theorize migration as having a "deeply disjunctive relationship" to technology, politics, and finance.[20] The logic of migration is thus still yoked largely to the inequities of the global system and to the uneven global distribution of resources and capital. As a result, the number of Pakistanis migrating to Great Britain still far exceeds the number of Britons (including those of Pakistani descent) migrating to Pakistan. Theories of globalization need to incorporate continuing (and often deepening) postcolonial disparities and unequal accumulation and access.

Some "prophetic criticism" also prematurely sounds the death knell for the nation state. There are many challenges to the status of the nation state: transnational forms of political organization, transnational capitalism, diasporic population flows, electronic capital transfer, global communications, local and primordial forms of identity. However, most transnational activity is predicated on the continuance of nation states as a critical level of organization, and most movements of primordial identity have some form of statehood as their goal. With no practical replacement in sight, nation states should be with us — meddling in the flow and accumulation of global capital, power, populations, and information — for a good long time.

I have digressed a bit in order to rein in some more prophetic aspects of contemporary critical theory concerning globalization. My point is that globalization theory must account for continuing asymmetries in flow and accumulation, for the continuing role of the nation state, for the reconfigured and less reified cores and peripheries, and for the stubborn grip of Western (read: American) cultural imprint on the new globalized world of consumption.

The Problematic of Place

Although ownership and control of the major transnational corporations is still located almost exclusively in Europe, the United States, and the newly industrialized nations of Asia, "place" is no longer as solid a phenomenon in contemporary transnational capitalism as it once was. The relationship of the local to global circulation and vice versa could be said to be the central problematic of contemporary capitalism. In this section of the essay, I would like to tease out how transnational industries are variously imagined to be located in global spaces and how they in turn imagine the terrain of their operations.

An example of the complexities of place in financial transactions was provided by one of our consultants, Mark Edmiston. Edmiston, who advises publishing firms in acquisitions and mergers, counseled a European company called Euromoney Limited (whose magazine of the same name provides information on world financial markets) on the purchase of an American firm whose principal asset was its access to information on the availability of large bank loans. The consultation was transnational, the purchase was itself transnational, and the magazine's subject matter, the financial market, was the classic case of transnational integration: the global electronic flow of capital.

The recent spat between France and the United States over the GATT (General Agreement on Tariffs and Trade) — ostensibly over the competitive edge it preserved for American commercial "monoculture" and the interest in the French Ministry of Culture in defending French cultural space — obscured the emerging international character of the infotainment industries. Many of the corporations that have the greatest cultural impact, especially in the so-called "infotainment" industry, are themselves owned by interests based outside of the United States. To wit, in the period pre-ceeding the GATT fight, the French company Studio Canal Plus bank-rolled *Terminator 2*, while one of the presumed worst American cultural imperialists, MGM Studios, was owned by a French bank, Credit Lyonnais. Likewise, Columbia Pictures was a division of Sony and the entertainment giant MCA was owned by Matsushita Electric Company.[21] In a more his-torical vein, German subsidiaries of Ford were producing for the German war machine well into World War II; similarly, Coca-Cola bottling fran-chises in Germany were distributing free Coke at Nazi youth rallies before the War and displaying the swastika at bottling conventions.[22] It may be best to view transnational corporations as being situated generally in the advanced industrial political economies but with little patriotic affiliation to any given state, at least when place functions as an impediment to capital accumulation.

Sonesta hotels attempt to demonstrate local good citizenship (Sonna-bend: 52). For reasons of public relations, it is important for transna-tional corporations to exhibit a sense of belonging to the locales in which they operate. Canadian subsidiaries of U.S.-based transnational corpora-tions typically incorporate maple leaves into their corporate logos; Parisian McDonald's restaurants serve wine; Toyota U.S. advertises a deserted fac-tory on the weekend, proving that Toyota workers get time off, too ("We Are Driven," a former corporate slogan, was used by the United Auto Workers to disparage Toyota's personnel policies).

Countering efforts to patriate themselves in the countries in which they do business is the trace (positive or negative) of their country of origin that transnational corporations carry in the opinions of their local audiences or clientele. Coke is "immediately identified as a piece of America," according to Ike Herbert (8). Moreira agrees that coke has "all this excitement of this Western world they've discovered in the last three generations in a big way."[23] As a result, Coke ads in Japan always contain some words in pseudo-English that advertisers call "Japlish." But Moreira also points out that Coca-Cola has stopped "leveraging the Westernness of the brand" as stud-ies show that Japanese actors in ads sell more product these days. Thus, as cultural nationalism has intensified in Japan, the Coca-Cola Company has successfully repatriated or indigenized its advertising appeal to consumers. Levi Strauss (indeed, all jeans manufacturers) has benefited from the strong linkage between their product and a widely held image of American free-dom and youthful rebellion. At the same time, Euro-Disney is saddled with the "ugly American" image in France, despite the beret worn by Mickey

Mouse. In a challenge to Disney, a French corporation has opened a theme park based on the venerable French comic strip "Asterix." Sonesta Hotels was formerly called Hotel Corporation of America, but changed its corporate name in 1970 in part because it had amassed international holdings and because the association with the United States was a liability in "the Vietnam years [when] Americans were not looked upon so favorably abroad . . ." (Sonnabend: 34). The emergence of transnational capitalism has, naturally, been haunted by the ghost of corporate nationality past, but transnational corporations have long sought ways of strategically positioning their "nationality" to maximize their appeal in global markets. Locally owned subsidiaries, globally traded shares of publicly owned stock, franchises, and other tactics allow transnationals to transcend their national origins in the quest for global free flow.

A classic example of this kind of strategy is the franchise strategy of the Coca-Cola Company. Coca-Cola has always been marketed and sold through independently owned, local franchises, "marketed and developed and invested in by mostly independent businessmen who are indigenous to the country in which we are marketing. You have Germans running the German operation, you have Frenchmen running the French operation, et cetera" (Herbert: 4). The origins of these franchises were in the mobile bottling plants that Coca-Cola developed to supply the Allied troops during World War II with Coke. "Everything that was done, all promotions, all activity, all packaging, all sales activity, all social activities, the image of the Coca-Cola bottler as a leading citizen of the local community, has all been keyed on a local basis, overlaid with an umbrella of the global strategy" (Herbert: 6–7).

Fordist Accumulation and the Rise of Global Brands

What David Harvey calls "Fordist" accumulation was arguably the dominant economic model in the West through much of the twentieth century. In Fordist-style production, rationalized factories and their assembly lines turn out mass-produced products for mass consumption. To maximize sales of standardized products, tastes are standardized through advertising in the mass media. The post–World War II "Pax Americana," reinforced by American military power and by the centrality of the dollar as the guarantor of international exchange, helped to secure global markets for this system of production. Industries hoping to operate on a global scale simply exported their standardized brands and products. These products were priced competitively against local products because of the enormous advantages afforded by their economies of scale. The result was a Fordist concept par excellence: the global brand. Fordist accumulation was indelibly linked with a sense of increasing global uniformity, standardization of meaning, cultural convergence, and homogeneity. Speaking of the experience of the Coca-Cola Company, Ira Herbert said, "In terms of our target group, which is really thirteen to twenty-nine, we have found that there are so many more similarities worldwide than differences that we can almost ignore the differences. That's what made our global pattern advertising successful, that recognition that in the last ten years, teenagers in Great Britain or Germany or the United States or some other place, had much in common" (15). I am impressed that Herbert saw this as a historical process ("in the last ten years") and as a process that hinged on the consumption patterns of youth ("teenagers").

Classic examples of global brands in the entertainment media include television sit-coms and Hollywood movies. The enormous capital expeditures for these products require that they be distributed and syndicated internationally to attain profitability. Television scriptwriter David Kendall develops sit-coms for a *domestic* audience, collects his residuals from foreign distribution, and claims never to consider the foreign markets in the creative process: "It is sold internationally as an American product and I have felt no effects of globalization. It's just 'Sell us some sitcoms' " (69). Strauss Zelnick of Twentieth Century Fox said, "The bulk of our [international] market is culturally similar to the United States, except for Japan" (22). Both individuals think similarly to early Coca-Cola executives in relationship to global brands: develop a product that sells well in the United States and simply distribute it worldwide, expecting its success to travel.

Concessions to locality on the part of the "global brands" may include simply dubbing or subtitling the finished product. International release and syndication is so common in contemporary entertainment deals that interviewee Victoria Traube described a clause that she includes in her "checklist for acting deals" guaranteeing an actor's control over the process of dubbing and subtitling his or her own performances in international distribution.

Language-driven texts (advertisements, films, television shows), however, do present more intractable problems for universal consumption than do material consumer products. As Zelnick comments, "Anything that is really verbally driven won't work [in an international market], especially comedy. You can translate most dramas, but not all. *Ordinary People*, for example, was a huge hit here. It didn't work at all overseas because everyone thought it was really stupid. They couldn't imagine what all these rich Americans were upset about. *Kramer vs. Kramer*, same thing" (22). He provided some insight into why some films succeed overseas and others don't. Twentieth Century Fox's *Rising Sun*, for example, was created to generate revenues in the foreign market through internationally sensitive casting and its Japanese subject. *White Men Can't Jump* couldn't jump into international markets because it relied too much on African-American street jargon and inside humor. Note the projection of audience tastes in Japan by Zelnick: "People in Japan do not tend to go see a movie with black stars unless it's an action movie . . . our black subculture, which is reflected in most of our movies, makes little sense to the rest of the world" (22). His testimony squares well with the industry figures for overseas releases, which show an enormous demand for action films (*Jurassic Park* or anything starring Schwarzenegger, Van Damme, or Stallone). Much of this anecdotal evidence becomes the received wisdom of the global cultural industries. That *Rising Sun* was crafted with an international market in mind demonstrates that foreign markets are beginning to have an aesthetic effect over the shape of Hollywood's cultural products, but they are still more closely akin to global brands than to customized products.

As the conflict between the United States and China over intellectual property rights and unauthorized duplication has revealed, it is still predominantly American cultural products that are marketed and pirated globally, just as it is still American commercial cultural products that form the core repertoire and product base of even foreign-owned multimedia and infotainment conglomerates. American songs do well in world markets, in part because their producers and artists continue to innovate technically in recording and production values (also a strong drawing card for American action films with their highly touted special effects). Speaking specifically of television advertisements, Oakes said, "Our production values are still looked at as being a model. It is just the etiquette, the social concerns, that differ" (85). Production values in cultural texts—whether in television, advertising, sound recordings, or films—are a means by which transnational culture industries maintain market share dominance in cultural production. While artistic creativity and sheer productivity may reach impressive levels outside of the industrialized countries, the returns on capital generally haven't resulted in the upgrade of technology to maintain parity with Hollywood, Tokyo, London, or Nashville. Try as they might, cultural workers in the rest of the world have been structurally prohibited from achieving the same results as state-of-the-art studios in the West (and

Japan) — that is, unless they turn over an essential stage in the production process to the transnationals.[24] Global commercial culture and its advertisements form a kind of code or language spoken best by the transnational cultural industries, for whom it is a language of origin.

By exploiting the fantasy visual world of animation, Steven Oakes imagines creating an advertising "language" that is not verbally driven and that is thus more potentially global, a "global brand" of advertising. He agreed with our suggestion that "One thing going on in the contemporary discourse of advertising is a lot of talk about globalization. Firms say that they are in pursuit of a language that can transcend national boundaries and speak to audiences on a transnational basis. Animation itself would seem to be a really good place to find that construction of a transnational language" (84).

Global audiences, with all of the residual and asserted cultural differences they represent, form a stunning challenge to the imagination of cultural industry advertisers and marketing specialists targeting local markets with global brands. There are numerous anecdotes about global brands that didn't make it for failure to read cultural and linguistic difference: the French pantyhose called Dim (pronounced "deem" in French) encountered a dim reception in Canadian markets. Likewise, the French computer company called Bull was unable to establish a trustworthy reputation for its information hardware among English speakers, even with a "Glo-Bull" pun on its transnational ambitions. And nearly everyone has heard how the General Motors Nova ("no go" in Spanish) got a "no go" in the Latin American market.[25] Linguistically, at least, difference is deeply entrenched and requires sensitive multicultural attention.

Flexible Accumulation: Toward Customized Products and Texts

Globalization unravels residual social and cultural differences among local systems even as it constructs and incorporates new forms of asserted difference. Despite the homogenizing influences of global culture industries on cultural geography, many centrifugal forces tear away at the notion of an increasingly homogeneous world culture: hybrid cultural forms proliferate, new local cultural forms arise, governments erect barriers to foreign cultural "pollution," and states are being torn apart by conflicts of identity and religious belief. As a result of increased economic, political, and cultural integration into the world system, social groups have struggled with questions of ontological security, individual and collective identity, and cultural authenticity. From Serbia to Cambodia, these conflicts have given way to movements based on essentialist or primordial identity. The coexistence of homogenizing and heterogenizing trends does not constitute a paradox or contradiction; rather, the two processes are inextricably linked: globalization generates its own local diversity, particularity, difference.

Because the world's regions and locales are in active competition to attract capital and investments, many have taken to emphasizing their competitive distinctiveness, or what Robertson calls their "global calling."[26] David Harvey claims that the global mobility of modern capital has resulted in "the active production of places with special qualities . . . variegated spaces within the increasing homogeneity of international exchange."[27] This view that locality and globality are interdependent and mutually defining has taken hold in the last decade and is expressed in various ways. Stuart Hall has emphasized the role of global capitalism in this process, "wanting to recognize and absorb those differences within the larger, overarching framework."[28] Culture industries have learned to exploit local "addresses" and to market the signifiers of locality and difference globally.

Tourist industries, of course, rely on the allure of locality. Peter Sonnabend of Sonesta Hotels emphasizes that his company's hotels "will reflect the area, the community. For instance, in Aruba, Curaçao, or the Middle East, the hotels . . . are going to feature elements from the community and from the area of the world where those hotels are located, either through decor or through facilities" (37–38). Sonnabend lists tropical colors, cuisine, local entertainment, local art, and transportation to local attractions as possible signifiers of locality to a global audience of travelers. "We are selling experience. When you go to Aruba, you don't want to think that you're in New York; you want to be in Aruba. You are going for an exotic experience (38). The quest for touristic experiences with exaggerated signifiers of place is a product of globalized modernity.[29]

The marketing of local distinctiveness propels the market in the West for non-Western musics, dubbed "worldbeat." I have described elsewhere how the deterritorialized consumption of these musics is related to the requirement that they carry the "grain of the locale": "Worldbeat recordings, in their sound structure, packaging, and promotion, privilege the marks of difference and authenticity and signifiers of exotic locales. Promoters of worldbeat music typically derive ancient histories for what are essentially contemporary musics."[30] An example of the latter might be the marketing of a Bulgarian television and radio choir as the "Mystères des Voix Bulgares." One of the more blatant local authentications of global cultural flows occurred in the years surrounding 1990 when two French entrepreneurs bought the rights to songs that were being marketed under the name "lambada" in Brazil; formed a group in France of African, Caribbean, Brazilian, and French performers; and launched an international dance craze sponsored by the French soft drink manufacturer, Orangina.[31] The original musical material, far from being "authentically" Brazilian, consisted of Caribbean recordings that were being played at sound-system dances in the north of Brazil, and also included Caribbean-flavored covers of other Latin American popular songs. Popularizers of the dance created an origin myth claiming that the lambada appeared forty years ago, only to be censored for its erotic appeal.

Expanding markets for worldbeat recordings (especially those emphasizing the music's spirituality or physicality) are a sonic corollary to expanding tastes in the West for ethnic foods, the increasing popularity of subaltern literature, and the increased visibility of the tourism industry, all of which cater to the burgeoning Western market for "difference" (i.e., the new and exotic). But the recording of music from non-Western artists was far from a recent phenomenon, even for the commercial industry. In 1901, at the dawn of the recording industry, the Gramophone Company sent Fred Gaisberg on his first expedition to record music (primarily courtesan songs) in India. The results of this and many other similar expeditions were meant to serve as "software" advertising for the gramophone — a means of inducing locals from the middle class and elite to purchase a phonogram or phonograph player. Culture industries are in the business of servicing markets like these all around the world, and the music industry happened to get a very early start. In more "flexible" modes of production and accumulation, industries have found technologies that allow them to exploit the opportunities that segmented markets offer. Flexible accumulation corresponds with a shift toward information technologies, mobile capital, floating exchange rates, and market research (the latter providing rapid feedback concerning local patterns of consumption). In this way, flexible production and accumulation have made it much easier for industries to cater to niche markets.

Edminston (136) spoke of "selectronic" binding for magazine and newspapers, which allows printing presses to assemble different versions of their publications for given regions, submarkets, or even individual subscribers. This has already become an issue of cultural conflict between Canada and the United States after *Sports Illustrated* was accused of assembling a so-called Canadian sports magazine from American copy and Canadian ads (masquerading as a national magazine for tariff purposes while taking away advertising revenues from home-bred Canadian sports magazines). The technologies (especially computer data templates) for customizing products on the assembly line provide an edge for the transnationals in their ongoing battle with local products because they are able to distribute products that enjoy economies of scale formerly reserved for global brands even as they compete with local products at the level of "local flavor" and cultural specificity.

Although selectronic binding and variable computer templates for the production line provide examples of extremely flexible forms of customization, the concept of customization can be applied to a host of strategies to vary products or texts for globally heterogenous markets. Stephen Oakes spoke of customizing ads to local conditions, citing his experience with Pillsbury Doughboy commercials in Great Britain. "British TV in particular needs to be more entertaining because their commercials are all in a block of time, so there is a tradition of more entertainment value and less hard sell" (80). Research showed that British women responded poorly to a boy's voice instructing them in cooking, and thus the British Dough Man has an adult voice (and British accent). According to Oakes, companies interested in transnational sales "want to be sensitive to the local market, so they will do their research. P & G will not boast as much in Japan as in the United States, because to talk about your product as being better is objectionable" (85). Similarly, note the manner in which Sonesta International Hotels pictures the needs of — and caters to — various national markets (in the following three quotes): "Europeans are used to larger bathrooms than Americans are. If you really want to sell the Europeans on the luxury level, you've got to have spectacular bathrooms" (Sonnabend: 51); "If your market is Americans, you have to serve hamburgers" (Sonnabend: 50); and "We know from experience that people from South America are looking for different kinds of experiences than people from the Northeast. Shopping is very important, and playing the casino in Aruba and Curaçao is very important for Latin Americans" (Sonnabend: 51).

As I have suggested earlier, Coca-Cola marketed a global brand using a global strategy through locally owned bottling franchises. As O'Barr makes clear,[32] until 1979, advertisements were designed with the American market in mind and distributed globally to interested bottlers. At most, an overseas franchise might reshoot the American ad locally with local actors, but the ads themselves corresponded to the notion of a global brand. The problem was that Coca-Cola had designed its American advertising campaigns to increase Coke's edge over Pepsi in the domestic market — to trump their rival in the "strategic tripod of taste, thirst, and refreshment"[33] — but this wasn't the same challenge that faced them in the global market, where Coke enjoyed an overwhelming competitive edge, but where per capita consumption was still low.

The so-called "global era of Coca-Cola" that followed featured advertising themes designed with the world in mind. These themes specified the feel and structure of commercials; they were what Herbert calls "patterned advertising" (5) that could be "adjusted to fit the local culture, the local language, and could be changed or edited as long as the concept wasn't changed — as long as the feel wasn't changed — as long as the sound wasn't changed." The onset of the "global era" coincided with the birth of the InterNational Team at Coca-Cola's advertising agency, McCann Erickson. The InterNational Team's goals were to "generate centrally designed and centrally executed advertising that will solve the problems of most [franchises] and establish quality standards for the remainder . . . The benchmark comes from the center and anybody that needs to produce locally, for a cultural reason, a legal reason, a religious reason, or a marketing reason, has to beat it."[34]

In 1993, Coca-Cola began to break up the feel of their commercials, allowing for very different executions aimed at particular markets (maintaining only the "Always Coca-Cola" meta-theme). "The company has moved to a more fragmented approach, based on the assumption that media today are fragmented and that each of those groups that are targeted by that media core should be communicated to in their own way with their own message, with their own sound, with their own visualization" (7). In the Coca-Cola example, we are presented with the simplest of global brands, a product that remains unaltered to fit local conditions. What have been changed are the strategies for the texts used to sell Coke: from the franchise approach, to the global patterned approach, to the decentralized multicultural approach. In its advertising, although not its brand, Coca-Cola demonstrates an increasingly customized strategy.

The movement toward niche marketing and production, flexible accumulation, and customized products would seem to dovetail nicely with the emphasis in Michael Curtin's essay on the move toward corporate structures that can capitalize on "elaborate circuits of cultural production and reception" by leveraging copyrightable material all the way through the value chain (Curtin: 190). The niche markets that both of us are talking about are sites of creative talent and highly specific audience identification that can be mined by culture industries as profit sources for both production and consumption. The worldbeat phenomenon that I discussed earlier is in part an encounter between these underserved niche markets and transnational infotainment industries in search of copyrights and consuming publics.

Conclusion

What are the effects of globalization on the world's cultural diversity? This is not as self-evident a question as it first may appear. Without a doubt, the range of cultural variability narrows as societies are progressively integrated into a global political economy. They are homogenized *at a certain level* while they are synchronized and ordered into a common historical timeline. The cultural differences that persist or that endure from premodern times might be called "residual difference" — cultural differences among hunter-gatherer bands, transhumant pastoralists, agrarian empires, or feudal peasant societies; differences characteristic of human society before the ascendence of the "culture-ideology of consumption" and capitalist modernism. Yet there are many ways in which globalization has resulted in a heightened or exaggerated sense of locality, local identity, and local cultural distinctiveness, and I have resorted to calling these emergent patterns "asserted difference."

With access to technologies of flexible production, transnational culture industries have become more sophisticated at customizing products and texts to adapt to local cultural differences (including asserted difference), even as they have succeeded in achieving a "common meta-culture of social modernity"[35] across the globe. These technologies allow transnational corporations to maintain economies of scale while responding flexibly to cultural preferences. Customization can be applied at the level of product design (as in Basmati Flakes), brand name, or packaging, or simply of marketing and advertising in those cases where the product works fine as a global brand.

Transnational corporations have never been able to eliminate risk and uncertainty from their activities in national markets; operating in *global* markets, they have been forced to negotiate increasingly complex cultural landscapes, work within new sets of rules, and risk colossal marketing failures on a global scale. Our effort to peer inside decision-making processes of culture industries renders these industries a bit less monolithic and conspiratorial, revealing the insecurity and anxiety (and creativity) at the heart of the global reach of the transnational corporations. In their often (apparently) maddening efforts to read global markets and conditions, our consultants have brought with them all of their personal experiences, abilities, values, ideologies, and limitations, and one of the most interesting aspects of this project for me has been the glimpse into the personal dimensions of transnational bureaucratic organizations.

Like my fellow contributors, I have been intrigued by the question of agency on the part of our interviewees and their associates. I have been struck by the potential impact of individuals within these bureaucratic institutions to determine outcomes for their own organizations as well as for audiences and consumers across the globe. Dealing with such a vast canvas, our consultants expressed a surprising degree of confidence about their readings of world markets, yet, as Richard Ohmann notes in this volume, they generally disavow agency in relation to their ability to *manufacture* demand, values, tastes, or attitudes. They view themselves as imagining their audiences and incorporating the imagined, anticipated, or researched tastes of these audiences into the process of cultural creation. In the end, I am convinced that the process of imagining cultural similarity and dissimilarity across great spans of the globe on the part of culture industries has helped to shape the world's cultural configuration.

In general, our discussions with cultural producers have supported the view that strategies of flexible production, accumulation, marketing, and distribution (fed by sophisticated global market research) have joined mass consumption and Fordist strategies in exploiting the global market and may be in the process of displacing them as the more efficient means for exploiting markets that are simultaneously both more global and more segmented and local than those in the past. In the current period, transnational culture industries are proving adept at responding to and manipulating the cultural politics of local identity and difference. Not only have they targeted niche markets for customized products, but they have increasingly marketed the expressions of the new local "addresses" for global consumption. Look for Basmati Flakes, coming soon to a supermarket near you.

Notes

1 This marketing campaign was the subject of a report by Chitra Ragavan on *All Things Considered* (National Public Radio), 26 January 1995.

2 David Harvey, *The Condition of Postmodernity: An Enquiry into the Origins of Cultural Change* (Cambridge, Mass.: Blackwell, 1989), p. 293.

3 Stuart Ewen, *All Consuming Images: The Politics of Style in Contemporary Culture* (New York: Basic Books, 1988).

4 The already "classic" literature on this subject would have to begin with Jean François Lyotard's seminal *The Postmodern Condition: A Report on Knowledge*, trans. Geoff Bennington and Brian Masumi (Minneapolis: University of Minnesota Press, 1974). My own thinking on the issue has been challenged by works like Jurgen Habermas, "Modernity Versus Postmodernity," *New German Critique* (Winter 1981): 3–14; I. Hassan, "The Culture of Postmodernism," *Theory, Culture, and Society* 2, no. 3 (1985): 119–132; E. Ann Kaplan, *Postmodernism and Its Discontents* (London: Verso, 1988); Harvey, *The Condition of Postmodernity*; and Frederic Jameson's monumental *Postmodernism or, The Cultural Logic of Late Capitalism* (Durham, N.C.: Duke University Press, 1991).

5 Leslie Sklair, *Sociology of the Global System* (Baltimore: Johns Hopkins University Press, 1991), p. 7.

6 Anthony Giddens, *The Consequences of Modernity* (Stanford: Stanford University Press, 1990).

7 Sklair, *Sociology of the Global System*, p. 6, identifies the "culture-ideology of consumerism" as one node in a three-node model of transnational practices. The other nodes are transnational corporations and the transnational capitalist class.

8 Grant McCracken, *Culture and Consumption: New Approaches to the Symbolic Character of Consumer Goods and Activities* (Bloomington: Indiana University Press, 1990), p. 88.

9 Ibid.

10 William M. O'Barr, "The Airbrushing to Culture: An Insider Look at Global Advertising," *Public Culture* 2, no. 1 (1989): 1–19. The article consists of an extended interview with Marcio M. Moreira.

11 Domination of the global music business by transnational infotainment corporations has continued in a statistical sense, furthered by vertical and horizontal integration, diversification, subsidiary ownership, and the growth of multimedia conglomerates. In the 1980s, 50 percent of worldwide production was controlled by eight of these transnational corporations, all of which were owned and based in Europe, the United States, and Japan. This concentration of productive resources has been challenged by the emergence of cassette, video, CD, and software piracy, and by protectionist legislation in the Third World and in industrialized countries such as Canada and France.

12 For example, Herbert I. Schiller, "Transnational Media and National Development," eds. Kaarle Nordenstreng and Herbert I. Schiller, *National Sovereignty and International Communications* (Norwood, N.J.: Ablex Publishing, 1979); and Armand Mattelart, *Multinational Corporations and the Control of Culture* (Brighton: Harvester Press, 1979).

13 Stephen Gill and David Law, *The Global Political Economy: Perspectives, Problems, and Policies* (Baltimore: Johns Hopkins University Press, 1989).

14 Stuart Hall, "The Local and the Global: Globalization and Ethnicity," in *Culture, Globalization, and the World-System: Contemporary Conditions for the Representation of Identity*, ed. Anthony D. King (Binghamton, N.Y.: SUNY at Binghamton, 1991), pp. 19–40.

15 Immanuel Wallerstein, *The Modern World System* (New York: Academic Press, 1974).

16 For example, Arjun Appadurai, "Disjuncture and Difference in the Global Cultural Economy," *Public Culture* 2, no. 2 (1990): 1–24, and Frederick Buell, *National Culture and the New Global System* (Baltimore: Johns Hopkins University Press).

17 Buell, *National Culture*, p. 259.

18 Ibid., p. 297.

19 Anthony D. King, *Urbanism, Colonialism, and the World Economy: Cultural and Spatial Foundations of the World Urban System* (New York: Routledge, 1990), p. 46.

20 Appadurai, "Disjuncture and Difference," p. 9.

21 I discuss the patterns of ownership of culture industries in the past tense to situate them in the discussion over GATT and also in recognition of the fact that ownership of culture, media, electronic, and infotainment companies has been changing rapidly due to mergers and acquisitions in the quest for "synergy."

22 This incident was recounted in Mark Pendergrast, "A Brief History of Coca-Colonization," *New York Times*, sect. III (15 August 1993). The marketers were especially aggressive in order to counter a rumor that the Kosher sign on some bottles of Coke meant that the drink was a Jewish product. The health fad among Nazi youth and their disdain for caffeine also had hurt Coca-Cola sales. Meanwhile, back in the United States, Coca-Cola's involvement in the war effort won an exemption for the company from wartime sugar rationing.

23 O'Barr, "The Airbrushing of Culture," p. 11.

24 There are, of course, ideological-aesthetic responses to this that define a position of power for the margins. In many cases in popular culture, discourses of authenticity privilege products without "slick production values" and with a "grain" of the undercapitalized production process. Wealthy rockers fly to Jamaica to record in crude studio conditions to obtain an "authentic" sound. Likewise, successful rappers have been known to scour pawn shops for early-model, analog rhythm machines for a tinny, unsophisticated sound.

25 Unsuccessful global corporate naming strategies were enumerated in Naseem Javed, "Brand Names Can Flop on Global Stage," *Toronto Star*, 3 January 1994.

26 Roland Robertson, "Globalization Theory and Civilizational Analysis," *Comparative Civilizations Review* 17 (1991): 20–30.

27 Harvey, *The Condition of Postmodernity*, p. 225.

28 Hall, "The Local and the Global," p. 28.

29 See, for instance, Mariana Torgovnik, *Gone Primitive: Savage Intellects, Modern Lives* (Chicago: University of Chicago Press, 1990), p. 188, where she applies Georg Lukács' concept of "transcendental homelessness" from his *Theory of the Novel*, tr. Anna Bostock (Cambridge, Mass.: M.I.T. Press, 1971 [1920]); or Dean MacCannel's chapter "Modernity and the Production of Touristic Experiences," in *The Tourist: A New Theory of the Leisure Class* (New York: Schocken Books), pp. 17–38.

30 Gage Averill, "Haitian Music in the Global System," in *The Reordering of Culture: Latin America, the Caribbean, and Canada in the Hood*, ed. Alvina Ruprecht and Ceciliana Taiana (Ottawa: Carleton University Press, 1995), pp. 339–362.

31 Julia A. Searles, "Dance Madness: The Commercialization of Lambada and Its Popular Predecessors." Searles analyzes the lambada fad within a history of Latin-inspired dance crazes in the United States and Europe.

32 O'Barr, "The Airbrushing of Culture," p. 4.

33 Ibid., p. 5.

34 Ibid., pp. 14–17.

35 John Tomlinson, *Cultural Imperialism* (Baltimore: Johns Hopkins University Press, 1991), p. 55.

Richard Ohmann **Knowing/Creating Wants**

. . . .

Richard Ohmann is Professor of English at Wesleyan University and former Director of the Center for the Humanities. He is the author of English in America, Politics of Letters, *and* Selling Culture; Magazines, Markets, and Class at the Turn of the Century.

What do culture makers know about us? How can they use that knowledge to anticipate, shape, or create desires in us that will lead to consumption of products and experiences? These questions are as old as mass culture critique, the worry intensifying as techniques of data gathering and analysis have grown more sophisticated. Here is a more-or-less typical judgment, from Erik Larson's *The Naked Consumer*: "the technologies and techniques of mass surveillance allow companies to learn details we never would have told them if asked directly," give them "unprecedented power to muscle in on the 'sacred' corners of our lives . . . ; and to transform them into commodities for subsequent sale, rent, or barter."[1] The author writes mainly about the marketing of household goods, but comments along the way on the power of ZIP-code cluster analysis and scanner-based ratings to scope out the tastes and incomes of radio and TV audiences, and sell them to advertisers.

Mass culture critique brings together vague concerns, some of which are incompatible. Larson's exposé, for instance, expresses alarm at the ability of marketers to know in intimate detail how we differ from one another, the better to target us with socially specific goals. Niche marketing tends to take each habitus[2] as a given. Critique in the Frankfurt School tradition, by contrast, fears the ability of culture makers to level differences in taste, homogenizing all but educated elites into a narcotized mass. The first anxiety concerns the invasion of privacy, the second its effective erasure. Yet both camps share a conviction that advertisers and others in the culture industries can powerfully know what people are like, and so reorganize their consciousness, or at least redirect their acts.

Do culture makers themselves believe they have such powers? Through "surveillance" and analysis, can they dissect people's minds and there implant alien needs and desires? The interviews collected here reveal no such confidence. To be sure, any conclusions drawn from this evidence must be tentative. These informants work in very different industries: managing a chain of hotels is not the same as advertising Coca-Cola or packaging entertainment deals. Our interlocutors also carry out very different tasks within their industries, from creative work to the management of talent to central administration. Some make key decisions about what to produce; most do not. Only a few are close to the apparatus of market research. In addition, our conversations were informal and unschematic. Finally, their academic context — at a Center for the Humanities! — may, along with publicity and critique in recent years of media mergers and centralized control, have prompted modesty in some of our visitors about their exercise of social power. For all these cautions, threads of similarity across many of the interviews may reward examination, and contrast with attitudes of cultural producers at an earlier time.

To begin with, interviewees in businesses that offer a product or service or experience have a good deal of information about who uses and doesn't use it. "Who" translates chiefly into some conventional demographic categories: men and women; adults and children; age cohorts; families and single people (and, in the hotel business, honeymooners); people in different cities or regions or countries; blacks and whites (Latinos would seem to have a more liminal status in market research); people educated to one or another level; people in various income groups and occupations. Although the last two measures have much to do with social class, explicit references to class are casual, as one might expect: the *New York Times* is read by "a major class" (Edmiston: 135); Coca-Cola is "the great middle class" (Herbert: 13). Nor do other categories appear that are more complex, less visible or measurable: conservative and liberal, religious or secular; lesbian and gay or straight (see Kendall: 59). Working classifications build on the sorts of data amassed by the census.

Producers also feel secure in a good deal of knowledge about how much people like and don't like existing products (a movie once it's made [Zelnick: 24], a new song on the playlist [Pearson: 121]); about who will or will not consume them; and about what groups of people want in a product or advertisement (diet drinkers, mainly women, want no calories, and don't care about taste [Herbert: 9]; Europeans want "spectacular bathrooms" in their resort hotels [Sonnabend: 51]; "British women don't want to be talked down to by a little kid" in a Pillsbury commercial [Oakes: 80]). The instruments of knowing range from Coca-Cola's sixteen thousand interviews a year ("We are very, very determined researchers" — Herbert: 6) and Broadcasting Partners' weekly telephone surveys, at one end of a spectrum, to Sonesta's poolside queries and comment cards in hotel rooms or National Public Radio's attention to listeners' freely volunteered criticism. One way or another, our interviewees who are concerned with marketing — not the creative people — rely heavily on such information about consumers' specific likes and tastes.

Beyond these relative certainties, the producers have little faith in research as a guide. Indeed, some — especially but not only in creative phases of the process — are fairly contemptuous of it. Oakes' remark about the Pillsbury doughboy and British women implies that this is the sort of trivial consideration "some market research" can put up as an obstacle. Kendall is openly dismissive: "research is one tool and very limited" (67); "research for the most part is useless and based on self-fulfilling prophecies" (66); it is "the agreed-upon fiction of our industry" (55); "People who do research for a living tell you things like" who stays home which nights of the week (58). The manager of Broadcasting Partners' Michigan station thought audience research a "waste, and had to be pressured into having studies done.[3]

Even those who depend heavily on research see some of it as unreliable. Bennet discovered staffers of NPR accepting the verdict of "derivative, commercial broadcast research," wrongly predicting that NPR listeners wanted classical music, news, and nothing else (170); Herbert thinks "attitudinal" research "thin," and "wouldn't identify it as a success" (14). Similarly, Zelnick says there is "pretty good" research on a film's "playability" (who will and won't like it), but not on its "marketability" (who will go see it); and it is useless to "research concepts" in advance of making a movie, in search of a formula for success: "all you will find out is that they will pick the concept that they are most familiar with. That doesn't tell you anything about making a movie" (24).

A fairly clear boundary appears. Producers can know who consumes a product, in what contexts, and for what purposes; they know whether people like it and perhaps what they like about it; they know a good deal about specific tastes. But they cannot empirically know much that is useful about people's deeper needs, their unmet wants, the ways they understand their lives and create meaning around consumption. This means that producers cannot empirically know what *new* films or television shows will succeed, what resort hotels to build, what new musical styles are likely to catch on, how to "reposition" a magazine and attract a new audience (see Edmiston: 136, 138–39). They do not believe they can create needs and desires. The one time that issue explicitly arises in the interviews gathered here, Dennis Robinson will allow that cultural producers can create a generalized need — for example, to "look good" — and shape it, but rejects the possibility of creating needs where none exist, or of creating markets, or of creating specific needs.

Producers often decline to venture into this unresearchable territory; they may do what seems safe: remake essentially the same movies and TV series that have worked in the past, stay with tried and true formats and styles. It is obvious to all students of commercial culture and to our informants that most decisions are made in precisely this way — hence the repetitiveness of what producers offer to the public. That repetitiveness can be read sympathetically, as giving sovereign consumers the dependable satisfactions they want, or it can be read critically, as manipulative, stupefying, antithetical to creativity, destructive of independent thought, and so on. Though not adherents of the Frankfurt School critique, the producers with whom we talked share some of its disdain for repetition: for the "scared and insecure" network executives who "try and clone" previous hit shows; for studios that would make movies by "formula"; for movie scripts written on spec that are "exactly like something else that had just been a huge success"; for ad agencies that "don't want to rock the boat" by departing from "traditions in product categories" or creative "stereotypes"; for "the need for audience homogeneity" and the "incredible narrowness" it produces in "use of the radio broadcast spectrum"; for the need to "maximize" the audience, which forbids giving listeners to adult black radio stations music they say they don't want, like jazz; for hotel "franchises" that "get chain feed" and offer travelers entirely predictable experiences (Kendall: 62; Zelnick: 19; Traube: 101; Oakes: 81; Bennet: 168; Pearson: 115; Sonnabend: 48). Even those whose businesses demand repetition would prefer freshness and variety.

Most believe they achieve it, and all see their work as requiring creativity. Research may be its foundation, but research cannot by itself ensure correct decisions. Herbert and his colleagues at Coca-Cola "read the research right" on what people wanted in a diet drink; on another occasion they "read the research wrongly" in concluding that "the American palate was going for lighter, sweeter drinks" (10, 16). Enormous consequences — the success of Tab and the failure of New Coca-Cola — followed from acts of interpretation for which no rules offered guidance. Pearson, whose company also does intensive audience research, speaks of a partner's strength in "the structuring and interpretation" of it. This man "is like a conductor with a score, and his score is the research, the raw data. He is very good at hearing in his head what the research is saying the audience wants to hear. That's more of a gift than a skill, frankly" (124). Knowing what the Chicago or Charlotte audience will want in music is a matter of "taste" and "judgment"; the Charlotte music director is "very intuitive" (121, 123, 124).

Such language often comes forward when producers tell how they decide what audiences will want and like. People on the business side of cultural production, who tend to assign research some weight, join with people on the creative side in privileging intuition when it comes to *interpreting* research and basing decisions upon it. Bennet rejected the request of NPR's research department to do electronic testing on candidates for a job as host of a show: "We're not going to hire people that way around here. We value intuition" (176). Picking art for Sonesta hotels is "intuitive" (51); Kendall says the networks rely on research "because they have no faith in their own guts, in creativity, or in anything else" (66); Traube says agents "have to think that they can recognize" the potential to be "a great performer": "Sometimes you just know" (100, 99); Zelnick trusts neither research nor formulas in choosing among proposals for movies: "it all comes down to reading a script and making a decision" (19). Similarly, intuition seems to underwrite assertions about the more basic desires of audiences, as opposed to superficial preferences. Research may identify an aversion to rap or a taste for sweetness in soft drinks, but when the producers talk about the fantasies of travelers or sports fans or magazine readers or kids, they call up resources of informal knowledge no different from yours or mine.

And in fact there is often an etiolation of difference among people, at this level of conjecture about desire and satisfaction. Doubtless, most would second Robinson's warning that "you don't do marketing research on yourself: 'This appeals to me, therefore it is going to appeal to everyone in America'" (159). Yet much of the talk about people's deepest needs and about what will respond to them reaches toward affinities that transcend the demographic particulars and that do indeed bring producers and consumers into equivalence. Robinson himself thinks of sport as "the great equalizer" (153, 161), and posits a human need for "affiliation," for feeling "like part of a group," for having "pride in something," that involves people in sports "no matter what socioeconomic class they belong to" (153).

Those who produce for large audiences, especially, tend to universalize. Zelnick holds that "people smell quality," that they "tend to agree on what a good movie or a bad movie is," that "people go to good movies," that "you get the broadest possible market by making movies that are great stories" (22, 24, 23). Kendall is explicit about this principle: "What television does best is finding what is universal. Even though people have different values, there are some common things," things "that are universal to a family or a workplace" (59, 63). Oakes knows what adults want that is different from what children want (82); Sonnabend knows that "image is important" to people when they travel (46); Herbert speaks of "the mind of the consumer" (16), Traube of spotting talent that all will recognize (99–100). Even those with narrower audiences may lay claim to "a sense of what is going on in the public mind" (Bennet: 173), or explain fragmentation itself by a generalization about Americans today: "Now each person thinks of himself or herself as virtually unique" (Edmiston: 136). Pearson, acknowledging that his company furthers the process of division into niche audiences, nonetheless wistfully thinks there are "ways to nurture cultural awareness in the broadest possible sense" (129). The yearning for commonalities is strong, as is, perhaps, the wish to make significant judgments and deploy insights, beyond what the research authorizes.

Be that as it may, the pattern I have sketched from these interviews is clear enough. With the aid of empirical instruments they think reliable, producers know a good deal about the habits, tastes, and preferences of demographic groups. For more doubtful knowledge of people's deeper needs and values they rely on intuition, which opens out for some into beliefs about the makeup and desires of people (or of Americans, or of adults, etc.) in general. I note that between the first area of knowledge and the second lies another wide range of activity and experience that also figures but little in the producers' practical understanding: the interests and principles of citizens, conflicts among groups, the ways those conflicts play out in historical process, the differences of power across social groups that give decisive historical agency to some, to others very little. In short, a silence closes over much of the social realm — that which we may call "politics," in the broadest sense of the term (though of course the producers speak much of the politics internal to their own organizations and industries). National Public Radio, one of two nonprofit organizations represented here, has an explicitly political "mission," which includes transforming its audience by educating it. Otherwise, the political enters these conversations occasionally as a concern about diminution of the public sphere or of cultural common ground (Edmiston, Pearson), against which these people feel powerless to act, *as* cultural producers. More frequently, they represent politics as a process occurring elsewhere, to which their work only responds. They don't create values, opinions, trends, needs, and so on, but reflect them. This reticence has nothing to do with the commitments of individual producers, many of whom take a lively interest in social and political process. It follows instead from the business imperative that requires them to think and know about us *as consumers*, faced with an array of choices in well established markets.

That imperative partially explains, I think, not only the muting of comment on social progress and conflict, but the narrowness of claims to knowledge about people, and the virtual absence of claims to power over our needs and desires. Yet just a hundred years ago, when cultural producers first organized millions of people around the country into audiences and groups of consumers, thus creating the system within which our informants now work, no such modesty was in evidence. I will set up the contrast, then comment upon it.

In the late 1890s, several monthly magazines attained circulations of five hundred thousand to a million, far larger than any had reached before. At ten cents an issue or a dollar a year, they sold for less than it cost to produce and distribute them. Publishers made their profits by selling the attention of readers to advertisers, with the price of ad space directly proportional to circulation. Advertising agencies, previously little more than space brokers, mediated this process by helping invent brand names and logos, devising slogans, writing copy, providing visuals, doing market research. In short, they first assumed their modern form and functions at this time. Together with the magazine editors and publishers they created what I believe to have been the first fully developed, national culture industry.[4] A historically new social relation was at its core: one group of businessmen (publishers) gathered large audiences and sold their attention through a second group (advertising agents), which organized and directed that attention to commodities produced and offered for sale by a third group (manufacturers).

As before, I examine this as a relation of *knowing*. Magazine editors claimed to know what articles, stories, illustrations, and features would draw a large group of readers able and ready to buy brand-name products. Ad agents claimed to know what words and images would make those products attractive to a particular audience, and they claimed to have useful knowledge about the habits and wants of various groups. Market research, new (and primitive) at this time, backed up the claim. It began plainly enough with a study the N. W. Ayer agency did in 1879 for a threshing machine company whose account it was trying to win. By 1900, agencies were claiming also to understand human nature — or rather, consumer taste. About it there was little consensus; where some saw rational *homo economicus* others saw emotional, "grown-up children" or "fools" driven by "credulity" and "*gullibility.*"[5] But a conversation had begun in which some people theorized others, behind professional doors and with no riposte from those being theorized. This relation is characteristic of the twentieth-century politics of social knowing.

Of more interest than the ad men's debate over human nature is their effort to identify and characterize particular groups. Already in the 1890s, agents sought to know the habits and tastes of old and young, urban and rural, male and female people. (Not black and white; African Americans had too little money to figure as significant consumers, and to be worth figuring out.) As an example, take social class, of which ad men offered an understanding as a key part of their expertise, far more explicitly than did our interlocutors at Wesleyan.

J. Walter Thompson, especially, insisted on the centrality of class. That was natural since he trafficked in magazines, and since magazines far more than newspapers or billboards aimed at particular social groups. He instructed potential clients that they must "know how people live . . . You must understand exactly how a man can support a family on ten dollars a week — and you must also know how a thousand-dollar-a-month family spends its income." Such claims made elementary business sense, for an agency specializing in consumer groups. Thompson had to know which magazines reached people of each sort, in order to promise: "We can insure that automobiles shall not be extensively advertised to the working classes nor bargain jackknives to the well-to-do" (this was in 1901). He used these kinds of knowledge early on to promote his lists of magazines. He divided farmers into "two classes — one a shiftless ne'er-do-well; the other the bright, sharp, shrewd, and intelligent man, who is wide awake to his own interests" (1888?). The latter, Thompson went on, bought the same manufactured goods as city people, and could be reached through the agricultural magazines to which he subscribed. For an affluent audience, Thompson recommended trade journals: "the combined wealth of the individual readers of Trade Journals exceeds that of [sic] the entire wealth of the balance of [the country's] population" (1889). He understood well the dollar value to advertisers of a class analysis: a circulation of a hundred thousand in a

sensational, trashy weekly story paper is not worth, to a legitimate advertiser, one-tenth as much as an equal circulation in a journal of a high character, that has entrance into the *better class* homes . . . The great bulk of business, aside from the necessaries of life, comes from people of moderate or independent means associated with at least fair refinement and culture . . . Hence, judicious advertisers seek to reach people having both TASTE for their goods and the MEANS to gratify it.

Could there be a clearer articulation of class consciousness right down to typographical emphasis? — and precisely at the point where the agent invited manufacturers to conceive and plan informed campaigns.[6]

Others in the trade wrote similarly. Earnest Elmo Calkins made a far more elaborate analysis of class and buying habits than Thompson, arguing, among other things, that it was pointless to aim ads at the Morgans, Astors, and Goulds, because their *servants* decided which soap and cereal to buy. He, too, connected the analysis to specific magazine audiences, setting off the *Ladies' Home Journal* against *Comfort*, for instance, as representing "two extreme types of magazine and their respective constituencies; the one, the highest type of an advertising medium, . . . reaching well-educated, well-to-do, intelligent American women; the other, poorly printed, . . . and reaching an uneducated and credulous class." The latter, nonetheless, was worth reaching: "Its readers buy only the most inexpensive things, but large numbers of them do buy, so that the space is worth what it costs the advertisers."[7] Class was a matter of practical knowledge, not high theory.

For magazine publishers, too: they collaborated with agents in this anatomy of the public along class lines. That Calkins should contrast the two magazines thus, in 1905, was no accident: Cyrus Curtis fought a relentless battle from the 1880s on, both to secure for the *Journal* a toney readership and (probably with a good deal of hyperbole) to convince advertisers that he had it. He wrote to doubters that most *Journal* readers were suburbanites, churchgoers, professionals.[8] Other publishers, some with an initial advantage over Curtis, also profiled their readerships in class terms. The *Atlantic* claimed to reach "persons of highest cultivation"; the *Forum*, readers of "culture, taste, enterprise, and the means to gratify their many wants"; the *Illustrated Home Monthly*, "intelligent, cultivated, and well-to-do families."[9] Later, some undertook research to back up such claims. *Ladies' World* photographed the homes of subscribers in a few towns, and showed the photos to advertisers. *McClure's* listed all its subscribers in Cleveland and found out their occupations, to show "how many of the professional class, how many of the leisure class and how many of the working class" read the magazine.[10] Most publishers identified their audience as "the professional class," for obvious reasons, but not all did. *Frank Leslie's Popular Monthly* said it reached the "great masses"; *Woman's Argosy* may have been putting the same case more politely in saying it entered "the homes of the people."[11]

There was of course some confusion, along with much puffery, in such talk. Thompson held in 1909 both that the ten-cent magazine "appealed to the masses" and that it was "high class" (*Blue Book*, as reprinted in *Advertis-*

ing Age, 7 December 1964, p. 20). But I hope I have shown that an energetic discourse of social class developed right along with modern advertising. As early as 1891, *Printers' Ink* ran articles with titles like "The Class of Readers Addressed" (15 April), and stated in an editorial that agents could "cover almost any particular class or locality" (25 November). This should not surprise anyone; consumption is class specific, and advertising had to be so, too. It had to know, or claim to know, who read what, who bought what, and how class figured in desire. (Walter D. Scott, author of the first book on the psychology of advertising, included the desire to be like more privileged people in his 1903 list of ruling interests and motives, along with health, possessiveness, and so on). Ad men both took class as a given, and helped to construct it, as they segmented audiences and spotted likely markets.

Not only did they profess dependable knowledge of class and desire; unlike our interlocutors they claimed the ability to create desire. Theirs was a historically new project that, unlike management of the work force, did not allow direct command and discipline as means of shaping people's conduct. How do you get people to do something they did not intend to do, yet without exercising power over them? Change their intention. If the desired act is purchase of a product, you must create a want for it. Frank Presbrey, the first major historian of advertising, wrote in 1929 that by 1905 agents and manufacturers alike realized that progress in national brand advertising lay not mainly in selling things "already established in the mind as wants," as was and is the case with much local advertising; rather, it entailed "creating wide desire for articles of utility or pleasure which among the majority of people would not be regarded as needs until advertising pictured their desirability."[12]

Much testimony from the period supports his point; the pioneers of national brand advertising were clear about the need to alter consciousness in this way, and confident in their ability to do so:

- Advertising is a "powerful force whereby the advertiser creates a demand for a given article in the minds of a great many people or arouses the demand that is already there in latent form" (Calkins and Holden, *Modern Advertising*, p. 4).
- Advertising aims to teach people that they have wants, which they did not realize before, and where such wants can be best supplied. If the merchant were to wait nowadays for people to find out for themselves that they needed his wares he would have plenty of leisure and plenty of nothing else" (*The Thompson Red Book on Advertising*, 1901, p. 12).

- [The advertiser] takes the vague discontent or need of the public, changes it into want, and the want into effectual desire (Emerson P. Harris, 1893; quoted by Presbrey, *History and Development*, p. 347).
- "[My aim in advertising] was to do educational and constructive work so as to awaken an interest in and create a demand for cereals where none existed" (Henry P. Crowell, on his success with Quaker Oats[13]).
- "The modern advertisement is not intended for the man who wants the thing already. It is for the one who don't [sic] in order to make him" (Edwin G. Dexter, Professor of Education at the University of Illinois, in *Printers' Ink*, 1904).[14]
- Advertising is "literature which compels Action . . . [and] changes the mind of millions at will" (Lord & Thomas, Chicago ad agency, 1911; quoted by Pope, *Making of Modern Advertising*, p. 13).
- "Advertising modifies the course of a people's daily thoughts" (Calkins and Holden, *Modern Advertising*, p. 7).
- Advertising is "the artificial creation and stimulation of wants" (N. A. Lindsey, *Printers' Ink*, 25 November 1891, p. 623).

Some of these writers qualified their claims in various ways, but evidently they all thought they could reach into the "mass mind," and alter its desires. Could they? In certain circumstances they could and did, as is proven by the campaigns that established needs for packaged crackers (Nabisco), safety razors (Gillette), brand-name soap (Pears', Ivory), breakfast cereal (Quaker Oats, Cream of Wheat), and many other products. Of course there were failures, too, and my main point is that these cultural producers had entered into a new social relation with the public, one in which, with ever-growing resources, they bent their efforts to creation of wants, and believed they could accomplish that transformation in audiences whose psyches and social motivations they understood.

That social relation, a hundred years later, is still much the same for culture industries like newspapers, magazines, TV, and radio that bring audiences into the presence of advertising's words, sounds, and images. The other culture industries — movies, books, video, sports, etc. — are also in the business of assembling audiences, and are also in one way or another closely bound up with advertising. As the whole system of media and entertainments has grown in complexity and ubiquity, its practitioners have far surpassed Edward Bok and J. Walter Thompson in the sophistication of method they bring to the study of audiences, and of consumers generally. Yet those with whom we spoke seem to think they have far less power to know and change people than was claimed by their turn-of-the-century counterparts. Why this decline in boldness, in spite of a great increase in means, sophistication, and share of GNP? Granting the penchant of frontiersmen for tall tales and rodomontade, and granting also that the very amassing of technique of which our interlocutors are beneficiaries may have fostered a skeptical reserve about its capabilities, and granting also that the necessity and power of marketing are everywhere accepted now, so that it would be redundant to insist on that power: still, the slim evidence of our interviews does point toward a shift in attitude. I offer three historical conjectures that may help account for it.

First, advertising agencies did take part in the successful launching of very many new, brand-named products during the fifteen years or so after 1890, and in the establishment of many product *categories* such as those mentioned earlier: breakfast cereal, packaged crackers, bar soap, safety razors — and also soft drinks (including Coca-Cola), cigarettes, cleaning powders, dentrifices, bicycles, automobiles, cameras, canned foods, and so on. One often hears how few new products make it today (Schudson *Advertising*, p. 37, cites estimates of from 10 to 23 percent). Not even rough estimates are available for the 1890s, but I feel certain that the rate of success was much higher then, and many of the successes more spectacular. They built whole new corporations, and made giants out of faltering ones. The same holds for the magazines that carried the ads — the 1890s equivalents of television. They gathered national audiences of unprecedented size very quickly, and not by deftly occupying niches of demography and desire. The four leaders on which I have focused my own study (*McClure's, Munsey's, Cosmopolitan, Ladies' Home Journal*) opened broad swaths among the middle class, building on very different formulas, or no formula at all beyond a certain buoyant triumphalism. It must have seemed in those fresh days of mass culture that almost any idea would work, if pursued with zeal. Pioneers of the consciousness industry had tangible results to fuel their sense of mastery.

Second, their new practices accumulated into a new economic system, which we now refer to as advanced capitalism, consumer capitalism, corporate capitalism, monopoly capitalism, and so on. The names reflect different emphases and understandings but designate the same set of transformations: the rise to dominance of large, vertically integrated corporations; intensification of and control over the sales effort; elaboration of media and popular genres into a national mass culture; the proliferation of brand-name consumer goods and their auras; the commodification of entertainment, of leisure, and of audiences. Some entrepreneurs understood clearly what they were helping to create, as did J. Walter Thompson, who wrote in 1909 that advertising was "part of the existing commercial universe," and "could not be abolished or reduced to any noticeable degree without changing the entire economic aspect of life."[15] He noted that capitalism's earlier work had solved the problem of production but not that of distribution, which had been brought under control only by the new system of brand names and advertising.[16] Few had the prophetic vision of Thompson, but many knew they were participating in deep social change, not just individual success stories. They would not have described their work as political, but they knew they were remaking the social order. Theirs was a justified feeling of historical agency not reasonably available to cultural producers today, within a system fully in place yet riddled with competitive uncertainties. (Or perhaps the latter *are* midwifing the birth of a new, global, information-based "regime of flexible accumulation"; if so, that seems not a matter of conscious intent or vision. See the essays by Averill and Curtin in this volume.)

Third, tectonic plate shifts of the 1890s included the consolidation and empowerment of a new, professional-managerial class. Most pioneers of advertising and magazining were of or close to its ranks; equally important, most magazine readers and users of name-brand commodities who constituted the base of this economic movement were of, or aspirants to, the new middle class. If I am right, it is reasonable to suppose that the confidence of cultural producers around 1900 rose partly from their participation in the making of an influential class, and their felt affinities with others who shared its modernizing zeal. Certainly the "needs" they felt able to foster and shape were at a deeper level and in specific ways historically produced — the needs of suburban and urban people, separated from the means of agricultural as well as industrial production, dependent on commodities, and eager to embrace an efficient, progressive, healthy way of life, represented to them also as stylish and enviable in the advertising pages of magazines that celebrated their class outlook and identified it with the well being of the whole society. No such closeness of social location binds most of the cultural producers who joined in conversations with us to their segmented but now universal audience (Bennet of NPR and Sonnabend of Sonesta may be exceptions). Nor is it possible to understand their work as contributing to a common project of class formation that builds upon and throws up new, historically produced, common needs.

If cultural producers generally were to share the reserve displayed by our

visitors, should that fact allay the concerns about surveillance and manipulative power with which this essay began? To some degree, yes, in my
view—at least insofar as the fear is of corporate big brothers gathering
banks of information about us individually and collectively, and able to
target us with smart-bomb accuracy. Apart from the annoyance of junk mail
and the quite genuine erosion of privacy, this seems to me the wrong
anxiety for people who (like the editors of this volume and like many of our
visitors) cherish democratic hopes. To be sure, capital and the profit motive
will intrude on private lives with whatever means can be devised and kept
legal. But the main impediment to democracy thrown up by commercial
culture is probably the basic relation of unequal knowing and selling established a century ago, and so deeply familiar now that its masters have far less
sense of mastery.

Notes

1　Erik Larson, *The Naked Consumer; How Our Private Lives Become Public Commodities* (New York: Henry Holt, 1992), p. 208.

2　Pierre Bourdieu's term, from *Distinction; A Social Critique of the Judgement of
Taste*, trans. Richard Nice (Cambridge, Mass.: Harvard University Press, 1984).

3　Such skepticism is well documented in, for instance, Todd Gitlin, *Inside Prime
Time* (New York: Pantheon, 1983), pp. 42–46; Michael Schudson, *Advertising,
The Uneasy Persuasion; Its Dubious Impact on American Society* (New York: Basic
Books, 1984), pp. 56–58; and Herbert J. Gans, *Deciding What's News; A Study of
CBS Evening News, NBC Nightly News, Newsweek, and Time* (New York: Pan-
theon, 1979), pp. 230–236.

4　For an argument in support of this claim, see my *Selling Culture* (London: Verso,
1996), from which parts of the following pages are excerpted.

5　Merle Curti traces shifts between these poles from 1890 to 1950 in "The Changing Concept of 'Human Nature' in the Literature of American Advertising,"
Business History Review, 41 (Winter 1967). The contemptuous phrases are quoted
by Daniel Pope in *The Making of Modern Advertising* (New York: Basic Books,
1983), pp. 246–247.

6　*The J. Walter Thompson Book* (1909), p. 43; *The Thompson Blue Book on Advertising*
(1901), p. 8; *The Red Ear* (1888?), p. 4; *Direct Acting * High Pressure* (1889);
J. Walter Thompson's Illustrated Catalogue of Magazines (1889), p. 12. These docu-
ments are in the J. Walter Thompson Company Archives at the John W. Hart-
man Center for Sales, Advertising and Marketing History, Special Collections
Library, Duke University, Durham, N.C., and are quoted with permission.

7 Earnest Elmo Calkins and Ralph Holden, *Modern Advertising* (New York: D. Appleton and Company, 1912), p. 73. Calkins wrote the book in 1905, adding Holden's name to publicize their agency.

8 Salme Harju Steinberg, *Reformer in the Marketplace* (Baton Rouge: Louisiana State University Press, 1979), pp. 3–5. Bok supported this effort by trying always to edit the magazine "on a slightly higher plane" than his estimate of readers' actual class and culture. See *The Americanization of Edward Bok: The Autobiography of a Dutch Boy Fifty Years After* (New York: Charles Scribner's Sons, 1921), p. 165. In 1915 he spoke quite precisely of his target audiences: first, families with incomes between $1,200 and $2,500; secondarily, those with from $3,000 to $5,000 a year (Steinberg, pp. 6–7).

9 Ads in *J. Walter Thompson's Illustrated Catalogue* (1887), pp. 40, 48, 56.

10 Calkins and Holden, *Modern Advertising*, p. 291.

11 Ads in *Thompson's Illustrated Catalogue*, pp. 38, 64.

12 Frank Presbrey, *The History and Development of Advertising* (New York: Doubleday, Doran, 1929), p. 526.

13 Quoted in Arthur F. Marquette, *Brands, Trademarks and Good Will; The Story of the Quaker Oats Company* (New York: McGraw-Hill, 1967), p. 67.

14 Quoted in Daniel Pope, *The Making of Modern Advertising* (New York: Basic Books, 1983), p. 68.

15 *The J. Walter Thompson Book* (1909).

16 *Advertising as a Selling Force* (1909). This document is in the J. Walter Thompson Company Archives, as described in note 6.

David Shumway **Objectivity, Bias, Censorship**

David Shumway is Associate Professor of Literary and Cultural Studies in the English Department of Carnegie Mellon University. He has written Michel Foucault *(Twayne 1989, University Press of Virginia, 1992) and* Creating American Civilization: A Genealogy of American Literature as an Academic Field *(University of Minnesota Press, 1994). He is currently working on a book on the discourses of romantic love (film, fiction, songs, self-help, etc.) in twentieth-century America and on a book of readings of major rock'n'roll performers from Elvis Presley to Bruce Springsteen.*

Most of us probably take for granted that there has always been news and are likely to recall the town crier as evidence. While the word *news* dates from the sixteenth century, what we think of as "the news" is in fact a relatively recent invention, coming into being only in the nineteenth century and gaining hegemony within journalism only toward the end of that century when journalism became professionalized and the culture industry was born. The news entails the idea that reality is being reflected or reported; opinion is not news. Many believe that the problem of media bias is a new one, or at least that it has been greatly exaggerated by the decline in the number of newspapers. Thus right-wing critics Bozell and Baker express nostalgia for the days when the *Daily Democrat* and the *Daily Republican* would take different sides on issues, and a reader could consult both papers "and figure out what was *really* happening."[1] While there may have been somewhat greater diversity of opinion in the heyday of newspapers, their insistence on presenting the news meant that significantly different perspectives were rare. Then as now, the presses were owned by rich individuals and corporations and the reality that newspapers reflected was theirs, colored to some extent by other perspectives needed to make the news salable to those who were not of that class. Nowadays, critics on both the left and the right dismiss the idea of journalistic objectivity, but, as I will argue, the claim of objectivity or freedom from bias is entailed in the news as a consumer good. Because of this, the charge of bias is an effective one, but it is also spurious. The question is not whether some partial or political conception of reality will dominate the news, but which. Both right- and left-wing critics struggle to achieve influence for their positions by the charge of bias. Such charges have also been leveled at the entertainment media. Our informants in the interviews contained herein provide useful clues to help us understand how the culture industry itself conceives of objectivity, bias, and censorship. Each term is in fact used to defend the industry against various challenges to its ability to make profitable commodities, even as it appears to be defending truth and freedom.

The term *objectivity* becomes common in English only in the late nineteenth century as the translation of the German *objektivität*. Though objectivity had been used in English since the seventeenth century, as a term for "representation of 'the actual facts,' uncolored by bias or preference — its appearance in English does not date before the late nineteenth century."[2] The importation of objectivity into American English reflects a number of cultural conditions of the period, including the development of the American research university, the powerful influence of German scholarship, and the popular worship of science. Interestingly, however, the term was not much used in connection with newspapers, even though late-nineteenth-century newspapers were obsessed with presenting the facts and avoiding opinions.

According to Michael Schudson, the first newspapers to claim to present "just the facts" were the penny papers of the 1830s, which "invented the modern concept of 'news.' "[3] Prior to that time, newspapers were not only associated with political parties; they were commonly subsidized by them. Coexisting with these party papers were commercial papers, which contained mainly advertising and business information. Both kinds of papers were priced beyond the means of most citizens. The penny papers not only sold for a penny rather than six cents a copy, but they were hawked in the streets rather than sold by annual subscription. Their circulations quickly dwarfed those of the older papers. The penny papers thus reflect the market revolution of the Jacksonian era in American history. Unlike earlier news papers, the penny papers claimed political independence. This was essential to their attempt to sell a new commodity, the news, which was to claim to be information of universal value. As purveyors of news, the penny papers claimed to present facts and not opinions because opinions had relatively limited exchange value. In order to provide such factual reports, the penny papers hired the first reporters, replacing the opinionated contributors who previously did the bulk of newspaper writing. The other papers made political debate or commercial information available to the elites that could use this discourse. The penny papers created what they claimed was a mirror of social reality, something everyone could use. They thus became the first mass medium.

The modern profession of journalism emerged at about the same time as consumer capitalism in the late nineteenth century. This new form of capitalism determined that "news" rather than opinion would henceforth define the newspaper. But the theoretical opposition of fact and value that defines objectivity was still not to be found in journalism. The reporters of the Progressive era "understood facts to provide moral direction of themselves and prided themselves that their own moral precepts grew naturally out of their association with the real world" (Schudson, *Discovering the News*; p. 87). For-profit newspapers of this era prided themselves on the facts they presented, but they did not all present the facts in the same way. The newspapers of Hearst, Pulitzer, and others of that style presented their facts in the form of entertaining stories. Such papers had by far the largest circulations of the era, but it was during this period that the *New York Times* developed with the aim of providing information rather than entertainment. It was the *Times'* conception of journalism that came to be associated with fairness, accuracy, disinterest: in a word, objectivity, though it was still not *the* word at this time. It is worth looking at Adolph Ochs' statement of principles to understand what journalism as information meant:

> It will be my earnest aim that *The New-York Times* gives the news, all the news, in concise and attractive form, in language that is parliamentary in good society . . . ; to give the news impartially, without fear or favor, regardless of any party, sect, or interest involved; to make of the columns of *The New-York Times* a forum for the consideration of all questions of public importance, and to the end to invite intelligent discussion from all shades of opinion.
>
> There will be no radical changes in the personnel of the present efficient staff . . . nor will there be a departure from the general tone and character and policies pursued with relation to public questions that have distinguished *The New-York Times* as a nonpartisan newspaper — unless it be, if possible, to intensify its devotion to the cause of sound money and tariff reform, opposition to wastefulness and peculation in administering the public affairs, and in its advocacy of the lowest tax consistent with good government, and no more government than is absolutely necessary to protect society, maintain individual vested rights and assure the free exercise of a sound conscience.[4]

This statement announces the adherence of the *New York Times* to what we would now call the conventions of objectivity, but it also reveals in the very next paragraph that the ideal was never meant to be taken literally, that information journalism was never assumed to mean value neutrality in the sense that the positivists demanded. The second paragraph tells us what positions the *Times* assumes as above or beneath partisanship. It is no co-incidence that these positions coincide entirely with the emerging corpora-tism of the Progressive era. They are the ground of agreement against which partisan differences stand out. The claims of the *New York Times* to present the news impartially would not have been understood to be under-cut by the statement of its political position, but that is because the news-paper's readers would have largely shared its assumptions.

According to Schudson, it was after World War I that *objectivity* first came into vocabulary of journalism. It did so as a response to skepticism rather than as a result of faith in facts. "While objectivity, by the 1930s, was an articulate professional value in journalism, it was one that seemed to disintegrate as soon as it was formulated. It became an ideal in journal-ism . . . precisely *because* subjectivity had come to be regarded as inevitable" (*Discovering the News*, p. 157). Schudson's point is that "relativism, a belief in the arbitrariness of values" is what the debate over objectivity assumed (p. 158). This analysis explains why it is that *objectivity* gets taken up as the name for the ideal of impartiality. The major threat to accurate reporting is not seen as stemming from interests, but rather from the inadequacies of the reporter. Just as modern science enacted safeguards against the subjec-tivity of the observer or experimenter, journalists sought ways to regulate their subjectivity. As one study proclaimed, "Since absolute objectivity in journalism is impossible, the social heritage, the 'professional reflexes,' the individual temperament, and the economic status of reporters assume fun-damental significance."[5] What this says, without saying it, is that it is the right kind of subjectivity that matters, one produced by social, professional, and economic status as well as by individual temperament. The effects of interests are acknowledged here, but only insofar as they may influence individuals. According to Schiller, this conception of objectivity served a distinct ideological function: "Subordination of journalists to an explicit objectivity established a new legitimacy for the entire news-gathering sys-tem . . . By charging individual journalists with responsibility for mistakes and prejudices, the systematic biases of news-gathering organizations . . . might be implicitly avoided and displaced" (*Objectivity and the News*, pp. 194–195).

While public opinion polls show that a large percentage of the popula-tion believes the news media to be biased, people also continue to believe in objectivity in the sense that they value facts about the world that they distinguish from mere opinion.[6] Moreover, they continue to consume news products on the assumption that such products do provide such facts. Objectivity is desired of the news media, but it is an obscure object of desire. Consumers confuse the reasonable acceptance of objectivity as a regulative ideal — which makes the news subject to standards of accuracy and provides for the possibility of rational debate — with objectivity as an attainable state. The claim to objectivity "ostensibly precludes the very presence of conventions and thus masks the patterned structure of news: it is an invisible frame" (Schiller, *Objectivity and the News*, p. 2). What is typically not understood is that journalistic objectivity itself can only be a set of conventions or rules that, far from guaranteeing the truth of what is reported, at best merely guard against specific sources of bias. In modern journalism, these can be boiled down to two: "*Depersonalization* demands that reporters refrain from inserting into the news their own ideological or substantive evaluations of officials, ideas, or groups. *Balance* aims for neutrality. It requires that reporters present the views of legitimate spokespersons of the conflicting sides in any significant dispute, and provide both sides with roughly equivalent attention."[7] Douglas Bennet invokes the balance convention when he denies bias against David Duke's point of view: "I would hope that David Duke would be covered no less sympathetically than any other candidate for public office. We struggle very hard to be sure that is true. You've heard more non-primary-party candidates on our air — they got their say, even if they didn't get covered as much as the major candidates" (173). In fact, Bennet claims greater objectivity for NPR by its including more spokespersons within the realm of the legitimate. The depersonalization convention is implicit in Bennet's dismissal of those who seek to discover bias by looking "at the age, sex and state of birth of our commentators: it doesn't prove much that Bob Edwards actually isn't from Washington, D.C." (174). Journalists and the public accept objectivity conventions as necessary controls upon bias, though the profession and public differ over the degree to which this control succeeds.

When Bennet was asked if NPR's news had a bias of any kind, he replied, "We struggle not to have bias. We struggle for objectivity, we struggle for breadth" (172). We see here in the repetition of the word *struggle* an acknowledgment of the impossibility of absolute objectivity, but there is also an affirmation of objectivity as something more than a regulative ideal. As he elaborates later, "I don't know that the world we are portraying is different from the world that is really there," but he allows that "We are portraying it — there is some shorthand involved in that" (174). Bennet thus believes that although NPR news is not reality itself, it is an objective representation of reality. Bennet, as a purveyor of news, has to believe this for the product "news" derives its value as such a representation. There is then a conflict in Bennet's discourse between a general acceptance that objectivity is impossible and the need to claim objectivity in order to be considered "news."

This conflict is behind the paradoxical fact that the public expects objectivity from the news media but also knows that it can't get it. The news not only claims objectivity, but it reinforces the claim by the very regularity and repetition with which the news is conveyed. To reject the view that the news represents reality is risky because the news is for many the standard by which reality is judged. And yet, a majority consistently believe that the media are biased. Bennet attributes this to the condition of mediation: "People view media as inherently prone to bias, unless it's C-SPAN or something, because they are intermediaries. Who knows what the intermediary may have in mind? Who knows whether that reporter is interpreting the event properly? So you start out with a degree of skepticism" (172). What this assumes, however, is that an unproblematic reality exists out there that each of us could know objectively if only we did not have to rely on misleading representations. The idea of bias as it is usually invoked entails this assumption. The term *bias* dates in English from the sixteenth century when it was borrowed from the game of bowls to mean an inclination, leaning, bent, disposition to, or prejudice. While many of these synonyms are value neutral — prejudice being the major exception — the *Oxford English Dictionary* examples suggest that bias has long had a bad reputation. In Holinshed (1577), for example, we find "They cease their crueltie for a time, but within a-while after fall to their bloudie bias." Blackstone (1768) tells us that "The law does not suppose a possibility of biass or favour in a judge." In 1662 it was possible to ask "if he was a Biassed or Partiall writer." Why does *bias* have a longer history than its opposite term? Because it has long been assumed that self-interest, invincible ignorance, or natural predisposition could cause individuals to distort reality or miss the truth. Previously, however, reality and truth were held to be ultimately guaranteed by God or other transcendental support. In this conception, it was possible to be unbiased. Objectivity came to be opposed to bias only when skeptical science became the privileged model of truth, and bias came to be regarded as inevitable.

As we saw, however, this inevitable bias was first associated with the inherent subjectivity of individual reporters. This conception did not entail the assumption of systematic bias, for individual reporters presumably had different political positions, class backgrounds, and idiosyncracies such that their biases would differ. Recent critique of the media, however, has alleged a systematic bias. The most well-known charge, familiar since Vice-President Spiro Agnew made it a personal hobbyhorse in the 1970s, is that the media have a liberal bias.[8] There is also a left-wing critique that holds that the media are biased in favor of capitalism in general and of corporate interests in particular. This critique may also note nationalist and statist biases.[9] What is interesting about these two critiques is that they are not necessarily mutually exclusive. While the two critiques are likely to clash over particulars, there is no logical reason why the media could not be at the same time liberal and procapitalist, procorporate, nationalist, and statist. Ironically, the familiarity of the Right's critique of the media is a result of the media themselves, which have given it extensive coverage while all but ignoring the Left's critique. On the one hand, this fact is evidence for the Left that the media are biased in favor of the political and economic power of the Right. On the other hand, the coverage of the Right's critique ought to mitigate the complaint, but it never even seems to be acknowledged in right-wing accounts. This suggests that the Right is not really interested whether the media observe the objectivity conventions of balance and personal disinterest. There is a much more profound charge that reality (as defined by right-wing ideology) is being systematically distorted by liberal ideology. The right presumes that its perspective ought to define the news; all others should be labeled opinion. In this we recognize that the right-wing critique represents a return to the epistemology of the nineteenth century, for it regards inherent limitations on objectivity as trivial.

Agnew did not invent the right-wing critique of the media, which had been around in sectarian journals since the 1950s and had attained some visibility in the wake of the 1964 election. Media coverage of the Vietnam War and of antiwar protests — both of which the Right blamed for growing antiwar sentiment — stimulated right-wing critique. The fact that support for the war and disapproval of the protests remained popular doubtless helped Agnew's attacks find an audience, and his emphasis on the control of media by an elite gave the right-wing critique a populist angle it had heretofore lacked. Moreover, by blaming liberal bias on an elite, Agnew produced a rhetorically powerful explanation for such bias.

It remained for *The Media Elite* (1986)[10] to offer an *argument* that there is a media elite and that it has a liberal bias. Actually, the book takes for granted the claim that there is a media elite, but it demonstrates that journalists at "America's most influential media outlets" have backgrounds that distinguish them from the average American: for example, 95 percent of such journalists are white and 79 percent are male (the authors make almost nothing of these figures), while 68 percent come from the northeast or north central states and 55 percent attended graduate school. These last figures and others like them demonstrate that journalists are different from you and me (yes, Julian, they have more education), though one would have thought it not terribly revealing to learn that 93 percent of leading journalists had a bachelor's degree or that 78 percent had a personal income above $30,000 (p. 21). These sorts of statistics do not demonstrate the homogeneity of background that would seem to be required for the strong claim that the book makes about the existence of an elite. The evidence is far more convincing regarding the political positions of the journalists studied: 54% regard themselves as liberal and more than 80% voted for the Democratic presidential candidates in elections between 1964 and 1976 (p. 28–30).

If we accept for the moment that *The Media Elite* demonstrates the liberalism of most leading journalists, we are still left wondering how such personal views translate into systematic bias. In fact, the book fails to demonstrate how this happens, relying instead on the assumption that the individual views of journalists will inevitably find their way into their reporting. At the core of *The Media Elite* argument, then, is the old assumption of the subjectivity of the reporter—which they name "the Rashomon principle" after Kurosawa's film that tells the story of a rape from the perspectives of four different characters (p. 132). This is, of course, a perfect reflection of conservative ideology, which makes the individual the source of all good and evil. As a result, systematic bias here turns out to be really just the concentration of like-minded individuals, and their like-mindedness is itself explained only by association. *The Media Elite* dismisses entirely the issue of media ownership, an ironic omission since it uses a survey of "business leaders" as a point of comparison (p. 36).[11]

We should be careful, however, even in accepting the claim that most leading journalists are liberals. When you break down the positions of the journalists on individual issues, you find that on economic matters they are hardly liberal at all. For example, only 13% believe that big corporations should be publicly owned, and 63% believe that less regulation of business is good for the United States (p. 29). This economic conservatism makes perfect sense if we keep in mind that it is business leaders who employ most leading journalists. The authors regard these statistics as expressing journalists' "acceptance of the economic order" while treating their favoring of abortion rights and the noninterference of government in sexual behavior as opposition to the social order (p. 31). Yet, as should be obvious, "less regulation" means a change in the economic order, while the right to an abortion is currently the status quo. The objective of *The Media Elite*, however, is to portray leading journalists as out of step with ordinary Americans, whom it defines as having conservative points of view — this in spite of the fact that polls consistently show that a majority of Americans favor abortion rights, oppose government regulation of sex, etc. This argument is surely exaggerated when it is not simply wrong, but it does point to a significant reason for the *perception* of media bias.

Bennet notes that "this is a very unsettled time. A lot of favored beliefs are turning out to not work very well, whether about families or Israel or whatever. It makes people nervous" (172). Under these conditions especially, a news story need not take an objectionable position on a subject in order to be understood as objectionable. Rather, the mere mention of homosexuality or the reporting of the views of blacks or Hispanics may seem threatening to the traditional audience, which feels that its assumptions can no longer be taken for granted. Bennet calls this problem "agenda setting," and he gives NPR's coverage of AIDS as an example: "We took an incredible beating because of our early coverage of AIDS. The charge of bias was the charge of agenda-setting. 'I don't care about this, I don't want to hear about it. And these guys are on there day after day talking about it. They must have their own agenda. They must have their own bias' " (172). During the period Bennet is discussing here, the disease we now call AIDS was known almost exclusively as an affliction of gay men. The cause of the illness had not been discovered. In this light it is easy to understand why people who find homosexuality to be immoral or threatening would be disturbed by the discussion of an illness that seemed to afflict only such immoral, threatening people. While in retrospect NPR probably now seems to most people — even many of those who originally objected — to have performed a courageous service in discussing this disease, some on the Right have continued to object that the AIDS crisis has been overblown. Agenda-setting is not covered by the conventions of objectivity, and one of Bennet's points is that NPR cannot be regarded as guilty of bias merely for discussing an issue. But that NPR treated AIDS objectively was of no consequence to its critics who objected to the very discussion of the issue.

Agenda-setting cannot be understood in terms of the opposition of bias and objectivity, since there can be no objective standard for what deserves to be covered in the media. And what gets covered is often of far more consequence than how it is treated. Coverage must be selective because there is a finite amount of space and time in which to present the news. All media decide what to cover — set their agenda — out of the conception of reality they assume. The issue here is not the one of multiple perspectives illustrated by Rashomon, but the differing lived relations to the real in which all subjects exist. Such lived relations entail differing assumptions and expectations which are not amenable to true/false judgments. This is reflected in the following exchange:

> Questioner: Obviously, you are biased. You have a bias in favor of liberal, secular humanism as opposed to Pat Robertson, right-wing Christianity.
> Bennet: He's the one with the bias.
> Questioner: You have a bias in favor of liberal policy regarding race, gender, et cetera. . . .
> Bennet: My answer is, if those are biases, then I'm very happy to acknowledge them. We are secular. On the question of the diversity of society, that is not a question of policy, it is merely a recognition of reality. There are some of us who greet it as desirable, and it goes along with a lot of federal legislation. I think if you are going to get tax money for anything that you have an obligation to reflect the society in your hiring practices. (173)

When Bennet remarks that Pat Robertson is "the one with the bias," the most common use of that term is invoked. Bias continues to be understood not as violation of objectivity conventions, but as an odd or wrong conception of reality itself. Secular humanism and right-wing Christianity construct vastly different realities. There is no third point from which the truth of these ideologies may be judged. Since the press as a whole tends to hold Bennet's position here, it is not surprising that the Christian Right or the white supremacists should feel that they are not adequately represented in the mainstream media. The point is that it would be equally impossible for secular humanism to be adequately represented in media dominated by right-wing Christianity, or for doctrines of racial equality to be adequately represented in media built on principles of apartheid — a condition that obtained in United States at least until the 1950s. As legal and public opinion changed, however, racial equality and the value of cultural diversity became a reality. Thus Bennet invokes legislation to justify his response to that reality. Those who see some essential American identity as the reality don't see diversity. Again, there is no neutral place here, as the issue of hiring practices suggests. A news organization must choose either to seek to represent cultural diversity or not.

Ideology at this level is not a simple matter of the reflection of class interests — or any "interests," for that matter. Much of what makes up ideology at any moment of history derives not from currently dominant interests but residual ones, surviving remnants of previous social struggles. Whatever their origins, ideologies cannot be set aside or bracketed so that the media can report the world as it "really" is. There is no "world" outside of ideology, no simple reality. Because of this, the media have little choice but to represent the dominant ideology most of the time since that ideology is the ground on which they walk and the air that they breath. Objectivity conventions most often adjudicate among relatively small differences within the dominant. Given this, the convention of balance makes sense since only a small number of positions need to be reflected. But the balance convention cannot help — and in fact actually may hurt — those positions which fall outside of the dominant because they are always already not legitimate. Lacking popular acceptance, these positions can be and usually are ignored.

The solution to this problem would seem to be the abandonment of the entire notion of news with its assumption that there is a reality that can be unproblematically reflected. What would replace the news in this conception would be explicitly marked representations of differing ideologies. While less news and more critique would undoubtedly be a good thing, such a proposal seems utopian because it assumes that the news itself exists outside of ideology such that it could simply be abandoned. The existence of the news reflects assumptions about the character of reality, assumptions that run counter to those entailed in the concept of ideology presented here. Moreover, given these assumptions, the news is a valuable commodity while critique that develops from other ideologies is not. This explains the collusion between the interests of the corporations that produce the news and public opinion. The news must be desirable; the public desires to have its construction of reality reinforced. As Entman argues, media coverage of events or individuals often seems to blow with the wind of public opinion, so that the media are more willing to present negative stories about an unpopular President than about a popular one (*Democracy Without Citizens*, pp. 46–47). The ideology of the media is not one it imposes on the public — or at least the majority — but one that is shared and negotiated between the two. The news bears this ideology not only because it is in corporate political interests for it to do so, but because the news would not be profitable if it did not. What Richard Hoggart observed of the popular press in Britain of the 1950s is true of the news media in general: though they make a "specialty of safe or pseudo controversy," they hate "genuine controversy, since that alienates, divides and separates, the mass-audience, the buyers."[12]

This point brings us to the issue of censorship and self-censorship and the matter of the politics of the non-news or entertainment media. The only one of our consultants who did not claim that his concern was to serve the market was Bennet, who claimed to serve the cause of providing better information. Bennet denied that the accusations of bias leveled by the Right have had any impact on NPR: "Do we feel political pressure that is couched in terms of bias? It's there but ineffective . . . we have continued to have federal appropriations that have increased ahead of inflation. So I don't feel vulnerable to this attack at all. It has no impact on our news department at all." This seems to portray NPR as an institution insulated from political or market censorship. Yet Bennet goes on to assert that "What does have an impact, and a profound impact, is grass-roots listener communications. When somebody says we have failed to treat a subject fairly, we take it very seriously" (172–73). Bennet is claiming sensitivity to the listeners' interests here, but these lines can also be read as an admission of the power of the market. News producers of all kinds and public media in particular are able to use their claim to be presenting the truth to insulate them to some extent from public opinion. NPR can claim a responsibility to deal with AIDS in spite of the reaction such coverage provoked.

The entertainment media, however, have no such insulation. Many of our consultants report the limiting effects of the market on their products. David Kendall is calling attention to this when he remarks that "I don't think people will watch a show that they aren't ready to see" (62). Earlier he had asserted that "what TV does best in the family sitcom is reassuring stories about middle-class family values" (58). In other words, audiences are not likely to watch shows that disturb or fail to conform to their construction of reality, but will watch shows that reinforce that construction. The market here very powerfully limits what can be said. Thus, even to "do a divorce" (presumably of a couple in whom the audience has developed an emotional investment) on a sitcom is impossible because it would be threatening, not reassuring (66). Like AIDS, divorce is very much a part of the audience's reality, but that reality is constructed so that divorce seems to be an exception to the norm if not to nature. Kendall's remarks reveal a high degree of self-consciousness about what can be profitably represented on television, and presumably this self-consciousness is indispensable to such producers. Kendall himself says that "most of the time you are pretty good at policing yourself" when discussing his relations with the network censors, and it appears that the same is true with regard to the market (68).

It is questionable whether such restraint merits the name self-censorship. That seems to imply that cultural producers such as Kendall are trying to express things that their superegoes won't let them, or that, in the absence of the market or the company censor, they would inevitably spring forth with all manner of heterodoxy. But cultural producers are as much the products of the culture in which they exist as are the goods they deliver. Just as the reality reflected in the news media is shared by producers and consumers, so the "reality" imagined in fictional narratives such as sitcoms or feature films is also of necessity held in common. If anything, heterodox realities are even more inhibited in mass entertainment than they are in the news, because the conventions of the news genres entail both controversy and warning. In fact, these elements are so powerful that those in power routinely complain that news media dwell on bad news and exclude most of the good (e.g., Agnew). For a large portion of the audience, entertainment is only pleasurable (i.e., really entertainment) if it is ultimately reassuring. Violence, horror, or other threats may be represented, but they must be contained. The content of entertainment is thus highly restricted by the market, but such restrictions are so naturalized that cultural producers usually experience them only at the margins of the production process, as in Kendall's account of his run-in with the network censor over the "drug" episode (68). It is because cultural producers take for granted the restrictions of the market that they see themselves as reflecting rather than shaping values.

The problem with this view, however, is that it masks the fact that to reinforce the dominant is to shape values.[13] The ritual denial by the culture industry that its products do anything more than reflect popular tastes or values is doubtless partly a defense against a long history of demands for censorship. The mass entertainment media have been regarded with suspicion ever since the fiction boom of the second half of the nineteenth century. Strauss Zelnick says of the film industry, "Some people think that what we do affects society's values. I disagree. I think we've become part of the cultural vernacular, but I don't think we create values" (28). This general point is later supported by this example: "Does someone who condemns adultery go to my movie and come out saying 'you know what, it is not such a bad idea after all'? I don't think so" (30). The example represents a typical move in such arguments, where shaping values is rendered, one, a matter of an instantaneous, radical change in behavior, and two, a process that occurs at the micro level, a single product changing the individual mind. Propaganda — material designed to change the individual mind — is thus the antithesis of what cultural producers think of themselves as making. The movie *JFK* is not regarded as political, but as "Pure entertainment. Specifically not propaganda, in my opinion" (Zelnick 29). Our interviewees' conception of these matters suggests both why concepts such as *ideology* and *discourse* are indispensable for cultural studies, and why they have been so vigorously resisted by the culture industry, especially the news media. Such conceptions displace the focus on the individual and treat values as cultural products. Moreover, the focus on the individual also reveals why censorship is the dominant way in which such matters are discussed. The question of censorship is a matter of whether an individual should be free to say or hear something. It distracts us from questions about the agendas of culture industry products and the relative absence from them of critical agendas.

While the consultants often speak of corporate censorship or other restrictions built into the production process, there is no mention of state censorship. Zelnick argues that "we have a First Amendment right to make whatever we want" (28), but for much of America's history, government censorship was the rule. A rather narrow range of political expression was understood to be protected by the First Amendment. Expression that was not deemed political was not protected. In such an environment, the representation of realities other than the dominant was quite rare. Because the history of the twentieth century has been marked by a series of battles resulting in ever-decreasing government censorship, we tend to assume that absolute freedom of expression is the ideal. But as Stanley Fish has argued, "All affirmations of freedom of expression are . . . dependent for their force on an exception that literally carves out the space in which expression can then emerge."[14] Fish's point is that what is permitted and what is denied is always a political issue. The cry "free speech" always serves to mask what is in fact a statement for a particular political position. The assumption of absolute freedom allows the political character of the choices about what gets said to be routinely misrecognized. For example, Nathan Pearson claims that the decision not to play the Prince song "Sexy Mother Fucker" was a matter of taste, not politics (123). Zelnick claims a moral responsibility for getting the right values into the movies he makes (28), but he makes no mention of the fact that such values are politically contested.

The point Fish makes about "free speech" is applicable to the cry of bias. Whenever bias is charged it is not some ideal objectivity that is being sought, but rather increased influence for the political position held by the speaker. Charges of censorship and bias work because impossible commitments to absolute freedom and objectivity are widely shared. And yet, we can't give Fish the last word on this point without some modification of his position. Neither freedom of speech nor objectivity is merely a move in a power game. Though free speech may never be absolute, there is a whole range of degrees of tolerance that Fish's conception cannot take into account. Historically, liberals have favored greater tolerance than conservatives, not — or not merely — because they had a greater need to use this move in support of their political positions, but because tolerance of (many, but not all) diverse positions is a liberal position. Objectivity, on the other hand, is a position that neither the left nor the right can do without. Both sides need to appeal to the fiction of a neutral reality, for how else can rational arguments be grounded? But most on the right and the left also continue to believe that there are degrees of accuracy or truth within their own discourses. The dismissal of objective journalism is not for either side a dismissal of objective reality, but rather a lament about the failure of an institution to capture that reality. The fact is that subjectivist or skeptical positions make political discourse more difficult.

The problem with the claim of journalism to objectivity is not in the claim but in the assumption of it as a norm. The news continues to appear as a mirror, even if most of us are aware that it is a distorting one. The news is not a mirror, but a politically invested representation. It will continue to present itself as a mirror as long as the attention of the audience can be gained by the device.

Notes

1 L. Brent Bozell and Brent H. Baker, Introduction, *And That's the Way It Isn't: A Reference Guide to Media Bias*, eds. L. Brent Bozell and Brent H. Baker (Alexandria, Va.: Media Research Center, 1990), p. 1.

2 Peter Novick, *That Noble Dream: The "Objectivity Question" and American Historical Profession* (Cambridge: Cambridge University Press, 1988), p. 25.

3 Michael Schudson, *Discovering the News: A Social History of American Newspapers* (New York: Basic, 1978), p. 22. On the penny press, see also Dan Schiller, *Objectivity and the News: The Public and the Rise of Commercial Journalism* (Philadelphia: University of Pennsylvania Press, 1981).

4 Editorial, *New York Times* (19 August 1896), p. 4.

5 Leo C. Rosten, *The Washington Correspondents* (New York: Harcourt, Brace, 1937), pp. 149–150.

6 Times Mirror, *The People and the Press* (Los Angeles: Times Mirror, 1986).

7 Robert M. Entman, *Democracy Without Citizens: Media and the Decay of American Politics* (New York: Oxford University Press, 1989), p. 30.

8 Spiro Agnew, "Speeches on the Media," in *Killing the Messenger: 100 Years of Media Criticism*, ed. Tom Goldstein (New York: Columbia University Press, 1989), pp. 66–85.

9 See Edward S. Herman and Noam Chomsky, *Manufacturing Consent: The Political Economy of the Mass Media* (New York: Pantheon, 1988); Martin A. Lee and Norman Solomon, *Unreliable Sources: A Guide to Detecting Bias in News Media* (New York: Lyle Stuart, 1990); Michael Parenti, *Inventing Reality: The Politics of the News Media*, 2nd ed. (New York: St. Martin's, 1993).

10 S. Robert Lichter, Stanley Rothman, and Linda S. Lichter, *The Media Elite* (Bethesda, Md.: Adler & Adler, 1986).

11 The authors describe business executives in one place as a "traditional conservative elite" (p. 32), but they do not typically refer to them as an elite, while they habitually refer to leading journalists as such. Such rhetoric is designed to promote populist opposition to the journalists, while "business leaders" are portrayed (though without much statistical support) as being more or less like average Americans.

12 Richard Hoggart, *The Uses of Literacy* (New Brunswick, N.J.: Transaction, 1992 [1957]), p. 133.

13 See Michael Parenti, *Make-Believe Media: The Politics of Entertainment* (New York: St. Martin's, 1992), pp. 2–3, for a list of the dominant values popular entertainment products typically reinforce; for example, "Individual effort is preferable to collective action"; "Affluent professionals are more interesting than blue-collar or ordinary service workers."

14 Stanley Fish, *There's No Such Thing as Free Speech: and It's a Good Thing Too* (New York: Oxford University Press, 1994), p. 103.

UNIVERSITY PRESS OF NEW ENGLAND

publishes books under its own imprint and is the publisher for
Brandeis University Press, Dartmouth College, Middlebury College Press,
University of New Hampshire, Tufts University, Wesleyan University Press,
and Salzburg Seminar.

Library of Congress Cataloging-in-Publication Data
Making and selling culture / Richard Ohmann, editor . . . [et al.].
   p. cm.
  Includes bibliographical references.
  ISBN 0–8195–5300-x (cloth : alk. paper). — ISBN 0–8195–5301–8
(pbk. : alk. paper)
   1. Culture — Economic aspects — Congresses. 2. Popular culture —
Economic aspects — Congresses. 3. Mass media — Marketing —
Congresses. I. Ohmann, Richard M. (Richard Malin), 1931– .
HM101.M23773 1996
306.3 — dc20   96–22546